BARE FEET

TO RUNNING SHOES

BARE FEET
TO RUNNING SHOES

ERNEST ANDRUS

Deeds Publishing | Athens

Published by Deeds Publishing in Athens, GA
www.deedspublishing.com

Printed in The United States of America

Cover design by Mark Babcock. Text layout by Matt King.
Cover photo courtesy of *The Brunswick News*

ISBN 978-1-947309-61-6

Books are available in quantity for promotional or premium use. For information, email info@deedspublishing.com.

First Edition, 2019

10 9 8 7 6 5 4 3 2 1

Dedicated to my family and the thousands of people
who have supported me in my run across America

CONTENTS

ERNEST ERVIN ANDRUS;

BORN AUGUST 19, 1923 TO ERNEST EZRA ANDRUS AND MARGARET VIOLA MCCARTHY ANDRUS.

PART I

MEMORIES OF THE FIRST SIX YEARS OF MY LIFE...

I WAS BORN IN THE ANDRUS FARM HOUSE, WOLF RIVER TOWNSHIP, NEAR SEVERANCE, KANSAS. This was grandpa and grandma William Wallis Andrus and Allie Candace Burell Andrus' farm. My mom, dad, and older brother had just moved into the smoke house.

We lived in the smoke house until my dad got possession of a farm on the Missouri River, a few miles from Troy, Kansas.

I still remember, all these years later, my little brother, Warren Lee, was born when I was almost two—June 30, 1925. Perhaps my memory is that I was told of his birth, but I feel like I remember it. My mother said I stood up at eight months and didn't walk but ran, and I have never quit running. While still a toddler, I fell down the stairs into the cellar and got a big cut on my forehead. I carried the scar all my life, but it is hardly noticeable now with all my other markings that go with being my age.

I remember that my older brother, John, and I got Chicken Pox. We were miserable. Our little brother, Warren, got one little sore and it went away. We thought it was unfair that he got off so easy while we suffered so much. In another incident, Warren didn't fare so well. I'm not sure how old he was but he must have been around two or three. We were playing with the corn sheller. John was feeding corn cobs into the sheller

3

and I was turning the handle. Little brother got his thumb in the cogs. He went through the rest of his life with one thumb.

When we were out running around the farm, John and I would run off and leave Warren. He moved too slow! One day our mother, whom we always called "Mommy," said, "You two have got to promise me you won't run off and leave your brother or you're going to have to stay in the yard all day." We made the promise. While crossing over some plowed ground, however, Warren was having a hard time keeping up. John said, "We promised not to run off and leave him. We didn't promise we wouldn't walk off and leave him," so we just picked up our pace. Goodbye, little brother.

When John started school, Dad bought him a pony. He didn't like being tied up at school all day so he would invariably break loose and run back to the barn. I was five years old and decided to get him out of the barn and ride him. We never heard of a saddle on the farm. We just rode bareback. I managed to coax him past the house and to the top of a little hill. He decided to go back. He started at a walk, then a trot, and then a full gallop. I could not slow him down. Just as we were passing the house, my dad started up the corn sheller. It backfired. The pony made a sudden stop and I landed in the front yard. I went into the house screaming. I have stayed off horses ever since.

We had another house on the property that we called the "brown house." It was sometimes occupied by family, sometimes it was empty. My dad decided to convert it into an incubator to raise chicks. He cut a hole in the floor to let the heat from the basement come up into the living room. It worked fine until the heat from the furnace caught the house on fire. Everyone grabbed a bucket and we had a bucket brigade from the creek to the house to put out the fire. Fortunately, the house was saved, but we were out of the chicken business.

In my pre-school days, I knew very little about money. Very few people had any. An aunt came to visit and gave me a nickel. I had never seen one before and had no idea what to do with it. An older cousin came to visit and I showed it to him and asked him what I could do with it. He said, "You know what you can do with a penny?" I said, "Yea! I can buy candy." So we made a trade. He gave me a penny for my nickel.

I started school in a one-room school house that had one teacher, eight grades, and about 20 students. School started in those days when you turned six and you went into the first grade. The first day of school, our teacher, Mr. Thompson, explained a few rules. The toilet was an outhouse so he explained if you need to go to the toilet hold up one finger for urinate, two for the other. You must get permission. I had to go real bad, but was too shy to hold up my finger. Being my last name started with "A," I was right down next to him, second seat from the front. Pretty soon, a river was running toward the teacher. He scolded me and said, "Never let it happen again." The next day, guess what... it happened again. He kept me after school and convinced me it was less embarrassing to hold up a finger than to flood the floor.

In those days, small farmers could not afford to pay the taxes so after a few years the government would foreclose on the farm and put it on the auction block. My dad and his brothers kept it in the family. After every foreclosure, another uncle would buy it back for less than what the taxes would be.

When my dad was plowing, he would pick up Indian arrowheads. They came in handy during the depression, when he sold most of them to buy a car. He kept a few and gave them to me before he died.

To get to the field on the other side of the creek, my dad built a swinging bridge. One day a couple of men showed up at the house and said, "There's a guy in St. Joe that pays $10 for wild mules. We rounded up three and have them roped on the other side of the bridge but they won't cross the bridge. They asked, "Is there any other way to get across the creek?" Dad said, "No, but I can get them across the bridge." So they made a deal, "You get them across and we split the $30 three ways."

My dad made $10, which was probably the most money he'd ever had. I asked him how he got them across. He said, "With a mule you got to get his attention, so I just took a 2x4 and did my best to kill him. Works ever time."

When the duck hunters came down to the river, my mother cooked for them. I think she made more money feeding duck hunters than my dad did farming.

My dad built a bunk on the side of the wall in a very small area of the farm house. That's where I slept. Every night, Mommy would come to tuck me in. She would have me kneel beside my bunk and she would recite the, "Now I lay me down to sleep" prayer and have me repeat it after her. When she came to the, "If I should die before I wake" part, I thought she was saying "fi-sha-die." It must have been a couple years before I figured out what "fi-sha-die" meant.

I loved my grandma. I thought she was the greatest person in the world. She probably was. I don't remember this but my aunt told me this so many times it seems like I remember it … Grandma came to visit and asked me, "What are you boys going to be when you grow up?" I said, "John's going to be a preacher, Warren Lee's going to be a doctor, and I'm going to be a grandma." Grandma Andrus had nearly 400 direct descendants when she died at 99, and they all loved her.

Just a little something here to show how old fashioned Grandma was. When she got too old to run the farm, she leased it out and moved into a house on the edge of Troy. Her son Lloyd's wife had died and all his kids had left the nest so he moved in with her to look after her. He wanted to build her an inside bathroom. She said, "No one's going to the toilet inside my house."

Dad was hitching up the team to take the wagon into Troy. John was going with him. I said, "Can I go with you?" He said, "If it's all right with your mother." I ran into the house and pleaded with Mommy. She finally said, "All right, if it's all right with your dad." I ran back outside. They were gone. Out of sight. I started running after them. I must have been about a third of the way to Troy when I met them coming back. This was my first 5K!

That pretty much covers the first six years of my life, at least what I can remember of it. Little did I know that I'd be running my whole life.

MEMORIES OF MY PRE-TEEN YEARS ...

WE LIVED ON THE FARM BY THE MISSOURI RIVER UNTIL WE LOST THE FARM. WHEN I WAS SEVEN years old, we moved onto what we called the Schroder Place. I think the nearest town was Wathena, KS. I attended a one room school with eight grades. The teacher was Miss Spate. I can name every kid in the school. The first year I was in the second grade. There were five students: Gertrude Groniger, John Andrus, Ernest Andrus, Mary Trompeter, and Johnny Trompeter. The next year Gertrude graduated and Warren Lee Andrus started. The school bell was a cow bell. The door had no lock, just a piece of wood on a nail you could turn to keep the door closed.

Here are some of the incidents I remember. We three boys were always roaming the farm and nearby woods seeking adventure. My dad was hauling a wagonload of hay across the farm. We kids climbed on to go for a hayride. Something spooked one of the horses and we had a runaway. The wagon scraped the fence and dumped us and a lot of hay over the fence. A damaged wagon, a damaged fence, and three shook up boys, but no one was hurt.

Another time, we were hiking in the timber along the creek when we spotted a hornet's nest. Now when you spot a hornet's nest, it's not a question of "Do we or don't we throw rocks?" It's just something that's gotta be done. The question was, "Where do we go to get away from the hornets when they come after us?" I decided we should take off all our clothes, blast that nest with some rocks, then run for the creek. A whole swarm of hornets came after us. We made it just in time and dove into the water. We would hold our breath as long as we could, and every time we came up for air, here came the hornets. We were in that water for a long time before the hornets gave up and went away.

We were playing in a shed filled with wheat. I got hold of a gunny sack and pulled on it. Turns out it was plugging a knot hole in the side of the shed and now the wheat was pouring out through the hole onto the ground. By the time we got around to where we could plug up the hole, there was a lot of wheat on the ground. Since my dad had borrowed a horse from one of his brothers, the horse came over and started eating the wheat. I was really worried! "What are we going to do?", I said. John said, "Dad and Mommy are getting the fishing gear together, and we're all going fishing. By the time we get back, the horse will have eaten all the wheat and we're home free." When we got back, that horse was swollen up like a balloon. My dad worked for hours with that horse just to keep it alive. Boy, did we get a thrashing for that one.

The day my dad became my hero was when Warren Lee was four, I was six, and John was seven. We were walking across the pasture when a bull charged us. We ran for the nearest fence. I was just starting up the fence and John was already at the top. John looked back and said, "Warren's not going to make it!" The bull was gaining on him and his little legs weren't moving fast enough. Little brother dove under a hedge bush. Hedge bushes have thorns. Every time the bull's nose hit the thorns, he'd back off, paw the ground, snort, and try again. John stayed at the fence trying to draw the bull's attention away from Warren.

I ran up to the house for help. Mommy said, "Go get your dad. He's in the barn." Our Aunt Lilly, who was visiting, started running to the scene. I don't know what she was going to do besides getting herself killed. She got straddled on the barb wire fence and froze. She couldn't go any farther.

Before getting to the barn there was a large wooden gate. I always went over that gate by hitting it at full speed, put one hand on the middle board, the other on top, and vaulted over it. So that is what I did. When I told Dad, he grabbed a pitchfork and took off at full speed. He wasn't slowing down for the gate and I was wondering what he was going to do carrying that pitchfork. He hurdled the gate then hurdled the fence. When he reached the bull, he was really traveling. He hit that bull with the pitchfork right in the rear end. The bull turned on him. He grabbed the ring in the bull's nose and gently led him away. Little brother was shaken but unhurt except for a few cuts from the thorns.

Most farm boys learned to work the farm at a very young age. My dad wanted to put us kids to work, but Mommy wouldn't let him. She claimed that we were too young and little boys need to play.

We did have our chores, which we rotated doing. I remember the two most important ones that we never failed to do—first, bring enough water in from the well to last all the next day and second, bring in enough wood to last until the next day. I don't remember what all the other ones were but we did have to keep enough wood stacked in the wood pile, feed the chickens, slop the hogs, and sometimes pick fruit.

Dad got up at 4:00 every morning and got a fire going in the wood burning cook stove. If it was winter, he also got a fire going in the heat stove before he milked the cows and went to the fields. He usually took a lunch pail with him. Sometimes he would come in for dinner, which is what we called the noon meal back then, then back to work. Mommy was up early and worked hard all day. She did the evening milking and sometimes even helped Dad in the field. The farm was self-contained. The things a farmer and his wife had to do is too much to list here. They grow, cook, and can fruits and vegetables; raise and butcher their own livestock; make their own butter; make their own soap; make most of their own clothes; and grind their wheat. Those are only a few of the many things that had to be done.

My dad purchased three sickly lambs from his brother and gave a lamb to each of us kids to raise. They needed to be bottle fed and needed other special care. When they were grown, he took them to St. Joe and sold them for $10 each. This was in 1929. My dad said that people were getting rich on the stock market and he sure would like to get rich, but Mommy would not let him invest. She maintained, "We don't gamble." Dad took the money the dairy had paid him for milk, took some livestock into St. Joe, and accumulated $100. He added our $30 to it and invested $130 in the grain market. Guess what… the stock market crashed and he lost it all. Mommy said, "You owe the boys $30." He said, "I don't have $30." She said, "You'd better find it."

My dad sat us kids down and said, "I lost your money on the stock market. The only way I know to get it back is you can take your choice of a little pig or the new born calf. You kids raise it and when it's grown, we may be able get your money back." We loved that cute little calf, so that's what we chose. The calf grew up fast and was pregnant. He sold her for $30. We now had a bank account and would never be broke again.

We were walking through a neighbor's corn field. John stripped a stalk of corn so I did the same. We wound up stripping a whole row of corn. The neighbor had no trouble figuring out who did it so he told our dad. Dad said, "You kids did a bad thing so I've made a deal with our neighbor." He gave us a hoe and said, "In order to repay the damage, you boys are going to keep the weeds out of his corn field until harvest." We learned a lesson there—vandalism does not pay. This same neighbor had a haystack at the intersection. We used to play in it on our way home from school. One night someone lit it on fire. He came to my dad and blamed us kids for the fire. My dad asked us, "Did you boys do it?" We said, "No!" My dad went back to him and said, "My boys said they didn't do it, so they didn't do it."

Our family couldn't show a profit on the Schroder place, so my dad signed on with George Prawl. George had married Dad's school teacher, Enid, in Severance, Kansas. Enid was also my mother's teacher in high school. Enid and Mother had become lifelong friends.

This is how my parents meet. While working her way through school, my mother took a job as maid for Candace Andrus. My mom and Candace, whom everyone called "Daci," adored each other. Daci wanted my mom for a daughter-in-law and my mother thought it would be great to have her for a mother-in-law.

William and Daci had five sons. Mom dated the eldest, Henry, once, but even though she highly respected the man, she had no particular feelings for him. Daci said, "Wait till Ernest comes home from college, he's the good looking one. You're going to like him." Shortly after Ernest, my dad, came home from college, he married my mom.

Dad did some farming in Missouri until their first born, John, arrived. A short time later, Mom was pregnant with me. Dad's father was not well and needed extra help on the farm, so they moved back to the homestead. My grandpa William said he wanted to live long enough to see the baby, which of course was me.

After I was born they fixed up the smoke house and we lived there for about two and a half months and then Grandpa died. We then moved to the farm on the Missouri River.

Now back to the Prawl farm ... I was eight-years-old, my brother was nine, and the four of us had some real good times together.

We envied the Prawl boy because he had things we could never afford, like his own pony, an air rifle, and nice clothes. It was two miles to school and two miles back over dirt roads and of course lots of trees to climb, a creek to wade in, snakes to kill, etc. We'd reach home with dirt and mud from head to foot. All our clothes had to go into the laundry. The Prawl boy, however, arrived in his neatly pressed clothes, without a smudge on them. We hated him sometimes because of this! Mommy would say,

"Why can't you be like him?" I keep calling him the "Prawl boy" because I don't know how to spell his name. It's pronounced "A'mal." By the way, I paid him a visit once in his old age. There he was at the senior club playing pinochle, wearing his neatly pressed pants, shirt, and tie.

The Prawl boy and I were playing cops and robbers, running around in the barn looking for places to hide from each other. I had a forked piece of a tree branch for a gun. He had his air rifle. He spotted me and wham... shot me in the arm. No more cops and robbers with this guy.

One day he showed up with a handful of rifle bullets and a hammer. He said, "Come on, let's go have some fun." Of course we were all for having some fun, whatever he had in mind. He placed a big rock at the corner of a shed. We all went around the corner and took turns putting a shell on the rock, stuck our head around to watch, and hit the bullet with the hammer. You'd hear a shot, a whine, and the bullet hitting the side of the barn. Fortunately, no bullet headed toward that stupid head peaking around the corner.

John was a real dare devil. One thing he liked to do was grab a snake by the tail and snap off its head. We were walking to school, just approaching the bridge at the bottom of the hill, when a beautiful snake started across the road. John rushed down, grabbed it by the tail, and snapped off its head. A bunch of little snakes (it looked like a hundred of them) flew out onto the road, running in every direction. Boy, did we take off running in the other direction.

The next summer we moved a short distance to the Corbet place. Grandma and Grandpa Corbet had a huge farm. They lived in the big house but had another house on the property. They adopted two boys, Shorty and Pete. I think their last name was Colsen. They had a son named Guy. Guy married Mable. My mother and Mable were best friends. Grandpa Corbet had died, so Guy raised his family there, helping on the farm until he took a job driving a truck for the dairy in Hiawatha, and his family had out grown the farm. They had seven boys.

They moved into a mansion in Highland, leaving Grandma Corbet rather short of help. We moved into the smaller house so my dad could help on the farm.

I built myself an obstacle course, which I loved. No one else would run it for two reasons. First, there was a log across the quick sand which you had run across and then a narrow path with a bank on one side which had a drop off into the quick sand on the other. Second, there was a barbed-wire fence where you would have to dive through a tire which was tied to a tree branch hanging just above the fence in order to get across. You had to run in order to dive through the tire. I found it not too difficult, but no one else wanted to try it.

School was two miles away, and no matter how early I started, I could never get there on time because there were too many things to distract me on the way. But when school let out, it took me 20 minutes flat to cover the two miles of dirt road because I couldn't wait to run my obstacle course.

I loved to do chores for Grandma Corbet. She would make donuts, and when you finished your chore, she'd let you eat some of the donut holes. She sent me out to gather eggs. I wanted her to be proud of me so I searched everywhere through the barn and sheds for eggs. When I returned, she said, "Great, you found twice as many as the other kids." But when she started cracking them, she was finding little chicks in some of them.

We went into Highland to visit the Corbets. The adults and some of the older boys had gone into town, so there were just my younger brother, who now went by Lee because he said he couldn't spell "Warren", and four Corbet boys. We were playing in the yard when one of us found a bullet. The oldest boy, Murl who was nicknamed Dick, said, "Bet this will fit in the gun over the bathroom door."

One of us ran in and got the gun. Dick put the bullet in the gun and kept trying to fire it, with no results. He didn't know the bullet had to be in the chamber. Finally, he said, "I think I got it." I turned around and said, "Got what?" Just then the gun went off. The bullet passed through my hand and lodged into the calf of my brother's leg. I took off as fast as I could go, screaming. I left a trail of blood clear around that house. As soon as my brother took a step, the bullet fell out of his leg. Now we were in deep trouble. We had stopped all the bleeding with pressure, returned the gun to where it was, but what were we going to tell our parents?

We came up with a story and we all had to stick to it. We picked the location as next to the laundry room because there was concrete there. We said Dick dropped the bullet and it went off. Good story. Hope they buy it. Our parents arrived shortly and rushed my brother and me to the doctor. After the doctor cleaned up my wound, he told my mother to put me down for some rest because I had lost a lot of blood. I'm laying there in bed when my mother sat down and said, "Your brother's going through a lot of pain because the doctor has to probe, just in case the shell is in there because no one can find the shell." Now, not wanting my brother to go through any more pain, I had to think of something real quick. Being too stupid to know that the shell was still in the gun, I said, "We didn't want Dick to get in trouble so we said he dropped the bullet. What really happened was he threw the bullet against the house and it went off, so you're looking in the wrong place for the shell. Try the other side of the house."

My mother shook her head and said, "One lie leads to another." Vern, the oldest of the Corbet boys, came home, went straight to the bathroom, took a whiff and said, "This gun has just been fired, and here's your shell." After that, Dick got a new nickname. His brothers called him "One Shot." That lie bothered me the rest of my life. We boys were always very careful to not lie to our parents. The one time I tried it was a disaster.

I am a very slow reader. The teacher would make me sit with the girl in the seat next to me because there were not enough books to go around. In the first place, I was not used to being around girls, and I was very shy. This little girl would want to turn the page and I'm still on the first paragraph. I'd motion go ahead.

I had no idea what we were reading so I'd be looking out the window at the squirrel playing in the tree. The teacher (I think her name was Miss Kieff—a wonderful teacher) came over, tapped me on the forehead, and said, "If you don't read the book with this end, I'm going to teach you to read it with the other end." I tried, but soon I was watching the squirrel again. She took me by my collar, grabbed the book, and led me to the basement. She said, "How would you like it if I did this to you?" Then she'd hit the vent with the book. It made a terrible noise you could hear all through the school. I was so scared every time she hit the vent I hollered. When we came up, I was scared and crying. All the kids looked as scared as I did. They said, "It sounded like she was killing you."

We were wading in a beaver pond when we saw a water moccasin swimming toward us. John waited till he got close then grabbed him by the tail and snapped off his head. Immediately, we saw about six more coming toward us. Lee and I backed off, but John waited for them, grabbed the nearest one by the tail, but before he could snap off its head one bit him on the ankle. We took off as fast as we could upstream, staying in the water because we had been told that's the best thing to do because the water will help to dilute the poison. When we got home, I don't know what Mommy did, but she seemed to know exactly what to do because he had very little reaction to the bite.

One time John picked a bunch of cherries, squashed them, added something, and said he was making some cherry wine. He placed it in a jar and buried it. He left it there for a long period of time, then dug it up, scraped away all the mold, and put it through a strainer. Worst stuff I ever tasted.

In those days, most animals had a bounty. We decided to go into business and set traps all around the farm. The only thing we caught was a skunk. We couldn't get near it because of the smell. Dad said, "Leave it there to rot." Mommy said, "The boys went to all that trouble. Now you have to go get the pelt or whatever off that skunk and collect their bounty." I think it was about ten cents. Dad put on some old overalls and did as he was told. Afterwards he buried his clothes and went down to the creek and bathed … and bathed … and bathed.

KANSAS CITY MEMORIES – THE EARLY DEPRESSION YEARS ...

HERE WE WERE, A POOR FARMER FAMILY WITH NOTHING, PRACTICALLY NO INCOME, AND THEN along comes the Great Depression. My mother's sister, my Aunt Sadie, was the hostess for Fred Harvey's at the Union Station, Kansas City, Missouri. She said to my mother, "Come to Kansas City. I'll get you a waitress job as a Fred Harvey girl. This way you'll always have an income."

We moved to Kansas City, on Woodland Avenue, right across the street from Mercy Hospital. We boys were enrolled in Woodland Grammar School. This was during the Tom Pendergast Regime. The city was run by Pendergast, the police department was part of the mob with Harry Truman as the mob's accountant. Most of the kids wanted to grow up to be gangsters because they seemed to be the only ones with money.

My Aunt Lilly moved in with us for a while to help with the rent. Dad, Aunt Lilly, and a couple of Aunt Lily's friends went together and opened a little restaurant. As soon as they opened for business, a couple of hoods showed up and told my dad he had to pay for protection. He said he couldn't afford it, and he didn't need any protection. They said, "You will if you don't pay up." He refused. The next morning Dad was walking along the street, getting his keys out of his pocket to open the restaurant, when a limousine drove by and fired shots over his head. He went out of the restaurant business.

Dad then got on the WPA. It paid a dollar a day, but there were so many people there looking for work that they couldn't use everyone. Both my mother and Dad were approached and told they had to register as a Democrat and give them permission to vote for them by proxy or they would not be able to work in Kansas City, Missouri. My dad did not always vote Republican, but never Democrat. My mother never agreed with Dad on anything, so she had no problem with this. Dad signed in order to get work, but stayed registered in Kansas, and went over there to vote so as to kill the vote in Missouri.

Woodland School discovered I had a reading problem and gave me an eye test. They found I had a lazy left eye. I knew I couldn't see well out of that eye but figured that was normal for a right-handed person. They had me go once a week to Mercy Hospital for eye exercises.

The school had a swimming pool but the water was always so cold that the kids hated it. Everyone had to take swimming lessons anyway. I never once saw the teacher in the water. After a year of swimming lessons, I still hadn't learned how to swim. One day the teacher lined us all up and said everyone had to dive off the diving board. I couldn't swim and the water was deep out there. I was scared to death. When a kid went in and couldn't swim, the teacher stuck a long bamboo pole in the water for him to grab hold of. I got to the end of the board and froze. I just couldn't do it. He stuck the pole in my back and shoved. I dove straight for the side of the pool. I no sooner had I hit the water and my hand was on the side of the pool. During summer vacation, we went to the farm to visit Grandma. My uncle Carl was Doniphan County's champion swimmer. He had scooped out a nice swimming hole on the creek. I told him I had a year of swimming lessons and still couldn't swim. He said I can teach you to swim in five minutes. We went down to his swimming hole and he taught me to swim in about five minutes.

We moved to the other side of town where we had room for Aunt Sadie and could split the expenses. She had the front part of the house and we shared the kitchen and bath. We lived upstairs. I have several memories of our time living in Kansas City....

I was out playing on the terrace and found a twenty-dollar bill. I took it in the house and went back outside. A young man came by, looking like he was searching for something. I said, "Did you lose a twenty-dollar bill?" He quickly said, "Yea, did you find it?" I ran into the house and got it for him. I hope it was his.

After we moved, Mercy Hospital was a long way away, but the street car stopped right in front of Lincoln Avenue grammar school, did a loop through town, and went right past the hospital. Street car fare was five cents each way so I was given two nickels once a week to go for my eye treatments. I decided if I took Woodland straight through, it wouldn't be too far and I could walk back and save a nickel.

Missouri is a southern state, so Kansas City was segregated. The blacks stayed pretty much in their area and the whites stayed pretty much out of their area. I had never lived in the South, so I didn't understand segregation and just ignored it. I had to walk right through the black section. I got nervous because people were staring at me, and pointing. I realized later that the black adults are not going to bother a white boy walking through their town, and the younger ones were in school, so I was pretty safe. It took longer than I thought, so it was too late to go to school. I didn't dare tell Mommy what I did so I had to think of something. I decided to tell her I was sick and stayed home. The thought of lying to my mother upset me so bad I actually got deathly sick and went to bed. When Mommy got home she said, "Why aren't you in school?" I said, "I'm sick." And that was no lie.

We attended a Christian Church regularly. I was eleven, John was twelve, Lee was nine. John went forward and made a profession of faith. He said he believed and wanted to be a Christian. He was going to be baptized the next Sunday. He asked me if I'd like to join him. I declined. Lee said, "I'll go with you." After they were baptized, I said, "You guys have just made a commitment I hope you can live up to. I'm not ready for that yet." I didn't see much change in their lives, but that wasn't my problem. I hadn't made any promise to God so I could go on doing as I pleased.

The hospital gave me glasses and a ruby lens to wear over my good eye to force the other eye to work. I didn't like not being able to see, so I hid the lens under the porch and told Dad, "I think I lost it." He said, "They cost twenty-five cents, so you'll have to wait till payday and I'll buy you another one." Just before payday, I'd conveniently find the lens, and then lose it again after he spent all his salary. I was good at math and I figured I'd be sixty-five before going blind. To a ten-year-old, sixty-five is forever.

I always looked up to John. I thought he knew about everything, and John thought so, too. We were living in a town run by gangsters. The kids all thought they had to be tough and mean. John said when a kid comes looking for a fight, never show fear, never back down, and remember a bluff is always better than a fight.

One day he had a chance to demonstrate it. We had ventured into a neighborhood on our roller skates where there were some steep driveways we could skate down. Four boys about our age approached us. The leader flashed a knife and made some remark. John said, "Are you looking for a fight?" He said, "Yea!"

John stepped right up into his face and said, "Well, you got us a little out-numbered right now, so I'll tell you what we're gonna do. You get your gang together, we'll get our gang together, and meet you on this corner at five o-clock tonight, and we'll have a real good fight." You can be sure no one showed up on that corner at five o-clock. I've followed that advice all my life, and it's worked almost every time. I found if you don't show fear, you overcome fear.

John developed a tumor on his right elbow. It was diagnosed as Sarcoma which was at that time always fatal. They tried a couple operations, but it came right back. On a Sunday, my dad said, "We're going for a drive, John where would you like to go?" John said, "Over to the Kansas side to see all those new homes they're building. Someday there is going to be a city over there just like over here, only newer."

While driving through the new housing developments, Dad said, "John, the doctor said your tumor is terminal, and you only have three more years to live. He wants to amputate your arm. He said it's never worked, but there's always hope." John said, "Tell him to amputate." I about fell off the back seat. How could he let them do that?

A boy my age named Vernon Smith lived next door. I admired him for his guts. We'd go into a store to buy a penny's worth of candy or just to look around. He'd walk out with his jacket filled with candy bars and gum. I always wished I had his nerve. On the last day of school, because we were moving back to Kansas the very next day, I was walking to school alone and decided that this was my last chance to prove to myself that I've got the nerve to steal something. I went into a Piggly Wiggly and started looking at the candy bars and gum. I stayed there way too long trying to get up the nerve. Finally, I slipped a Dentine gum into my notebook and turned to walk out of the store when I felt a hand on my shoulder. It was the store manager. He said, "Give me the gum." He gave me a good scolding and I walked out of there shaking. I was so glad we were leaving town the next day because I just knew the police were going to be watching every move I made.

BACK TO KANSAS – MORE DEPRESSION YEARS MEMORIES

I WAS GOING ON 12 WHEN WE MOVED TO HIAWATHA, KANSAS. MY DAD AND UNCLE CARL GOT A sheep shearing machine, towed it behind a Model A Ford pickup, covered the pickup so they could sleep in the bed, and traveled to Nebraska and South Dakota shearing sheep. We moved in with the Corbet family on the edge of Hiawatha. My mother was only on a short vacation, then back to her job at the Union Station so she could be near Mercy Hospital, knowing John would be getting treatment there often. John was in the hospital getting his arm amputated.

I went to a grammar school there for a short time until the Corbets moved into town. My brother Lee and I stayed with them and had to change schools. When John got out of the hospital, he joined us. Here we were, Mable and Guy Corbet and 10 boys, all living in the same house, then Mable gave birth to a beautiful little girl. Boy! Did we love that little girl whom they named Donna. One whimper out of her and 10 boys were right there ready to spoil her.

When the doctors could do no more for John, mother left Kansas City and took a waitress job at a service station café. We rented a small house with enough property to raise our own food and raise chickens. It was much like living on the farm, except there was a pump in the kitchen so we had fresh water. Mother made seven dollars a week, plus tips.

Our rent was ten dollars a month, so there wasn't much spending money. While here I entered junior high school at Hiawatha High.

One day on the way to school, two Corbet boys, Lee and I were having a contest to see who could jump over the most sidewalks. I spotted a house and thought here is where I win. There was a sidewalk going around the house. If I hurdle the steps and then jump that sidewalk, I'll be one ahead of everybody. I was pretty good at hurdles, but had never learned the proper way. I always bent my knee under me to go over the hurdle. I overlooked a mud scraper on the edge of the step. My knee hit the scraper and I rolled out onto the lawn screaming. The wound opened so you could see my knee cap. Someone got ahold of Mother and Mable. They got me to a doctor. There was no such thing as Novocain in those days, and Mother said while the doctor was sewing me up everyone in town could hear me screaming.

I got up before daylight one morning to help one of the Corbet boys deliver newspapers. He said, "The first one up has to fix breakfast for everyone. That's us." He took a big wash tub, filled it half full of water, put it on the stove, lit a fire under it, dumped a great big bag of oatmeal in it, then dumped in a few pounds of raisins. He put the sugar bowl, a jar of jelly, and a loaf of bread on the table and said, "The oatmeal will be ready when everyone gets up, there's butter and milk in the ice box. We'll eat when we get back." I might add that there were never any leftovers.

One of the Corbet boys, Dale, was quite a bit older than me and he loved to tease me. He would sit next to me, grab the bread, and pass it the other way, knowing there wouldn't be any left when it got around to me. He'd watch my face and when the tears began to form, he seemed to get a big kick out of that. All the boys ate at a big table in the kitchen. The adults ate in the dining room. Mable baked a big beautiful cake that was setting on top of the stove. She said, "I'll cut the cake when everyone has eaten their supper." We were all eyeing that cake, couldn't wait to get at it. When Mable cut the cake, it was nothing but a shell. Someone had lifted it up and ate all the insides and replaced it on the plate in perfect condition. Everyone knew Dale was the culprit, but he never did admit it.

We knew that John's life expectancy was short, so why save his money for college? John came up with a plan. We all agreed that if we owned a bicycle, that would be just about the greatest thing in the world. Our plan was we would draw enough money out of the bank to buy a used bicycle. Each of us would own the bicycle every third day. We bought the bike and John took a calendar on which he put each of our names every third day so we knew which days we owned the bicycle. This plan worked great until one day…

It was Lee's day for the bicycle, but Lee and I were working on some kind of a project. I don't remember what the project was, but it must have been important to us because Lee decided he'd ride the bicycle later. We looked up and here came John, lickity-split down the dirt road on Lee's bicycle. Lee had the hammer in his hand so he ran out to the road. When John came by, he threw the hammer right into the spokes. John only had one arm now, so he wasn't in too good of control anyway, and John and the bicycle went end over end.

John got up, grabbed the hammer, and took off after Lee. Lee knew John could outrun him, so he headed across the garden to the nearest fence, knowing that John, with his one arm, would be slow getting over the fence and he could get away. I really believe John would have killed him. I think Lee believed it, too. After John cooled off and Lee came home, John said, "We need an arbitrator. You saw the whole thing, so you decide what should be done and we will abide by your decision." So I said, "John, you took the bicycle when it belonged to Lee, so on the next day when it belongs to you, the bicycle will belong to Lee. Lee, you broke the spokes, so it's up to you to replace them." Lee went right to work replacing spokes. I don't think we had enough spares, so he probably had to go buy some. I think they were a penny each. He may have gotten a quantity discount.

John was 12 years old when he was diagnosed with cancer. The doctor said he only had three years to live. The prediction was accurate. He died right after his fifteenth birthday. There couldn't be a more horrible way to die, he was in constant pain. He had taken so much morphine that it no longer had any affect on him. He just rotted away to nothing. The night he died, he said, "Mommy, I'm going to die tonight. Now there's nothing to keep you from moving to California." Right after the funeral, we got on a train and headed for California. I had my 14th birthday in Los Angeles.

CALIFORNIA, HERE WE COME – TEEN YEARS IN THE GREAT DEPRESSION

We moved to California and moved in with my uncle Charlie McCarthy in southwest Los Angeles. He was married to Elsie, a very beautiful woman. My Grandmother McCarthy was also living with him. It was a very crowded house until my mother could find a job. She took a waitress job downtown for 17 dollars a week, plus tips, and rented a house on 48th Place. The 17 dollars seemed like a lot of money, but the rent was 30 dollars.

This was 1937, still in the Great Depression. Employment was easier to find in California, so people from all over the US were moving to Los Angeles. There were more jobs and better climate. The influx of people created competition for jobs so it was still hard to make enough money to support a family. In 1939, things started to improve. We were producing war materials for our allies.

I have lots of memories from those teenage years in Los Angeles ....

My uncle took us to the Beach in San Pedro. We had never seen the ocean so this was very exciting. We knew nothing about sunburn. We spent a lot of time in the water. In our bare feet, wearing nothing but swim trunks, my brother and I ran all the way to the end of a rock pier and back. That night my skin started to burn, I ran a high fever, got chills, and was shaking. All night I kept getting cramps in my legs. Then came the blisters. Every part of my body, except where the trunks had protected, had blisters. When the blisters busted and the peeling started, the itching was unbearable. Fortunately for my brother, he didn't go all the way to the end of the pier, so he wasn't suffering as much as me.

We were new in town so my brother and I decided to take a walk around the neighborhood. As we approached a group of kids playing baseball in the street, remembering how things were in Kansas City, I told Lee, "Don't show any fear, but be prepared to bluff or fight. We are greatly outnumbered here." One of them came walking toward us. I walked right up to him just to let him know he didn't scare me. He said, "Would you like to join us in a game?" We declined and said, "We're new here and just checking out the neighborhood." As we walked away, I told Lee, "We sure ain't in Kansas City anymore."

Lee enrolled in the local grade school and I enrolled in John Muir Junior High. Mr. Smith was my homeroom teacher. He was also one of the coaches, a fabulous man. You couldn't help but like him. In the seat behind me was a boy who had just arrived in town from Iowa, by the name of John Donald Allensworth. He always went by Don. We quickly became best friends. He gave me the first gift I ever received outside of the family. He said, "Here, I got you a present. It fits you perfectly." It was a screw and a ball pin. I cherished that pin. Wish I still had it. When young boys insult one another, it's a sign of affection.

The YMCA approached my mother and said they were getting up a group of boys for summer camp and asked if she would like to send us boys to camp. She said she'd love to, but couldn't afford it. They said they had a fund for that. They couldn't pay all of it but it would cover a large portion. They came up with a deal and Lee and I went to Little Green Valley camp in the San Bernardino mountains. Two things I remember about that camp. First, everyone had to memorize Psalm 23. When you memorized and recited it, you got a blue scarf and became a Blue Ragger. Everyone in camp was a Blue Ragger, except me. I tried but I just couldn't get it right. The last day at camp, the camp chief helped me through it and gave me the scarf.

Second, a kid in our cabin by the name of Chuck Hutton was a natural born comedian. When the other kids were hiking or swimming, we would stay in the cabin. I'd get him started talking and I'd laugh till my sides ached. After camp, I used to think of Chuck and wish I knew where he lived. One day I was walking up the street and here came Chuck walking toward me. He had just moved in a couple blocks from me. We became good friends. By the time I went into the Navy, I had become his hero. It remained that way until I married his fiancée and ruined that friendship.

I got a job selling newspapers. I'd stand on the corner until the signal changed, then walk between the cars hollering, "Herald Express, Evening News, get your latest race results." The Herald sold for five cents, the Evening news was three cents. I made two cents on the Herald, and one cent on the Evening News. We had to eat any papers we didn't sell, so sometime I made very little money. There were times I took a loss. We turned all our money over to our mother. She took three dollars a week to help pay the bills. On Sunday, she gave us back ten percent of our earnings to put in the collection plate at church. Every day she gave us a nickel for spending money. I always made sure I saved a dime for the Sunday movie. Any excess went into our bank account.

Next, I got a morning paper route delivering the Los Angeles Times. It paid $10 a month, selling papers every evening six days a week and delivering newspapers every morning seven days a week, 365 days a year. Not much free time for me, but I was on easy street and getting rich. One summer, the Times offered us a free trip to Catalina Island. You had to sell a certain number of subscriptions to the Los Angeles Times. I was a pretty good salesman so got a trip to Catalina and had a wonderful time. My brother wanted to go, but he just wasn't a good enough salesman, so I went door to door and sold enough for him and Mother to both go.

My brother Lee was two years younger than me, but always had a steady girlfriend. I'd never had a girlfriend. I was still very shy. His girlfriend had a very pretty girlfriend who wanted a date with me, so my brother talked me into double dating, which I agreed to. We went to a twenty-five-cent movie. This really upset me, paying fifty-cents to see a movie. I always went to the Reo, we called it the Rat House. Their price was only ten cents and they had a double feature, cartoon, a serial, and the works. Well, I was sitting there trying to watch the movie and get my money's worth. My brother and his girl weren't even watching the movie, they were just smooching away. My girl said, "Look at Lee and Mary." I said, "Ain't it disgusting," and went on watching the movie. As we were walking home, Lee and Mary were cuddling up real close. My date said, "Isn't that romantic?" I said, "if she gets any closer, she'll be on the other side." A little farther along she said, "I'm getting cold." I offered her my sweater. That did it, she never spoke to me again.

One day in junior high, I went to the agriculture garden on my lunch hour and filled a pocket with grasshoppers. The first period after lunch, I released the grasshoppers in the classroom. Grasshoppers were jumping everywhere. The girls were jumping up and screaming. It was hilarious, funniest prank I ever pulled. I never did tell anyone I was the one that released the grasshoppers, because this was my favorite teacher and I didn't want to get on her bad side.

Just before graduation from junior high, I was in a classroom where there was a beautiful girl I really liked. I think her name was Mary Davis. Now Carl Anderson sat right behind me and this guy had everything going for him. He was a tall, blonde, football player. He leaned past me and asked Mary to go out with him graduation night. She quickly said, "Oh no I can't. I already promised Ernie I'd go out with him. Isn't that right Ernie?" So, I went along with it. Now I'm getting scared. What if she was serious? As much as I'd like to date her, there's no way I'm going to spend my hard-earned money on a girl. On graduation night I got away fast for fear I'd run into her.

I went on to Freemont High School in Los Angeles. Every time I got a little money ahead, I'd either start up a crap game or get some kids together to match coins. I got caught gambling a couple times and got some demerits. One day, the Lone Ranger's side kick, Tonto, came to the school. The whole student-body was in the bleachers and Tonto on the football field giving a presentation. I got a few kids in the bleachers together and we were matching nickels. I got caught again. As soon as Tonto was through talking, the kids were swarming onto the field to get his autograph. I thought, what the heck, I might as well get his autograph. So I took a piece of paper out of my notebook and had him autograph it. While walking across the campus, a kid came up to me and said, "Did you get his autograph?" I showed it to him. He said, "Wow wish I had got one." I said, "I'll sell you this one for a nickel." He quickly forked over the nickel.

I thought, "Hey I've got something going here." I took the sheet of paper out of my notebook, tore it into six more pieces, signed Tonto's name on them, and sold them for five-cents each. I took my newly acquired wealth into the rest room and got up a crap game. As luck would have it, a teacher walked in. Now I'm in deep trouble for sure. The next day, someone came into the classroom and asked for Ernest Andrus, and I was off to see the principal. He gave me a good scolding, gave me a note to have my mother sign, and said "If you are ever caught gambling again I'm transferring you to a special school." I knew what school that was. It's Jacob Reese where all the troublemakers wind up. That would break my mother's heart so I really had to toe the mark, but I was so hooked into gambling I couldn't resist.

Sure enough, I got caught again. Now my brother was starting high school the next semester. We lived in an area where we were in two school districts. My brother chose the other, George Washington High, because they had an aeronautics class and Fremont didn't. So I had a plan. When they came and got me out of class the next day, I walked straight up to the principal and before he had a chance to say anything I said, "My brother's starting high school next semester and he's going to Washington. I think I ought to transfer to Washington."

He said, "Good idea." Washington High school was fine, but I couldn't get anyone interested in gambling.

I took a bookkeeping major because I liked working with figures, and math was the only subject I could get straight A's in. There was a math course that was compulsory for bookkeeping majors. The first day the teacher gave us the final exam. Two of us passed with 100%. The teacher said, "No need for you two to take the course because you already know everything I'm going to teach. I thought it interesting that we were both newsboys. The other boy was assigned to get the ice cream bars ready for lunch hour and I was assigned to get the candy bars ready. The rest of the hour was free time, which was good, because by this time I was up every morning at 4:00 delivering newspapers, selling newspapers on the corner in the evening, and then setting pins in a bowling alley until the middle of the night, so this was nap time. At the end of the semester, we took the exam again and were still the only ones to get 100%, so another semester of nap time. Can you imagine sleeping through class for two semesters and getting straight A's?

Music was a required subject, and I was stuck in a music appreciation class. I'm practically tone deaf, so most music sounds the same to me. I was sitting in the front row and when he started playing that Long Hair music, I could not stay awake. This is really irritating the teacher. He would play a record and ask us to identify it. I was just dosing off when he called my name. Knowing what one of his favorites was, I blurted out, "The Piano Concerto in B flat by Freddy Martin." All the students were laughing. I listened real careful and realized, no piano. Then it dawned on me that he was playing the Star Spangled Banner.

One day the teacher was standing up there swaying like an idiot, playing the Grand Canyon Suite, and said, "Can't you just see the donkeys?" I whispered to the kid next to me and said, "The only donkey I see is standing right there in front of us." From the look on his face, I think he heard me. It was obvious I wasn't going to make it through that class so I started ditching. I'd go to the auto shop, climb into a car and take a nap. I was the first student ever to flunk Music Appreciation at Washington High School.

In 1941, before the attack on Pearl Harbor, our social studies teacher had us write an essay. Mine was, "What I owe America and What America Owes Me." The essays were entered in the American Legion contest, and mine took third place for the State of California.

When I turned 18, I had accumulated a nice little bank account. I bought a 1930 Model A Roadster, with all the accessories, for $90. This car was like new, just like it came off the assembly line. The kids at school were astounded. Where in the world could any kid raise $90? They thought I was nuts to spend all that money on a Model A Roadster. The other kids were buying their Model A Roadsters from the junk yard for $5 and fixing them up for drag racing. This was 1941, the beginning of the hot rod—not like the expensive hot rods you see today. These were just souped up jalopies. People were talking about a Chevy that had just broken the speed record on the Utah Salt Flats hitting a fabulous 107 miles per hour. I was working in the bowling alley when someone came in and said that Chevy just pulled into the service station next door. I ran out to get a look at it. "I said that's not a Chevy." The owner said, "The frame is a Chevy. That's what they go by."

Now that I was 18 and had a car, my interest turned to girls. On Halloween evening, I was cruising Vermont Avenue with a couple of friends. We saw two girls walking. One was a gorgeous blonde. I pulled over, we introduced ourselves, and after a short conversation, offered them a ride. They declined. We turned down a side street to a park where they were having a bonfire. I said to my buddy, "Can't get my mind off that blonde. That was the most beautiful woman I have ever seen." He said, "Would you like to see her again?" I said, "Sure would." He said, "Well, here she comes."

Sure enough there she was, walking across the lawn, so we got better acquainted. I offered them a ride home. This time they accepted. This was my first real crush. I had a terrible inferiority complex. I put her on a pedestal and always felt like she was way too good for me. Her cousin was a photography student and used her as a model. She sent me some of the pictures and she was my pin-up-girl while overseas. After the war, I dropped by her house and her mother told me she was engaged to a childhood friend, so I never called on her again, but you never forget your first love.

I invited a couple girls I'd been driving home from school for gas money to go for a ride, and I'd bring my brother along for a double date. I had made a real noise maker out of my Model A. I installed several horns, a door bell, and a whistle. My brother and his girl were in the rumble seat, smooching away like a couple of lovers. I had installed a horn in the rumble seat area that went off like a fog horn. It started getting chilly so the two in the back had slid down underneath to keep warm. I pushed the button and that horn blasted. I heard two heads hit the overhead. I sure broke up that romance.

One day while cruising along Broadway with Don, we picked up a couple girls. We didn't really know these girls but we knew who they were. They were a year younger than me and in my brother's class in junior high. Before I left for the Navy, I introduced them to some of my friends, and during the war, they were dating them. More about this later.

On December 7, 1941, I was cruising the streets of Los Angeles with my buddy Don looking for chicks to pick up. The news came on the radio. Pearl Harbor had just been bombed. I said, "Where's Pearl Harbor?" Don said, "I don't know, but I think we are at war. Let's go join the Navy." We had a friend called Red, because he had red hair. Red had been bugging us to join the Navy and see the world. We had told him, "Wait till we get our high school diploma, then we'll consider it." We drove over to Red's house and said, "Let's go join the Navy." Red said, "Not me, I'll get killed. Wait till the wars over." We said, "We're going, with you or without you," so he went with us. They took Don and Red and turned me down because of my lazy left eye. I never gave up.

I would go to Los Angeles, get turned down, drive to Wilmington Beach, and get turned down again. On the sixth time, while standing in line, I noticed the Corpsman would say, "Cover your right eye and read the second line from the bottom, then cover your left eye and read the second line from the bottom." The line of volunteers was so long he was rushing them through as fast as he could, so I memorized the second line from the bottom. He said, "Cover your right eye and read the second line from the bottom." I read it off so fast he got suspicious and changed the eye chart, then said, "Cover your left eye and read the second line from the bottom." Now this is my good eye, so I read it off just as fast. That's how I got into the Navy.

MY PART IN WORLD WAR II

The war was raging on both fronts, and our enemies were advancing. Great Britain was being bombed. The Japanese were conquering island after island and had a stronghold in New Guinea. Both the east coast and west coast were blacked out. The US was all out for the war effort with factories across America producing war material. Troops were being shipped overseas as fast as they could be trained. I got my orders to report to the recruiting station in downtown Los Angeles. A few hundred of us boarded busses and convoyed to San Diego, stopping somewhere along the way for lunch at the government's expense. We arrived at bootcamp and got our hair cut. We went through a shower and were issued all new clothes, sea bag, etc., lined up for shots, and short arm inspection. I was immediately assigned to outfitting clothes for the new recruits. Bootcamp was five weeks. I spent the first two weeks outfitting clothes, then three weeks doing a little marching, practicing semaphores, and a little KP duty. That's all the training I got. When my unit went for the swimming test, I was in a crap game. I was hot and didn't want to quit. No one missed me.

I knew I couldn't kill anyone, so I wanted to be a Corpsman. A Corpsman is in charge of taking care of Marines. Don had been there ahead of me and volunteered for Hospital Corps. He instructed me on how to get what I wanted, and it all worked perfectly. Most recruits want to be either Motor Macs or Gunners Mates. Very few volunteer for Hospital Corps, one reason being that more Corpsmen are killed in action than any other position. So, when you take the exam, if you don't do too well in any field, you can volunteer for Hospital Corps and be pretty sure of getting it. Even though I had never taken Algebra or Geometry, I was the only one out of the 120 in my unit to get 4-0 on the math test, but I did poor on everything else, so had no trouble getting in the Hospital Corps.

I spent five weeks in Hospital Corps School at Balboa Park in San Diego. I had my 19th birthday there. They threw everything at you that a doctor learns in four years. Being a slow learner, I learned practically nothing. I wanted to go to Corona Naval Hospital for my training because I heard the duty there was great, and it was close to my home. Don told me how to arrange that. When you graduate, they give you a final exam. The ones with the highest scores get first choice. Most live in areas where there is no Naval Hospital close by, so they really don't care which one they train in. You know who the brains are, so you find two or three who don't care, and flash a $20 bill at them. Say, "If you pick Corona and trade with me, the $20 is yours." It worked. I was assigned to Bremerton Washington and traded it for Corona. No place in the Navy could you find better duty. When you went to breakfast, instead of getting green scrambled powdered eggs like you got in bootcamp, they had Filipino cooks that asked how you wanted your eggs cooked.

I spent about two months at Corona. Great duty, but really not learning much. I gave a few shots and felt sorry for the sailor I gave my first intramuscular injection to. I was nervous and tried to take it easy on him. Big mistake! I had to shove it the rest of the way into the muscle.

One of the Corpsmen got married to a girl in Riverside. I attended as a witness. The other witness was the bride's sister, a senior in high school. We hit it off real good, so I dated her while stationed there. She wanted to go to a movie. I think it was "Three Coins in a Fountain." She told me she was Pentecostal and didn't believe in going to movies. I said, "Then why did you ask me to take you?" She said, "I'm a back-slider."

I had 30 days of night ward duty. Every night duty, and every day liberty. A good sailor never turns down a liberty, so I was getting very little sleep. My dad had taken a job in Nevada and left his 1937, either a Chevy or a Plymouth, for me to use. If I got sleepy, I'd drive barefooted with the wind-wing open blowing wind into my face. Once in a while, I'd stop the car, get out, and run around the car a couple times to wake myself up. One night, coming back from Los Angeles, I had my girl-friend with me. She was asleep with her head on my shoulder. I didn't want to disturb her so I didn't open the wind-wing.

While driving through the canyon, I dozed off, crossed over, and hit the tool box on the running board of a Model A pickup coming the other way. The light switch was the pull-out type and the collision had turned out the lights. I had the brake on and was moving very slow, but the car kept moving. Through the wind shield it appeared like I was going through a jungle, knocking down trees. When the car finally stopped, I got out and what looked like trees were very tall weeds. The reason the car wouldn't stop was we were going almost straight down over a bank. My bumper was against a rock wall and beyond the wall was about a 20 foot drop off. Just before reaching the wall, there was a cable stretched along the wall. I guess it was put there knowing, sooner or later, some fool like me would come over the side. My front wheel had come off and my axel was caught in the cable holding me there. When the tow-in arrived, I showed him the insurance paper and he took my car to a shop in Westwood Village. Since my name is almost exactly the same as my dad's, the next day, I went to the insurance company in Los Angeles to file a claim and he didn't ask if I was the insured. He just said, "Are you Ernest E. Andrus?" I said, „Yes Sir." He said, "Sign here." I signed "Ernest E. Andrus." He said, "You're fully covered. There's no charge."

I called the shop in Westwood Village and asked when my car would be ready. He said, "I'll have it ready this week." I said, "I'll pick it up on Sunday." He said, "We're closed on Sunday. I'll leave the key under the floor mat." In the meantime, the insurance company called the hospital and left a message saying, "We cannot release the car to you. The contract shows the owner as 47 years old. You are not 47 years old." I went to the shop on Sunday, got the key from under the mat, and drove off. I never heard any more from them.

In November, 1942, a large group of us Corpsmen boarded a train. Destination — Oakland, California. We had a brief layover at the Los Angeles station. It seems we had the least priority of all the trains on the track. It took us three days to get from Los Angeles to Oakland. We were bussed from the train station to the ferry, crossed on the ferry from Oakland to San Francisco, put up overnight in some barracks, and bussed the next morning to Treasure Island.

After a few days, about 20 of us went to Goat Island to pick up our orders, then bussed across the Oakland Bay Bridge back to Oakland where we went aboard the USS Rochambeau (AP63), an old luxury liner that was being converted into a troop transport. It took about a month to get the guns installed. They didn't have time to install radar. Then we loaded supplies, cargo, and troops. Among the troops were the rest of the Corpsmen from Corona. Our Captain and the Captain of the USS Chicago were friends. The Captain of the Chicago said, "Delay for a couple days and I'll be ready and I'll escort you across the Pacific," so we shipped out on New Year's Eve.

The night before we shipped out, a few of us each bought a fifth of booze. We were standing in front of the liquor store and I was showing them how to put the fifth under your jumper, pull your stomach in, and you could smuggle the booze aboard without being detected. Another of the Rochambeau crew was watching and said, "I wonder if I can do that." This guy had a pretty big chow gut, so I said, "Let's try it." We put the fifth under his jumper. I said, "Pull it in, farther, farther." Finally, I said, "I think we've got it. You can probably get away with it." All of us Corpsmen managed with no problem.

I was in the sick bay when two of the guys came in laughing. I said, "What's so funny?" They said, "Remember that guy with the big gut? He came aboard pretty drunk. Being the last night in port, most of the officers had gotten permission to go ashore. So, the Chief Boatswain Mate was acting Officer of the Deck. This guy came staggering up the gang plank, saluted, and said, "Permission to come aboard, Sir." Boats took his club and wham … smashed the bottle, returned his salute, and said, "Permission granted. " This poor guy came staggering aboard, soaked with booze.

The USS Chicago escorted us all the way to New Caledonia. A destroyer escort came out to escort us into the bay. The USS Chicago headed for Guadalcanal and was immediately sunk. She wound up in Davy Jones Locker on the bottom of the bay we referred to as Iron Bottom Sound. While we were offloading, there was a bunch of natives working on the dock. Our crew was throwing candy bars down to them. The Chief in charge of the work crew explained to them the way to say thank you was to hold up your middle finger and say "F*** you!" It was funny watching those big black guys with bushy hair with red on top that stood straight up, grabbing candy bars and waving their middle fingers and hollering "F*** you!"

We loaded up with troops. One of the troops was a Naval Officer by the name of Jack Kennedy. No one had ever heard of Jack Kennedy at that time, so it was no big deal. We went into Espirito Santo in the New Hebrides Islands. Our troops had just recently taken the Island, so we had to follow a mine sweeper in. We disembarked our troops there. I assume that's where Jack Kennedy picked up his PT boat, because it was sunk off the coast of New Guinea. Don't believe that song about

Jack Kennedy saving a crew member's life. That's just propaganda. What really happened was two Soloman Islanders saved Jack Kennedy's life.

We loaded up with some US troops and some Australians and went to Brisbane, Australia. We sailed up the river and as we got near Brisbane, the jelly fish were so thick we were just plowing through them. The Aussies had a net stretched around a large area to keep the jelly fish out, and were swimming. I loved Brisbane! It was a beautiful city which had a nice climate, and wonderful people. I went to a skating rink, picked up a girl, and took her to a movie. I was telling her about an Aussie sailor I had a conversation with on the ship, and when I used the word 'bloody,' she said, "Don't use that word, it's vulgar." She continually used the Lord's name in vain. I thought, "How strange, bloody was vulgar but she thought nothing of using the Lord's name." I guess it just depends on the society you grew up in. I walked her home and the good night kiss was a very passionate one. She made quite an impression on me. After 74 years, I still remember her name, Melba McDonald. She said she was named after a famous opera star.

We left Brisbane and headed for Melbourne with an Australian destroyer for an escort. I was sure glad we had an escort because as we were cruising down the coast I was topside enjoying the scenery when I saw a wake coming toward us. I hollered, "Here comes a torpedo and it's gonna get us." The Captain turned the ship and was heading toward the wake. I thought, "What is he doing, he's gonna get us all killed." Turns out he knew exactly what he was doing, because he was able to maneuver the ship so the torpedo crossed our bow and missed us by more than 50 feet. The destroyer dropped depth charges. No more torpedoes. When we docked at Melbourne Portside, we got liberty. We heard that cigarettes were a good medium of exchange, so we lifted our bell-bottoms and stuffed cigarettes in the top of our socks. As soon as we stepped onto the dock, here came a bunch of kids. They went straight for our socks. Good bye cigarettes.

While in port, I met some of the crew from the destroyer. They were a cocky bunch… claimed they were unsinkable. Their ship was the only one of the original fleet still afloat. The next day, we left for Wellington, New Zealand, with them for our escort. This area was known as torpedo junction, and for good reason. About halfway across, we spotted something on the horizon. They went to investigate. We picked up an SOS. The "unsinkable" was going down. We couldn't stop for survivors. We were loaded with troops and patients. We stopped zigzagging and went full speed ahead to Wellington. We heard that most of the crew were rescued, because we weren't too far from Australia.

I didn't get ashore in Wellington. We were busy loading about 3,000 wounded aboard to take them back to the good old USA. They were mostly patients from the hospital in Auckland. Most of them were ambulatory and didn't require much care. A friend of mine from my school days came aboard carrying a stretcher. It was so good to see someone from home.

When we left Wellington, the Skipper said, "We've lost both of our escorts. I'm a jinx. No more escorts." From then on, we sailed alone with no escort. We had a few patients we had to keep locked up in the psycho ward. One of them had a cast on his leg. He said, "If this ship gets hit, don't come for me with a stretcher, cause I'll rip this cast off and I'll be the first one over the side." Somewhere out in the middle of the Pacific, in the middle of the night, there was a big explosion. The loud speaker came on with, "Fire in the engine room, fire in the engine room." My first thoughts and I think most everyone on the ship thought, "We've got a fish (torpedo) in the engine room." What had happened was a boiler had blown up.

When I got to the sick bay, I saw parts of his cast on the deck. I found him leaning on the rail, ready to abandon ship. I said, "Come on, I've got to get you back to the sick bay." He said, "I'm not budging from here till I hear the all clear." I have never really known fear.

Maybe that's because I've never been through what this poor guy had been through.

The one thing I liked most about my duty on the Rochambeau was being topside when the Golden Gate bridge got in sight. Every patient that could be there was up there watching. Here they were getting home alive. When that bridge came into sight, I'd watch their faces and saw every emotion imaginable, weeping, cheering, laughing, dancing, and some heads bowed, apparently thanking the Good Lord. That was so emotional and even now, after all these years, I am having trouble holding back the tears while writing this.

I made three trips to the South Pacific and back, taking troops over, and bringing the wounded back, then I was transferred to Treasure Island. I had my 20th birthday there.

When we pulled out to sea on the Merchant Marine ship, I was thinking back on my first trip across the ocean. I was told at that time the odds of making it back were about 50/50. By now the odds were much better because there were lots more men involved. The number of deaths and wounded were more, but the percentage was less. Now that's good news, but this is my fourth time. I figured I'm bucking the odds, but I didn't let that bother me. Like most young men, I was indestructible. I'll just do my job and I'll do fine.

When we got out to sea, the crew turned the ship into a gambling ship. Wow! This was great. I'm on a pleasure cruise … until I went broke. I met a couple guys that were bootlegging brandy. I negotiated a deal with them. We agreed on a wholesale price and they supplied me with a few bottles. I was bunked right by the brig, so I sold brandy to the guys in the brig. As soon as I sold my supply, I went out of business and went back to gambling. I was never broke again for the whole trip.

These Merchant Marines knew how to make money. When we got close to New Caledonia, they came up with a bunch of nice knives. They convinced the boots, the new ones, that their chance of survival on the Islands depended on a good knife. They sold out real fast. A young sailor said to me, "I'm worried. I don't have a knife and I lost all my money gambling." It just so happened I had a beautiful knife stored in my sea bag which I had no use for. The ironic thing is I won that knife in a crap game the last time I was in New Caledonia. I didn't want to take his knife, but he said, "What do I need with a knife? I've been here for four months and have never used the knife. What I need is some money!" So I covered him with $5 and won his knife. I took out my knife and showed it to the desperate boot and said, "What do you have to trade?" He said, "I've got this Bulova watch." He was wearing a watch just like the one I was wearing, so I pretty much knew the value. I thought, "A $5 knife for a $20 watch." I said, "You've got a deal." I packed it away in my sea bag.

There were two Mobile Hospitals on New Caledonia. I was at one but I had visited the other because I knew some of the Corpsmen there and the other Hospital was right on a beautiful beach. Christmas down under falls right in the middle of summer, so I approached a friend (I don't remember his name but he was from Tylor, Texas) and said, "We need to celebrate Christmas by going for a swim, and I know the perfect beach." He said, "How we gonna do that? They won't give us liberty and there's a guard at the gate." I said, "No problem! There's only one guard on the fence and he sticks pretty much to this end so we go up toward the other end and over the fence." We grabbed our swim trunks and were off to the beach. I was out there riding the waves when my friend hollers, "Hey, Ernie! What time is it?" You guessed it. I was wearing my Bulova watch. The watch was ruined, but fortunately I had another in my sea bag.

There was a sailor on my ward being treated for a venereal infection. He saw a picture of my cousin, Madeline. He said, "I'd sure like to write to her." I said, "I think she'd like that, grab a pencil and paper and I'll give you her address." He said, "I don't know how to read or write." I said, "How in the world did you get in the Navy if you can't read nor write?" So he filled me in on his background. It went something like this. He lived on a farm in the hills of Tennessee. When he was about seven or eight years old, his stepfather pushed him out the door and told him to leave and never come back. He said, "If you try to come back, I'll kill you." He had never been to school. He had never been off the farm, but he knew which direction town was so walked in that direction. He got to town and was hungry. He was looking in the window of a restaurant. A well-dressed man parked his car and started for the restaurant. He looked at him and said, "Are you hungry, kid?" He shook his head, "Yea." The man said, "Come on in, I'll buy you some dinner."

While dinning, he explained what was going on. The man said, "I've got a nice home in Beverly Hills, California. You're coming with me, kid, and I'll see that you're taken care of." The man was so good to him, he gave him his own room in a beautiful home in Beverly Hills. He never sent him to school. The man just used him as a servant. The sailor was so grateful as that little boy that he never complained. Just as he turned seventeen, Pearl Harbor was bombed. He wanted to do his part. He knew the Navy took seventeen year olds so he decided to join the Navy, but first he wanted to see his mother so he bid his Beverly Hills home good bye and hitchhiked to Tennessee.

When he walked up the drive toward the house, his stepfather came out on the porch with a shotgun and said, "Turn around and go the other way," so he never got to see his mother. He walked back to the recruiting station to join the Navy. The recruiting officer said being he's only 17 years old, they need a signature from his parents. When he explained his situation, he said, "OK, we'll waive that part." He passed the physical just fine. The recruiter handed him some papers and said, "Read these and sign them." He said, "I can't read or write." The officer said, "You can't get in the Navy if you can't read or write." He said, "I don't need to read or write to fire a gun and I want to do my part for my country."

The officer just stared at him for a while and said, "Sonny, you just joined the Navy." At bootcamp, the Chief said, "You are doing great. I don't give a damn if you can read or write, but you're going to have to sign your name in order to get paid, so I'm going to teach you to sign your name."

So he learned how to sign his name, but nothing more. I said, "I can't be writing your letters for you, so I'm going to teach you to read." Either I'm a poor teacher or he's a poor learner. I couldn't teach him anything. I finally just gave it up. One thing I noticed about this guy, he always knew everything that was going on before I did. I depended on either reading or asking questions. One day we walked to the mess hall together. When we got there, he started filling me in all the latest scuttlebutt. I said, "How do you know all this?" I hadn't heard any of it yet. He said, "While we were walking to the mess hall, we passed a lot of people talking, and I just keep my ears open."

After I transferred, I never knew what became of this guy until on the way back to the States, he was on the same ship. I filled him in on what I'd been doing in the last year and a half. I said, "Well! You said you didn't have to read or write to fire a gun. Did you get your chance to fire a gun?" Every time he'd try to talk about it, he'd tear up and change the subject. I thought, "Here's a guy who can neither read nor write, has no home to return to, no idea of where to go or what to do when he gets Stateside, and has apparently been through hell defending the country he loves. Isn't it great to be an American?"

I was sent to the transfer unit for reassignment. A shipment of Australian lamb came in. They were serving lamb three meals a day. The smell was so bad you could smell it before you got to the mess hall. It tasted good, but the smell made it hard to swallow. After a few days, a Chief came to the barracks and said, "A group of LST's just arrived and you've been assigned to one of them, so get your gear packed and right after chow I'll be by with a jeep to take you to your ship." When he pulled up in the jeep, there was another sailor on board, a young man about 17 years old. We became pretty well acquainted on the way to the docks. Neither of us had the slightest idea what an LST was. All I remember about this sailor was what he looked like, and I went on the LST 124 and he went on another LST. Never knew what became of him until 50 years later. Stay tuned...

The Skipper of the LST 124 was Captain Bartose. He was Chief Boatswain Mate on President Roosevelt's yacht when the war broke out. Roosevelt gave him a commission and made him Captain of the LST. This was a wise decision because he knew all there was to know about ships and he knew how to handle men.

We had a landing craft lashed down on the top deck. I think it was an LCI. We took the LCI, it's crew, and a few Seabee's they had brought with them from the States to the Russell Islands. We emptied the ballast tanks on the starboard side so the LST tilted to port, un-lashed the LCI, and it slid off into the water. It is pretty neat how that works. We spent the rest of the war taking islands back away from the Japs. In addition, there was a lot of boring trips between islands haul-ing everything from shoes to troops, and even a tank deck load of tele-phone poles. I can't remember the names of all the islands we invaded, but here's some of them: Espirito Santo, Russell Islands, Guadalcanal, Tulagi, Bougainville, Munda, New Ireland, Emirau, Manus, Saipan, Tinian, Peleliu.

There wasn't a lot for me to do between sick calls, so the Captain was having me stand watches and do work details. The first-class Pharmacists Mate was a Jewish podiatrist by the name of Strouse who was from New Jersey, I think. He was one of the smartest men I ever knew. He knew how to get what he wanted and proved it many times for his own bene-fit and for the benefit of the ship. Strouse had one fault... he didn't care who he had to walk over to get what he wanted. Maybe that's not a fault? I'm not sure!

He said to me, "You are not part of the ship's company. Your orders come from the Bureau of Medicine and Surgery, Washington DC. The Skipper has no right to put you on watches and work details. I'm going to do something about it." I said, "Leave it alone. The only watches I stand are on the con. I lean against the bulkhead and take a nap. If the Skipper wants a cup of tea, I go get it for him. The work details are always supplies coming aboard. I'm going to turn to and do my part, whether ordered to or not." But he wouldn't let it go and he went over the Captain's head.

Two doctors came aboard to investigate. The senior officer told the Captain, "Andrus stands no more watches outside the sick bay and no more work details. I'm leaving this other doctor on board to see that these orders are followed." The other doctor was an intern right out of college and stuck on this LST for the rest of the war, so he disliked me right from the start, and it got worse as time went on. The Captain transferred Strouse off the ship and Freddie Heiber came aboard as a replacement. I was going to miss Strouse but Freddie was regular Navy and a pleasure to work with.

We were beached at Kucom Beach, Guadalcanal. One of the Seabee's we had dropped off on the Russell Islands came aboard. He was quite an entrepreneur. He had a bag full of rings. I knew he had to be good at something or he wouldn't be a Seabee, but these were beautiful gold rings with cat eye settings. They had to have been made by a professional. I said, "Where did you get these?" He said, "I make them myself." I said, "Where do you get the gold and the cat eyes?" He said, "There's a gold mine on the island, guarded by a native. I learned enough of their language to communicate with them. I bribed the guard to let me go in and help myself to whatever I need." I said, "What about the cat eyes?" He said, "There are plenty of those among the coral, but it's too dangerous to dive for them. Some of the natives are expert at this, so I hired me a couple natives."

While we're walking through the ship, we came to a crap game. The new Seabee started covering some bets. I knew all the odds and I watched him. He never covered a bet unless the odds were in his favor. If the odds were in his favor it didn't matter how small or how large the amount, he covered it. I learned something there that paid off in the future, but it sure takes the fun out of going to a Casino because the odds are always in their favor.

We were at New Ireland and the LCI that we had taken into the Russell's tied up alongside us. They said, "We've been doing ferry duty between Islands and we always help ourselves to a little of the cargo. We have plenty of beer, so any of the crew who wants to come over for a beer bust, you're welcome." I naturally joined them and drank all the beer I could hold. I always enjoyed a good cold beer, but it never had an effect on me except to make me spend a lot of the time in the head. When I climbed back on our ship, I said, "I need something to get a buzz on," so I reached into a life raft and grabbed a small bottle of brandy. When that brandy hit my stomach, I was loaded. They announced there was a movie on the Island so there was liberty for starboard side. I was port side, which meant I had the duty. I wanted to see the movie and figured that I wouldn't be gone long and nobody's going to need a Corpsman, so I jumped ship. Lot of good it did me! I was too drunk to enjoy it. I don't even remember what the movie was.

When I got back, a mess cook had cut his finger and found nobody on duty in the sick bay so he put me on the report. All he needed was a band aid! I was given a Captain's Mast. Our Skipper was lenient. He was a regular Navy man who came up through the ranks. He probably had done what I did more than once during his time in the Navy. He said, "Deserting your post when on duty is a serious offense. You will have to be punished. No liberty for three days." We were heading back to the Russell Islands and would be at sea for two days. Not much punishment.

When we beached at the Russell Islands, port side had liberty. I had one more day of restriction and couldn't leave the ship. Who cares! What is there to do on this desolate Island anyway outside of get your feet on dry land and maybe go for a run. When the crew came back aboard, there was a lot of excitement. There was a Red Cross nurse on the beach giving out coffee and donuts. Wow! I hadn't seen a woman in over a year. I just needed the assurance that there still is such a thing, not to mention the donut. I hadn't tasted any pastry for at least a month! If you bite into a cockroach, he crunches, and you know what you just bit into, so I tried breaking up the pastry to get rid of any cockroaches. While doing so I'd brush out all the weevil. By the time you finish, there's nothing left, so why bother.

The next day was starboard liberty, so I talked Pete into taking my watch. I just kept going through the line. About the tenth time in line a sailor said, "You sure like donuts, don't you?" I told him about the weevil and he said, "What do you think is in these?" I broke one open and, sure enough, lots of weevil. I said, "I think every man on the island is in line here and I don't think they came for coffee and donuts."

We went to Carter City, Tulagi for some repairs. Carter City was a bunch of Quonset huts set up as a boat repair unit. We went there often. The USS Hoel (DD533) pulled into the bay. My friend, Red Morris, was part of that crew. He's the one who wanted me and our friend Don to join the Navy with him to see the world. When Pearl Harbor was bombed, we went to Red and said, "Let's go join the Navy." He wanted to wait till the war was over because he knew he'd be killed. We said, "We're going with you or without you," so he went with us. I took a small boat over to his ship. Red was very depressed. He said, "You guys have been out here all during the war and never worried about getting killed. This is my first trip out and I'm going to die and I know it." I tried to get him to take a more positive outlook, but with no avail. He had this premonition and it wouldn't go away. He went to Leyte and went down with the ship. This was his first and last battle. A short time after the war, I was managing a Thrifty drug store on South Broadway in Los Angeles when his mother came into the store. Being I was the last one to see him alive, I thought she might like to have a talk, so I offered to come by her apartment after I closed the store. I knocked several times, but she would not answer the door. Don said, "I think she blames us for his death."

A refrigerator ship was docked at Tulagi, not too far from where we were. Any fresh meat would be a treat so we went over to see what they had to offer. Our supply officer, whom I think it was Don Van Nest, loaded up our reefer with New Zealand ox, beef, and pork. We no sooner got out to sea when the doctor went up to the galley to get a pork roast. He wanted to use it to give us Corpsmen a lesson in suturing. He said, "When a bunch of wounded come aboard, one man can't do it all." When he saw all that pork, he told the cook, "You're going to kill everyone on the ship. Do you know how many times that pork has set out on the dock in this heat before you got it into the reefer. Throw it all over the side. That's an order." As soon as I heard this I went up to the galley and said, "We need another pork roast. We need more practice." I cut that roast up into chops, got out our hot plate, and we had a pork chop feast.

I went ashore on Guadalcanal, and walked over to the Red Cross to glance at the registrar to see if there was anyone on the island I knew. There was the name Eugene Hathaway from Hiawatha, Kansas. Wow! This was my buddy when I was thirteen years old. We used to ride our bicycles all over town, singing at the top of our lungs. I stopped by his camp and this was a real fun time reminiscing. He said, "Every time a beer shipment comes in, they issue us each two beers. I don't drink beer and I have a lot of beer stashed in my locker." I always had a couple bottles of ethyl alcohol in my pocket for bartering. We didn't often get beer on our ship so I traded him two ounces of alcohol for a beer.

I don't care much for warm beer so I went back to the reefers and told the man on duty. "Let me have the key to the reefer. I need to inventory my penicillin." Those reefers have a very low overhead. You almost have to crawl in. I was checking around for a good place to hide my beer when I walked right into an electric fan and sliced my head open real good. The doctor and I were never on very good terms, so I didn't want him stitching up my head. I said, "Pete needs the experience. Why don't we let him do it?" I felt secure with Pete practicing on me. He was my best friend. When I went back to get my cold beer, it was gone.

We left Guadalcanal in a convoy heading for Pearl Harbor. A soldier came in with a very high fever. I checked all the symptoms and decided he had sun stroke. I went to get the doctor and said, "I have a patient with sun stroke." He said, "How do you know it's sun stroke?" I said, "He has all the symptoms." He said, "I'll do the diagnosing," He diagnosed the soldier with appendicitis. I'm standing there wondering, "What's going on here? I could be wrong about the sun stroke, but I know this guy doesn't have appendicitis." The only thing I could figure was he's just trying to tell me he knows more than I do. He covered himself by saying, "We can't operate because his temperature's too high. We're passing an Island in a few minutes where there's a Mobile Hospital. I'll go make the preparations for transfer." I hope he didn't send him with that diagnosis, or if he did, I hope they checked him out before they started operating.

We were passing an island covered with pineapple trees. The Skipper said, "We're going to have pineapples tonight." We broke away from the convoy. He sent a crew over on an LCVP to pick pineapples. This didn't surprise me because I knew he loved to pick fresh fruit. He told me once he didn't believe I was from California because I had never picked avocados. On Espirito Santo, he had me helping him pick plumbs. He said, "I discovered a plumb tree. I need a volunteer to help me pick plumbs. Andrus, you just volunteered, let's go." Now these guys in the LCVP were approaching the island when someone started firing bullets over their head. I think that plantation owner was just protecting his crop. I teased the Coxswain, told him he was a coward. He said, "Bullets are the best unwelcome sign I know of."

When we entered Pearl Harbor, the Skipper cruised right up next to the battleship Arizona so we could get a good look at it. At that time, the upper decks were still sticking out of the water.

May 21, 1944 is the saddest day of my wartime life. I was walking into Honolulu when there was a big explosion, followed by more explosions. I could see the smoke and fire. I know that large pieces of metal were flying through the air, up to one or two miles. I was far enough inland that I was out of danger. The scuttlebutt was that LST's were blowing up in West Loch. Someone assured me that our ship had moved out of the danger zone and where to find it when I returned. When I got back to the ship, I couldn't find out much of anything. There was a gag order. No one was allowed to mention it, not even among themselves.

The explosions continued all through the night. The newspaper played it down like a small mishap when actually six LST's, many small craft, ship loads of equipment and supplies, were all lost, plus over 500 casualties. They feared if the Japanese knew what really happened, they would know that something big was coming down and it wouldn't be hard to figure out what it was. They didn't want them to get there ahead of us, like we did to them at Midway.

No one heard about this because the gag wasn't lifted until the 1960's, which is ridiculous because once we invaded Saipan, there was no reason to keep it a secret. I didn't know much about our ship's part in it until years later at our reunions after the gag had been removed. Two books have been written on this subject. William L.C. Johnson PhM1/c was on one of the ships involved and wrote the first book entitled, *The West Loch Story*. The most recent book was written by Gene Eric Salecher, entitled *The Second Pearl Harbor*. I have both books, autographed by the authors. Salecher contacted me and told me he was going to write the book and wondered if I could give him any information.

I wasn't able to help much because I was on liberty at the time, so I referred him to a couple shipmates who were on board. My shipmate and good friend Leo Bednarczyk was a good eye witness and was involved in retrieving dead bodies. We are both mentioned briefly in his book. I have never tried to get Leo to talk about it because I know it's hard for him. When Leo and I get together, we talk about the good times. He was our Oil King and he calls me Pill Popper. He tells everyone I saved his life because I gave him a shot once. I tell them I saved his life twice, once when I gave him the shot and again when I took him to the Grand Canyon and didn't push.

The author of *The Second Pearl Harbor* did a lot of research and I learned a lot about the disaster that I didn't know. I knew some soldiers were passing ammunition from a raft onto an LST and I always suspected one of them dropped a shell. After reading his book, I'm convinced it was a cigarette butt. Everyone smoked back then and if you read his book you'll see why I've come to that conclusion.

My battle station was sick bay, so the only way I saw the fireworks was to open the hatch above the sick bay and stick my head out. Saipan was the biggest display of fireworks I had ever seen. I said, "Lord, what am I doing here? A monkey could do what I'm doing with a little training. Just get me home alive." Then a message came over the loud speaker, "Corpsmen to the tank deck, Corpsmen to the tank deck, wounded coming aboard, wounded coming aboard." I rushed to the tank deck, grabbed the foot of a stretcher holding a Marine who appeared to be dead. We got him to the sick bay and when we put the stretcher down, he moved his head. The doctor checked him out and said, "No vital signs, he's dead come help me with the others." I said, "No he's not, he moved his head." He checked him again and said, "He's dead" and walked away.

This doctor was my commanding officer and we never liked each other. I knew if I didn't follow his orders, I could be court-marshaled, but do to me what they want, I wasn't going to let this guy die. I poured blood plasma into him unit after unit for what seemed like all night. There was no place to hang the bottle so I held it up with one arm until the bottle was empty, snap on another bottle, and switch arms.

When he came back to life, the doctor said, "Your patient's going to live. I need your assistance in an arm amputation." We had converted a mess hall table into an operating table with a flood light over it, knowing that sooner or later we were going to need it. He had a Marine on the operating table, a good looking young man around 18 years old. We gave him a spinal and told him to start counting. When he got up to 20, the doctor started cutting. He continued counting to nearly a hundred before he stopped. I was taking his blood pressure. When the doctor started sawing through the bone, he gave out a yell, swung his head around, and vomited all over me. I jumped back and the doctor said, "Keep taking his blood pressure." The doctor said, "We need type O blood right now." I said, "I'm type O, take mine." Every few minutes he'd say, "We need more blood." I kept saying, "Take some more, he needs it more than me."

Fortunately, word got out that we needed type O blood and sailors were lining up by the sick bay wanting to give blood. Now I hadn't had any sleep for 96 hours, I'm covered with vomit, I'd given away most of my blood, my arms felt like they were going to fall off from holding that blood plasma above my head all night, when the first class pharmacists mate, Freddie Heiber, said, "Here, get rid of this," and handed me the arm. When I took the arm and saw that hand hanging down, my stomach did a flip. I said, "What shall I do with it?" He tossed me a towel and said, "Wrap it in this and throw it over the side. There's so much flesh in the water, a little more won't make any difference." I felt so sorry for this Marine. I was thinking, "What's he going to say when he wakes up and sees his arm gone?"

When he woke up he looked over at where his arm should have been and said, "Thanks doc, I can go home now." He also said, "Whatever that was you gave me, sure was good stuff. I only counted up to six and I was out."

We went back to my patient and the doctor said, "He's going to live. He has an arm and a leg that need to come off, but if we amputate now he won't make it." I had to open my big mouth and irritate him more than I already had. I said, "Good! I didn't keep him alive so you could take his arm and leg. If it was my arm and leg I'd say leave it alone. I'll take my chances." It was obvious I didn't approve of him being so quick to amputate. This hurt his ego, I'm sure. I think he thought I was acting like I knew more than he. In this case, he was wrong and I was right. There's no way he was going to court-martial me now, because I just saved a man's life.

I was not smart enough to know how much blood you can give and still live. I looked it up later and discovered I gave more than the limit. This doctor knew that and he didn't try to stop me. He must have hated me even more than I hated him. I went back to my patient so tired I was about to drop. All he did was complain, complain, complain. I smiled at him and said, "I wish I'd let you die." I knew that all this complaining was a good sign. That morning I thought to myself, "Thank you, Lord! Now I know why I'm here." I never lost a patient during the whole war, but this was the only life I actually saved.

I had another patient who was caught in the same machine gun fire. He had more than one wound but the one that really concerned me was where a bullet had gone through his head and he was having brain seepage. I knew that if he went to sleep he would not wake up, so every chance I had I'd go over and talk to him to keep him awake. He didn't seem to be in much pain, but he had trouble talking because he couldn't recall some words. He couldn't say water, so it didn't take long to realize when he said milk he wanted water. On June 17, a hospital ship arrived.

I put all my patients on an LCVP (Landing craft vehicle personnel) and took them to the Hospital ship). On the way, a tanker signaled us. They had a patient and asked if we would take him with us. They lowered him down into our small boat. He was Japanese, in a coma, and had no medical care. I couldn't keep the Marines off him. They kept reaching out of their stretchers and taking a poke at him. When we reached the hospital ship, a doctor came down the gang plank. I said, "Take this one first, he's in the worst condition." The doctor said, "That's a Jap, leave him till last, and if we're lucky he'll fall overboard." I thought, "What hatred war creates."

Just recently, I got a Facebook message saying, "You were at Cherakano Saipan? My grandfather was there. He was shot through the head and taken aboard an LST. He died on the Hospital ship on June 19th. I'm not surprised that he didn't make it, but I had hopes. If they could have just kept him alive, the brain has a way of healing itself, just like any other part of the body. The remaining part of his brain would just have to learn what he had lost. Life is worth living, regardless of the condition."

I think the worst thing about death is the heart break to the loved ones. I can still hear my mother's screams when my older brother died of cancer at the age of 15, so if you love your mother, you just gotta outlive her.

We were stuck on the reef and couldn't get off until the tide came in. Now when you're on an enemy beach, you want to off-load, on-load, and get off there as fast as you can. This is not a very safe place to be. When the tide came in, we still couldn't get off. Some LST's and some tugs offered to pull us off. The Skipper was a stubborn man, declined the help, said he could do it himself. A couple incidents happened while we were stuck on the reef that are worth writing about. First, a seaman came to me carrying two machine guns and said, "Let's go ashore and look around." Anyone who knows me knows I can never resist a new adventure, so off we went holding the guns above our head because the water from the reef to the beach was chest deep. When we reached the beach, my shipmate started to put the clip into his gun. I said, "Put that back into your pocket. We're not going to kill anybody. My job is to save lives, not take them."

We rounded a corner in Cherakanoa and he quickly brought his gun into firing position, but he couldn't fire because there was no clip in his gun. I said, "What are you doing?" He said, "Those look like Japs." I said, "Those are Japs. Take a better look and you will see a soldier at each end of that long table. They are getting ready to feed the prisoners. Good thing that gun wasn't loaded or you would have killed someone for sure."

We started up a dirt road out of town, here came a couple soldiers with a herd of prisoners. We moved into the ditch to give them room. A prisoner broke ranks and was running down the ditch straight toward us. We aimed our Tommys at him. He slid to a stop and got back in line.

Later, when we got back to the LST, I was top side and saw a plane coming low over the island. We had our bow doors open and the ramp down. It looked like he was heading straight for our tank deck. This was before suicide planes (Kamikazes), so his intention was probably to drop a torpedo or a bomb. It seemed every gun in the area opened up on him and he headed straight up and got away.

Another time, a Marine came aboard, scared to death, shaking and crying. I couldn't calm him down so I sent for the doctor. He talked to him, gave him some Phenobarbital, and calmed him down. I got him to open up and tell me what his problem was. His story, as well as I can remember it, is that it all started at Tarawa. He was so scared he couldn't get over it. I said, "If you were at Tarawa and weren't scared, you just weren't human." He went on to say he was in such bad shape they sent him to Pearl Harbor to recuperate. They would give him guard duty. Here he was on a friendly Island standing guard duty, scared and shaking.

He was put on an LST for the invasion of the Marianas. His LST was one of the LST's that blew up. He landed in the water, was rescued, scared but unhurt. They put him on another LST and he went ashore at Saipan. As soon as he hit the beach, a machine gun opened up on him. He dove under a tank, a bullet came through his helmet, whirled around inside the helmet a few times, and stopped. He showed me his helmet, the bullet was still there. He left his gun under the tank and waded out to our ship. While he's telling me his story, some of the crew came through the sick bay, laughing. I asked, "What's so funny." They said, "You know the little black Stewart Mate, Taylor? He was setting out on deck having a cigarette. A plane came over and strafed right above his head. That little black boy turned white." They thought it was funny. Being he didn't get hurt, I thought it was funny, too.

I looked at my patient. His eyes got big and he said they're out to get this ship and they are going to get it. He took off and I never saw him again. I worried about him because he's out there running scared with no gun and no helmet. I kept the helmet until I got my orders to go home. I left it with a few other neat souvenirs I didn't want to get caught with that might keep me from going home.

The Captain promoted me to PhM2/c. Before the day was over, the doctor took it away from me. He went to the Captain and said, "He's not ready for second class. I'll promote him when he's ready." This gave me even more reason to hate that doctor. He was right, I was not ready, but being a depression kid, that money meant a lot to me.

He said, "I'll give you an exam. If you pass, you can have the rate back." I said, "What's the test on?" He said, "The book." I said, "What part?" He said, "All of it." I said, "When's the test?" He said, "Tomorrow." I'm a slow reader and it's a big book. I knew I could never pass the test, so I flunked it. Never did get my rate back.

The Captain looked at my records and said, "They're rotating some of the crew back to the States after so many months of sea duty. You had more sea duty than they have when you came aboard. I'm going to get you rotated." Good news! I waited. We were still Island hopping. Finally, we got a message, "Your replacement is in Pearl Harbor. We're going to get him a flight as soon as possible." Weeks went by, no replacement.

Finally, a message came, "Your replacement was flown into Guadalcanal." We were nowhere near Guadalcanal. We pulled into Espirito Santo. His gear came aboard. No replacement. We made a few trips between Espirito Santo and New Caledonia, even made a trip to Wellington, New Zealand. (Great Liberty). I was just leaving the ship, walking across the pier, when they announced "President Roosevelt just died. America is in mourning. All establishments serving alcohol is off limits until 1600 (4 PM)."

My best friend, Peter George Nickelson, said, "What did you miss most in the last year?" I said, "Fresh milk, ice cream, and women, not necessarily in that order." He said, "Well, it's all available right here. Let's find a nice restaurant and start with a thick steak, milk, and ice cream." We went to a Greek restaurant and did just that. When we went to pay for our meal, a young man at the checkout looked at Pete and said, "You're Greek." Pete looked at him and said, "You're Greek."

The young man rattled off a name about a mile long and Pete said, "Boniotis Yode Papanicholouge." He took Pete to the kitchen to meet his parents. When they came back, he said, "Your meal is on the house." We bought a fifth of scotch, rented a room, and hid the scotch in a drawer, then went to a dance, picked up some girls, and after 4:00 PM took them to a night club. The Captain and some other officers were sitting at another table. One of my group heard the skipper say, "Who's that gal with Andrus?" I noticed he kept eyeing her all evening. She said she was a Wren and had to get back to her base. I made a date with her for my next liberty and promised to bring another sailor for her sister.

We never used the room but went up to get our scotch and someone had stolen it. On my next liberty, we were having a ship dance in a rented hall. I took her to the dance. The Captain kept cutting in. I know this was good for her ego with the Captain showing all that interest in her. I got disgusted and said, "I'm going back to the ship." She said, "I've got to get back to base," and we left together. I don't know for sure, but I've got a hunch she went back to the dance and the Skipper got what he was after.

A couple months went by, still no replacement. We pulled into New Caledonia. The Captain, the doctor, the first class pharmacist mate, and my striker all got rotated to go back to the States. The Executive Officer was promoted to Captain. He said, "I'm going to transfer you off the ship. They will have to send me a replacement because you're the only Corpsman left on board." The next day, Albert Anderson PhM1/c came aboard. I showed him where everything was, gave him the key to the narcotics, and was off to the same transfer unit where I was a year and a half before when I went aboard the LST.

I got a passport on an Army transport heading for San Francisco. Oh happy day! My friend Pete was on the same ship so I got out my little black book and as soon as we got to San Francisco I lined us up with a double date. We had one last liberty together before he caught a train to Brooklyn and I headed for Los Angeles. They gave me a 30-day rehabilitation leave, and then sent me to San Diego for reassignment. When they looked at my record, they asked, "What do you want?" I said, "Long Beach Naval Hospital." They said, "You got it, but we'll have to wait for an opening so just hang tight." After a few days, they said, "OK, you'll be on a bus tomorrow morning for Long Beach, so no liberty tonight." I went over to the pool for a swim and was lying there getting some sun when the broadcast "The War is Over" came loud and clear over the speakers.

I ran and changed my clothes. I just had to get in on this celebration, but I didn't have liberty, so it was over the fence and over the hill. San Diego would have been the best bet, but I figured if I got to Los Angeles, I'd have a car. I hitchhiked to Los Angeles, borrowed a car, picked up my cousin, Madeline, and we cruised downtown Los Angeles.

Never was there ever a celebration like this. The streets were crowded. Service men were kissing all the women. Streamers and confetti were flying out the windows of all the buildings. Now, I had to return the car quick and hitch a ride back to camp in time to catch my bus to Long Beach. I didn't want to blow this opportunity to transfer to Long Beach.

At the hospital, they took a look at my record and said, "What do you want?" I said, "Transportation." I picked transportation because I loved to drive and if you're in transportation you can bring your car on base. They said, "You'll have to wait. There's no opening right now." I said, "What do you have to offer?" They showed me a list. I picked Dermatology because I wanted the opportunity to work with this particular doctor. He was famous because while in the European theatre he'd developed a burn treatment that was saving lives.

The patients on this ward loved me. Every other Corpsman on the ward was inexperienced, right out of Corps school. There were several patients with third stage of Syphilis. Their poor butts looked like they'd been used for pin cushions from all the shots they'd had. I'd line them up in a row on cots then start a conversation about baseball. Everyone in those days was interested in baseball. While we're all talking baseball, I'd walk along, slap their butt, and hit them with a needle. The first time I did that, when I finished they said, "When do we get our shots?"

I had a problem off and on with an ulcer that was giving me trouble. I didn't want to turn myself in and miss out on my liberties, so I transferred to the ulcer ward. This way, I could treat my ulcer and still go on liberty.

Now people were getting out on the point system. I had more points than anyone there except the married men. They got extra points for being married. Someone came to me and said, "There's a married man in transportation that's getting discharged in about a week. I need a guard on the prison ward. If you'll take that job, I'll get you into transportation." This was an easy job. I'd just stand guard by the door. If a prisoner got permission to go to small stores or whatever, I was supposed to call for a guard for each prisoner, and they usually went in pairs. They would beg with me not to call for guards because everyone would know they were prisoners and that was embarrassing. I would say, "Give me your word you'll come right back so I don't get in trouble and I won't call for guards." This humane treatment had worked fine on the psycho ward aboard ship, so I figured it should work with prisoners. Not one of these guys ever let me down. The very next day after I transferred to transportation, two prisoners took the clubs away from their guards, beat them unconscious, took their clothes, and escaped.

In December, 1945, my points added up. I was transferred to San Pedro where I received my discharge. They were offering $50 if you would ship over. A lot of guys were shipping over just to get that $50. I liked the Navy and I liked sea duty, but I found that authority over me hard to take. $50 couldn't tempt me. Once you shipped over, you're stuck in the Navy for another four years, like it or not.

TRANSITIONING OUT OF THE NAVY INTO CIVILIAN LIFE

I WAS TRANSFERRED TO LONG BEACH NAVAL HOSPITAL IN AUGUST, 1945. WHILE THERE, WAIT-ing to be discharged, a lot of things transpired. Whenever I had over-night liberty, I'd spend the night at my mother's. I had a cousin named Frank. Frank and I hung out together a lot in our teens but Frank was an unusual young man. He had a stepfather named Larry. Larry was a big man, tough and mean. He was a hard worker, a chain smoker, a heavy drinker, and fought at the drop of a hat. Frank thought the world of his stepfather and wanted to grow up to be just like him. Larry drowned duck hunting when Frank was only thirteen. Frank's mother was an al-coholic. He grew up in poverty. He tried running away from home once, then decided he had to stick around to protect his two younger sisters from the cruel world and an alcoholic mother.

As soon as Frank was old enough, he followed me into the Navy. After the war, he shipped over. Life in the Navy was far better than what he was used to. When he had liberty, he came to my mothers. He said, "Wish she was my mother."

By the age of thirteen, Frank was hooked on cigarettes. While in the Navy, he was fast becoming an alcoholic. One night we both wound up at my mothers. He showed up with a black eye and a messed-up face. I said, "What happened to you?" He said, "I was in a bar and this guy was a lot bigger than me but I was uglier than him and thought I could whip him."

The next morning, he said, "I just got paid, let's go out for breakfast." He said to the waitress, "I'll have six eggs, six strips of bacon, fried potatoes, and toast." She said, "Are you serious?" He said, "I'm serious." She said, "How do you want your eggs?" He said, "Anyway I get them." She turned to me and said, "What would you like?" I said, "The same." I said, "Frank, I sure like your kind of breakfast." I could understand him shipping over. The Navy was good for him. He had no home to return to. My mother had taken in his oldest sister, Madeline, and his youngest sister, Lillian, was in a foster home.

I had a friend named Louie. He was in the Air Corps. He was hitchhiking from Idaho to California and found a puppy along the highway. He had trouble getting rides because she smelled so bad. He cleaned her up, had her spayed, got her shots, and gave her to me. I called her Princess. I loved that little mutt. I didn't even have to house break her. No one was home during the day. We would lock her on the screened porch. The first one home would open the door and she would dart out into the yard to do her thing. Never once did she make a mess on the porch.

She was easy to train, but I knew nothing about training a dog and everything I taught her I regretted later. For instance, when I came home, she'd come running for me. I'd pat my chest and she would jump right up against my chest so I would catch her. After a few times, I no longer had to pat my chest. Whenever she saw me, here she'd come, … wham … right up into my arms. If it happened to be a damp day, and her feet were muddy, and I was in my dress uniform … I had regrets.

After I bought my beautiful convertible, I said, "I'm not going to be opening the door for you," so I'd pat the top of the door. She'd run and jump onto the door and crawl into the passenger seat. Pretty soon, all we had to do was start for the car and away she'd go. It didn't take long until I was getting a lot of toenail scratches in my paint... regrets again. I found it's much easier to train a dog than to un-train one.

My friend from high school, Chuck Hutton, who sort of held me up as his hero during the war, was also the one that I had introduced the two girls to mentioned earlier. He was now engaged to Anna Mae Berger. Chuck had a beautiful 39 Mercury convertible. He took such good care of it that if anyone touched it he would grab a cloth and polish the spot they touched. He said he felt so proud cruising around in that car with this blonde sitting next to him. Chuck and I did a lot of things together. Anna Mae would get a girl friend to come along for my date when we double dated. I loved his Mercury and was in the market for a car, which was hard to come by at the time because none were built during the war. One day there was just Chuck, Anna Mae, and me in the car when he said he was going back east for a few months to try out a job opportunity and to start writing a book. He needed to sell the car. We quickly came up with a deal. I jokingly asked if the blonde came with the car.

Apparently, Anna Mae took this to mean I was interested in her. After Chuck left, I couldn't shake her. She would say she needed to talk to me. At first, I thought she missed Chuck and needed someone to talk to. We were seeing a lot of each other. Soon we were dating pretty regular. I knew she was dating other guys besides me and she certainly wasn't sitting home waiting for Chuck to return. I tried several times to break it off but she just wouldn't accept it. I really didn't like her because she was a spoiled brat.

I always felt that was no fault of her own because she had no upbringing. Her father committed suicide when she was very young and her mother was a wonderful woman but had no idea how to raise kids, so she just grew up without any discipline and learned how to get her own way by hook or by crook, or by throwing a tantrum. I found out years later that she told her best friend that all her girlfriends wanted me and she was going to prove she could get me. I think all this was just in her head, because if any of her girlfriends wanted me, it was news to me. We did eventually get married. She gave me three precious little girls, and I do mean "gave." She always maintained she didn't want them. When I got home from work she would say, "I've had them all day. Now they are yours."

She never gave a baby a bath, said she was afraid she would break them. Unless I was working late, I was the one who tucked them in at night. I loved doing all of this. I think one of the greatest feelings is sitting in a chair, holding a baby in your arms until you both start falling asleep.

The Bible says you are to love your wife. It even says you are to love your enemies. It's not difficult to do. It just means you only do what's good for them and never do anything to harm them; so you can love someone without liking them, but I don't think it's a good idea to marry them because they are not going to change. She liked dressing the girls to look pretty and then showing them off. She made sure the holidays were special for them and was compassionate for anyone who was sick. Outside of that, it was a miserable marriage, so when the girls were pretty well grown, I filed for divorce.

I was discharged from the Navy in December, 1945. I took a job with the U.S. Post Office delivering special Delivery. They paid 30 cents an hour plus 10 cents an hour while using my car. It was the holidays so special delivery was coming through faster than they could deliver. They didn't pay extra for overtime but I loved that 40 cents an hour and they loved me because I didn't desert them and leave them at night. They wanted me to stay on after the holidays, but I had enrolled at UCLA on the GI bill. I would be in class during the day. The Government only gave us $90 a month, so I needed an evening or weekend job.

My cousin Madeline had worked for Von's Market. One of the Von der Ahe boys was running the business and she said they were wonderful to work for, so I went to see him. I was a little afraid to tell him I was starting college, thinking he wouldn't give me a job, but I had to tell him because I'd only be available for part time. His reaction was opposite from what I expected. He said, "The job's yours if you promise you won't give up your education." I was working produce on Pico Boulevard in downtown Los Angeles. It was not easy getting from UCLA to the store on time. A couple times my car broke down and I was late.

The produce manager said, "I depend on you. You can't be coming in late. Which is more important, that car or your job?" I looked at him like he must be kidding. That car meant much more to me than any job, so I resigned. In the meantime, I got married to Anna Mae. She took a waitress job in Westwood Village, right by UCLA. They arranged her hours so I could drop her off before class and pick her up after school.

She kept this job until she got pregnant, then she got a job close to home. I think it was a sweat shop where she could sit down and use a sewing machine. There was another woman there about her age who was also pregnant named Betty Dalton. They became friends and remained friends all their life. Anna Mae made lots of friends but they were all party friends and fair weather friends. I think Betty was the only true friend she ever had. I felt then, and I still feel, Anna Mae was a very lucky person. How many of us have ever had a friend outside of family who stuck by us and is always there for us, no matter what?

I learned at a very young age not to get too close to anyone. This was during the depression. I'd make friends, then we'd move and I'd have to make new friends. Even in the Navy I tended not to make too much of friendships. You make a friend then one of you gets transferred or a friend could get killed and that's going to hurt. It seems things haven't changed, even in my 90's. I just ran coast to coast across the U.S. I made hundreds of friends along the way then ran off and left them. I'm not complaining, because I've been wonderfully blessed and I will not forget these friends until I take my last breath.

We were living with my mother-in-law, Lena, and brother-in-law,

Jack, because there was a great housing shortage. Jack was in high school and he couldn't remember his father, so he just accepted me like a big brother. I had a great mother-in-law. We had a lot of good times. Lena's income was about $15 a month from her husband's Social Security. Her step-father was a preacher and had his own church. He paid Lena a few dollars a month to straighten up after a service and to clean up and get it ready for the next service. I gave her $10 dollars a month and helped with groceries.

We argued over that a lot because Anna Mae said I should give her the $10 because she needed it more than her mother. I said, "I'm not going to sponge off your mother. She never asked for anything but I told her I'd give her $10 a month so she's going to get $10." She would go to her mother and get in a big argument over that $10. After hollering at each other for a while, Anna Mae would promise to pay her back, so her mother would give in and loan her the $10. I asked Anna Mae where are you going to get $10 to pay her back and her reply was, "Oh, she knew I wouldn't pay her back when she gave it to me."

I would save a little here and there until I got $10 ahead then go to Lena and say, "Here's the $10 Anna Mae borrowed. Don't tell her or she'll just borrow it again." I think that $20 a month it was costing me was the best money ever spent. Anna Mae had the pleasure of talking her mother out of the $10 every month and go on a shopping spree. Her mother saved the other $10, and when we got our own home and moved out, she took that money and fulfilled a dream she had for years, she got rid of the ice box and bought a refrigerator. I've never known anyone happier over a possession than she was with that refrigerator.

Here's a little about Anna Mae's grandfather. He was a Pentecostal preacher. They had a little group that met in a little hole in the wall on Vermont Ave. I think this may have been the beginning of the Pentecostal movement. As the congregation grew, he bought a small church just east of Broadway on 57th street, I think. Amy Simple McPherson was one of the group. She opened a larger church near Silver Lake and became the most prominent Pentecostal preacher in Southern California. Anna Mae's grandfather named his denomination "Religious Science." By the time he died, he had sold his original and started up two or three more around the country.

There's a lot of Religious Science churches in the world now. I don't know if they all came from Mr. Mickley (not sure if that's the proper spelling), because Religious Science is a religion related to Science of Mind founded by Ernest Holmes in 1927. Being Anna Mae had no male figure to teach her, her grandfather tried to be of some help. He did his best to get her to say please and thank you. Even though she respected him and considered him a sincere preacher, she apparently felt no obligation to mind him. He was not her real grandfather, he was a step-grandfather. She just refused to say please or thank you.

Several years after we were divorced, our daughter Cathy was having some real problems. I came forward, took over, and got her through her problems. Anna Mae called me and said, "Thank you." That had to be a first.

While living there on 70th Street, Carol, our first born, arrived. Boy, how we loved that precious little girl. She was the apple of my eye. She was so beautiful and people were making her pretty clothes and bringing her presents. Anna Mae liked to dress Carol up nice and show her off. As she grew older, Anna Mae told her, "You got to stay beautiful so the boys will like you." Vanity eventually killed her. More about that later.

Anna Mae was a good cook, but she would not do dishes or clean house, and at that time she would not do laundry. When I got home from school, there were always diapers to be washed. Anna Mae or Lena would rinse them in the toilet and throw them in the wash tub. I would fill the tub with water, take a bar of laundry soap, and scrub them on a scrub board, rinse them out, twist them to ring them out, then hang them on a clothes line in the back yard. Jack made a forked type thing out of wood in wood shop. He gave it to me and said, "This is for washing clothes."

Boy! What a blessing that was. I didn't have to put my hands in hot water. Just stand there and pound away. When my mother heard about this, she called my dad and said, "You didn't give them a wedding present, so now you're going to buy them a washing machine." She was no longer married to him, but seems she was still wearing the pants in the family.

That washing machine sure was a labor saver. When Carol was a baby and I had a late class or found some work that got me home late at night, as soon as I walked in the door, Carol would whimper. I'd pick her up, heat up a bottle, walk the floor with her, and sing her a little lullaby. She'd drink a little of her formula and fall asleep. She seldom slept through the night. I usually had to get up a couple times during the night and give her a little milk. Anna Mae accused me of waking her up when I came home, which wasn't true. She was just laying there waiting for that door to open.

Carol was a climber. Before she could walk, she would climb out of her crib, hang on the rail, and drop to the floor. She'd come crawling into the living room and climb all over the furniture. This was a small house, so the washing machine sat in the kitchen. One day we had put Carol down for a nap. I started up the washing machine and went into the living room. This machine was the agitating type with a ringer. It made a lot of noise, so when Carol got up we didn't hear her until she started screaming. We rushed to the kitchen. There she was in the washing machine with her head sticking out, screaming, and the agitator was knocking her back and forth. Scary, but funny. She had crawled onto a chair, onto the table, and into the washing machine.

While raising children I hated to go out to dinner. In those days, eating out was always something special, so it was difficult to train kids how to behave in a restaurant. It was something they weren't accustomed to. We were visiting my brother in Gardena and he told us about a nice restaurant. When we left, Anna Mae said, "It's going to be awful late by the time we get home. Why don't we try that restaurant Lee told us about?" We took a booth. I sat Carol next to me and told her to sit still. She slid off the seat, crawled under the table, and up onto the seat next to her mother. Anna Mae said, "Get back over where you belong." She crawled over the top of the table back to where she started. I said, "Do you see why I don't like to eat out?" She said, "I like to eat out, we just need a baby sitter."

I really needed more income. I was still going to school, so I decide to try Wild Catting on the week end which is shuttling passengers without a license. I would go downtown to the bus station on Friday night and pick up any service men heading for El Toro, Oceanside, or San Diego. I'd make a few bucks going down, then Saturday morning I'd catch the sailors going on weekend liberty heading for Los Angeles. I would load six sailors in my car at $4 each and drive 90 miles an hour all the way to Los Angeles. Sunday night I'd catch a load back to San Diego. I was clearing about $40 a weekend, which was pretty good money back then.

Someone told me, "Watch out for that cop in San Clemente. He sits around the corner at the signal. If you're speeding, he'll get you. He's got a little 36 V8 Ford and he's got it souped up." I was going through San Clemente, the signal changed to green, and I sped up to get through before it turned back to red. Sure enough, there was that little 36 V8 and he took out after me. I thought, "I can outrun him," so I floored it. I was doing well over 90. I looked in my rearview mirror and he was gaining on me fast. So I just pulled over and took my ticket.

With all the expenses I had, my money just wasn't lasting. The fine was $10. I didn't have $10 so I decided to appear in court. I could drive down on Friday, appear in court, and catch a load back on Saturday. The first thing the judge said, "The fine is $10, would you like to pay it now?" I said, "No, your honor." He looked at me sorta startled, like he thought that was what I was there for, to pay my fine and go. He said, "How do you plead? Guilty or not guilty?" I said, "Not guilty, your honor." I figured if I said guilty, even with an explanation, 90 in a 55 was not going to go well with him and then when I tell him I don't have the money, I'll get locked up for sure. He said, "If you plead not guilty, I have to have the officer here. He's out on the highway somewhere. I'll put in a call for him." I just sat down and waited. After he took his other cases, he said, "I haven't been able to locate the officer. If you'll change your plea to guilty, we can get this case over with."

I figured this judge is just trying to make money because I knew he hadn't put a call in for the officer, because he hadn't left the bench and he hadn't given anyone else an order, so I said, "I just can't plead guilty for something I didn't do." He said, "If you plead not guilty, I'll have to set up another date when the officer can be here and you'll have to come back." I said, "Your honor, I have a wife and child to support and my only income is the $90 the government gives me while I go to school on the GI bill. I took off school today and drove all the way from Los Angeles to appear in court. I can't afford to do it again."

The judge said, "If you continue to plead not guilty, I have no other choice but to set another date. But if you will change your plea to guilty, I will waive the fine and we can both go home." Whew! Close call!

One night I took a load of sailors from Los Angeles to San Diego. Then I went by the bus station to pick up some Marines going to Camp Pendleton. The Greyhound called the police, saying the Wild Cats were cutting into their business. Two policemen and an MP approached me as I was loading some Marines into my car. They shoved me into their car, along with two other Wild Cats. These other two had obviously been drinking. I tried to say something, and a policeman said, "Shut up. If I hear one more word out of you, I'll bust you in the mouth," so I kept quite.

They left me in the car and took the other two and threw them in the tank for the night, then asked me, "Ok, what's your story?" I said, "I was a Hospital Corpsman with the Marines. I brought a buddy back to the Navy Hospital last night. These Marines were friends of ours. I told them I'd give them a ride back to their base and to meet me at the bus station so if for any reason I couldn't make it they could catch the bus." The officer said, "Were they paying you anything?" I said, "They promised to fill my tank with gas to get me back to LA." The officer said, "I don't believe you, but I'll take you back to your car and you get out of town, OK?" Another close call!

I was cruising around the UCLA campus trying to find a vacant parking space when I blew a tire. I pulled over to the curb. It had a two-hour parking limit. I had a spare but didn't want to be late for class, so I put a note on the window "Blown tire, be right back" and went to class. When I came back, there was a citation on my windshield. I was going to have to appear in court in West Los Angeles and I didn't have any money. I explained to a couple Los Angeles Police my predicament and asked them for advice. They assured me that if I would plead guilty with an explanation, the judge will understand and there won't be any fine. While waiting in court, I met a very interesting teenager who had built a hot rod and was trying it out to see how fast it would go and got a ticket. When I pleaded my case, the judge said $2 or two days. I didn't have $2. The teenager stepped up and paid my $2 and said, "My mother came along to pay my fine so I asked her for another $2 for you. It's a loan." I got his address and got the $2 back to him the very next day.

I was coming back from San Diego and got cited for speeding through Laguna Beach. When the day to appear in court came, I told Anna Mae, "Get the baby dressed, you're going to love Laguna Beach. Let's make this a pleasure trip." When the judge came out, he looked at me and said, "Now, who is this young man with the beautiful wife and little baby." I gave him my name and he said, "If the rest of you don't mind, I'm going to take this case first. How do you plead, guilty or not guilty." I said, "Guilty your honor." He said, "$5." As I was reaching for my wallet, he said, "Can you afford the $5, or would you like to make payments?" I jumped at that opportunity. I said, "Can I send you a dollar a week?" He said, "I hear-by waive the fine and you take that $5 and take your wife and baby out to dinner," and that's just what I did.

After one year and a summer session in school, I decided I was wearing myself and my car out trying to make ends meet, and not doing well in school. It was time to change directions, so I started looking for a full-time job. I was driving past a Thrifty Drug store on Vermont Avenue. I saw a young man with his thumb up, so I gave him a ride. I told him what I was doing. He said, "Why don't you do what I did? I'm working at that Thrifty Drug Store as a prospective manager. Thrifty is the fastest growing drug chain in the country, and they have a contract with the government. It's an on-the-job training program for veterans. The government will pay you the $90 a month and Thrifty pays another $20, so you're making $110 a month while training. It's a three-year contract. You go from Prospective Manager to 3rd man, to Assistant Manager and at the end of three years you're supposed to get your own store as manager. There's an increase in pay at each promotion."

I went to work for them. They really knew how to make money. I went to a class in downtown Los Angeles once a week, which we called the Thrifty College, and then to work in a store. I worked six days a week, and long hours. I learned a lot from them on how to run a retail store at a profit.

One day a big tough looking guy came into the store. He said, "I need to talk to you, so let's go over to the soda fountain and I'll buy you a cup of coffee." He was with local 770 retail clerks union. He said, "You've been on the job for 30 days so you have to join the union. I need $20 from you." I said, "I don't have to do anything, and I'm not giving you any $20." He said, "We have a deal with Thrifty, they will not promote you until you join the union. When you get your promotion, you can take out a withdrawal and you never have to pay any dues." I said, "No deal." He looked me right in the eye and said, "I used to be a wrestler. I was always hurting people. I don't like hurting people, so I took this job where I can help people. Now let me help you, just give me the $20." I said, "No deal." He said, "You're a veteran, aren't you?" Of course I was a veteran, we were all veterans. "I can give you a veteran's discount. It'll only cost you $10." I gave him $10, got my promotion, and took out a withdrawal. My pay increased by $20 a month.

I was still living with my mother-in-law, Carol was over a year old. I figured I had a good job with a steady income so I should be able to get a GI loan. Living quarters were still scarce, but Kaiser was building some tract homes. We picked out a lot in Monterey Park. Thrifty gave me a letter of recommendation and the bank approved me for a loan. The government didn't have enough reserve to cover all the loans that were coming through, so I had to go for a combination GI and FHA loan. The extra interest on the FHA wasn't too high, so I figured I could handle it. Kaiser built us our first home.

We had to scrimp to make ends meet, but we were able to furnish the house. No luxuries. My aunt donated an old antique radio which worked pretty good. I put in my own lawn and did all the car repairs and maintenance myself. We were doing ok, except for one big thing… Anna Mae still had the attitude that she didn't have to pay her debts, so I took care of the finances or the bills wouldn't have gotten paid. She thought if she bought something with no down payment, it was free. If I came home and found she'd bought something new, I'd say, "Where did you get that?" She'd say, "It only cost me a dollar." I'd ask, "How could you get that for a dollar?" She'd say, "That was the down payment." When I asked, "How are you going to pay it off?" She'd just shrug her shoulders like it didn't matter.

On July 20th of our first year in our new home, Linda was born and was entirely different from Carol. The first night home from the hospital she took a full eight ounces of formula. She went to sleep and didn't wake up until morning. Our babies were all bottle fed because Anna Mae refused to breast feed them. Like most new born babies, she was not all that pretty. Anna Mae looked down at her in disgust and said, "She's got a double chin." Within a few days, she became a very beautiful little baby. Anna Mae changed her attitude and right away started planning how she was going to dress her and show her off.

We alternated shifts at work so I had two weeks opening and two weeks closing. I loved my day shifts. I couldn't wait to get home and take over with my two precious little girls. Two years had passed and I was still third man. I got to thinking, "They just opened store #76. There's four managers in each store. Only one year left on my GI contract. How many stores can they open in one year? There's no way I'm going to get a store of my own!", so I turned in my resignation. The personnel manager, Mr. Purser, called me in to his office and wanted to know why I was leaving. When I explained, he said, "Here's all the progress reports the manager sent in every month." I looked at the reports and saw that every report that Mr. Miller sent in showed everything as satisfactory and added at the end "Not ready for promotion."

I knew right away why the reports read that way. I always felt that outside of murder or pushing drugs, the worst thing a man could do was squeal on someone. I knew what was going on, and he knew I knew, and he knew I would never tell on him. He didn't want me to get transferred to another store because I always covered for him. He was doing a lot of drinking and womanizing and living beyond his means. When I took the day's receipts to the bank, he would hold one back, saying it wasn't ready yet. I knew he was lying because if I closed the night before, I made sure it was ready before I left the store.

Mr. Miller was an Officer in the Air Corps during the war, so when they finally discovered what he was doing, he re-enlisted in the Air Corps to avoid prosecution. Mr. Purser said if you'll just hang on for a while, I'll get you a store. You should be ready for a C store. I knew they had only one C store. It was in Pomona. I also knew they were getting ready to build a new super store in Pomona and they would transfer everything to the new store and close the other, then I would be right back where I started, so I said, "No thanks."

He said, "What do you want?" I said, "I want more pay, some weekends and holidays off to spend with my family, and no more working at night." He said, "I've got just the thing for you in our pricing department. It fits everything you're asking for. We had a meeting the other night at the Biltmore Hotel and our Comparison Shopper and one of our female Educators showed up intoxicated. We fired them both."

Mr. Purser always liked me. I think it was because when he was teaching at the Thrifty College, I was good with figures and I understood gross profits, which most people seemed to have difficulty grasping. He thought I would do well in the pricing department. I loved that job. I had my own office with my own secretary. I only went into the office once a week. I got paid by the month and it was considered a 40 hour a week job. I could get up and go to work whenever I felt like it and quit whenever I felt like it. I always made sure I put in my eight hours.

My routine was go to the nearest store to where I lived and pick up my interoffice mail. After going through my mail to see if there were any specific instructions for the day, I'd go through all the newspapers and check all the ads, including our own. Every one of our own stores I went into, I'd check to make sure there were flags on all items advertised to be sure we were meeting our own ads, and that we were not being undersold by any competitor in the area. Then I'd call my office to see if there were any last-minute instructions, and let her know where I was going. She could leave messages at the next store I was going to and I always called in to let her know where I was going next.

I would go to one of our stores and visit all our competitors in the area. If they were underselling us on any item, I would make sure we were meeting their price. I tried to put on as many miles as I could every day because I was paid four cents a mile for traveling expense. I carried all the tools I needed, so if I broke down, I could usually fix it and be on my way. I could put on a spare in five minutes, even break down a tire and patch a tube in 10 to 15 minutes. If I had a break down that I couldn't fix on the spot, I'd catch a bus or hitchhike to the next store to finish out my day. Many times, I worked on my car all night to have it ready for the next day.

We had no sooner got Linda off diapers, when Anna Mae missed a period. She screamed at me, "I don't want any more kids. Take me to the doctor and see if he can give me something to bring my period around." The doctor said, "You may be pregnant. I can't be sure." He took me to one side and said, "Your wife has had two children and two miscarriages. If she's pregnant, there's a good chance she will have another miscarriage. Would you prefer to save the baby or lose it?" I said, "Save it, by all means. If that's a precious little baby in there, it has a right to life." He said, "I'm going to write you a prescription for Stilbestrol. If she's not pregnant, this should bring on a period. If she is pregnant, keep her on this medication through the entire time. It should keep her from miscarrying."

I couldn't afford the refills so I told my cousin what I was up against. She was training at General Hospital to become a nurse. She supplied me with the medication. So Cathy was born. I felt so privileged to raise this precious little girl. She's all grown up now, but she's still my little girl, and every chance she gets she's here joining me when I do my runs.

I was under such pressure trying to hold down a job and pay all the bills that Anna Mae kept running up that my ulcer was hurting and I was losing weight. I cashed my pay check, handed her the money, and said, "Here, you take over and you lose the weight." She was glad to accept that responsibility. For a while it seemed like I had made the right decision. I was a little concerned about the letters we were getting in the mail regarding unpaid bills. Especially the doctor bill. When I asked her about them, she said, "Don't worry, I took care of them."

I was called into the office. My boss sat me down and showed me some papers. He said, "Your wages have been garnished. This collection agency wants their money. It seems you haven't paid your doctor bill. We cannot allow this. We don't want anyone working for us who can't handle their finances. If you don't clear this up right now, we will have to let you go."

I explained the situation and said give me 24 hours and I'll find a way. There was no way I could raise that much money so I went to my mother and she loaned me the money. She said, "When I loan money, I expect it to be paid back, but if you can't, no hard feelings. I never loan money I can't afford to lose."

I took over the finances again. Anna Mae felt no responsibility to repay my mother so it took me years to pay her back, but I made sure I did. I got a small raise in pay every year. I opened a separate checking account that she knew nothing about. I would cash the check and bring the stub home from the previous year. She never noticed the year on the stub so never knew about the extra income. I would put the extra money in the checking account. When a letter came in the mail from a department store, I would write them a check and write on the back "Endorsement of this check is an agreement not to allow any more credit to this person." It wasn't long till she was having trouble getting credit anywhere.

I went on a vacation and blew a motor. I managed to limp into Klamath Falls, Oregon. I needed a new motor. I went into Sears and explained my predicament. He said, "Have you ever had credit with Sears." I said, "Yes, but I don't think it's any good now" and told him what I had done. He said, "Let me call the Sears in Los Angeles." He came back and said, "Your credit is good. It's only hers that's not good," so I got a motor installed and was able to finish my vacation.

I made a lot of friends among my competitors. Most were very friendly. There were a few that gave me a bad time. I enjoyed that. It made the job a little more interesting. One day I was checking Pringle Drug Store in Santa Anna. Jim Pringle, the brother of the owner, approached me and said, "We plan to expand, you get around a lot, where is a good location to open a store?" I said, "Riverside! It's not far from here and it's wide open for a big self-service drug store. The only competition is a little hole in the wall Owl Rexall."

The next time I came into their store he said, "We took your advice and leased the Alfred M. Lewis building at 10th & Main St. right in downtown Riverside. How would you like to come and manage it for us?" We worked out a deal and I said I'll give Thrifty my notice and I'll be here next week.

I knew I would miss Thrifty, especially my secretary. She was good. I had to send in a report every night. She would type it up and correct all my spelling and send me a copy to help me with my spelling. It didn't do much good...I still use spell-check. I went into the office to turn in my resignation. I went to my superior and gave him a one week notice. He said, "I can't train anyone in a week, I need two weeks." I said, "When you go, tell Bill Henry I'm quitting. I won't even be here for a week. He's gonna say, 'Pay him off and when he walks out that door he don't get back in'." He said, "I don't do business that way." I said, "Bill Henry does, I've been with this company longer than you have. Just go and give him the news." When he came back, he laughed and said, "He said exactly what you said he would. I told him you gave me a week's notice." He said, "Give him a week's pay and he's out the door and he don't get back in." Bill Henry was the General Manager for the chain and the most brilliant retail operator I ever met.

I went to work in the Santa Anna store until we took possession of the store in Riverside. A lot of work had to be done to turn that empty building into a drug store.

BENEFITS AND HAZARDS OF STORE MANAGEMENT

I LIVED IN MONTEREY PARK AND COMMUTED TO SANTA ANNA WHILE THE RIVERSIDE LOCATION was being constructed into a workable retail store. I rented a house in Riverside and put my home on the market.

We had a warehouse in the basement of the store with a conveyer belt coming down from the alley, and another going up into the store. We could receive merchandise there, check it in, price it, and send it up into the store, and then stock the shelves. We advertised for help wanted.

Jim Pringle had a system. We alternated shifts in the basement. While receiving and pricing, we would take applications and do interviews. We would grade the applicants by marking their application the military way, 4.0 being perfect. Then we could go through the applications and pick the ones we felt most qualified. We had an agreement. If I wanted to fire someone he hired, I was not to do it until he agreed. And he would do the same for me. If I wanted to fire someone I hired, I had to wait 24 hours to cool off before making the final decision.

The Pringles were the greatest people I ever worked for. The owner, Ralph Pringle, was one of the kindest, most generous people I ever knew. He paid his employees well and treated them with respect, and he treated his customers the same way. I went to lunch with him and noticed he treated everyone that way. I had just come from a company who taught me the bottom line was all that mattered. The Pringles were Mormons. Ralph told me, "We don't want to make money. We just want to make friends. If we make enough friends, the money will come."

I had to learn a whole different means of operation. At Thrifty, if we ran a loss leader, we would advertise it, put a big sign on the window to get them in the store, then hide it under the counter so they had to ask for it, then limit them to one. The first time we ran Kleenex below cost, I asked Pringle how he felt about that. He said, "Make a nice window display. Make a big display in a prominent location, and no limit. We're only taking the loss to make friends. Let's see how many friends we can make."

I wasn't getting any offers on my house, so I leased it out for a year. Big mistake! The rent I collected that year was just enough to pay the rent where I was living. When my renters moved out, it cost me more to fix it up for resale than I had collected. I let a real estate company put up a sign and let it go on multiple listing. I wasn't getting any action. A Mexican real estate agent contacted me and said, "Let me put my sign in front of your house and I will get you a buyer."

I said, "I'm not signing any contract. I gave this last real estate company an exclusive and they did nothing." He said, "You don't have to sign anything. Just give me permission to go ahead. I will get you a buyer." I said, "Go for it."

Someone came into the store, I don't know who he was or who sent him, but he said, "Everyone looking at your home in Monterey Park is Mexican. Some of your neighbors are getting pretty upset because if Mexicans start moving into the neighborhood, their property value will drop." I said, "That's their problem." And he left.

Someone made an offer on my house. I never met the buyer but he had a Spanish name and he was a veteran and had qualified for a GI loan. I went down to check things out to make sure the house was still in good shape. The next-door neighbor was a policeman. He strapped on his gun and approached me. He said, "I understand you have a buyer." I said, "I think so! I hope so." He just turned around and went back in the house. I wondered, "Was he trying to scare me or what?"

It irritated me because it reminded me of something that happened while I was living at my mother-in-law's house. Two men knocked at the door and had a petition they wanted me to sign, thinking I was the owner. They had the same argument. They were trying to prevent the blacks from moving west of Main Street and were worried about their property value. The petition was an agreement not to sell, lease, or rent to a black person. I don't anger very easily but I got mad and I told those guys off. I said, "I just went through almost four years of a war defending our freedoms. I believe in our Constitution and our Bill of Rights. What makes you think you have the right to restrict any American citizen of his rights or freedoms?" I was not raised in the South, so I never understood prejudice.

When my house sold, I had a little reserve cash so I decided it was time to stop paying rent and buy another home. I went to the VA in Los Angeles to apply for a GI loan. A very nice young lady at the desk explained there are only two ways you can reuse your GI loan. First, a doctor orders you to move for health reasons, or, second, your job transfers you to a new location. She said, "I think you should qualify under #2. Your job didn't transfer you, but you moved to take a better paying job with a better future."

She typed up a nice letter of explanation. She said, "Now I'll take your application upstairs and put it on the desk. This guy is a real jerk so it's a tossup whether he'll approve or disapprove. If he approves it, I take it around to each of these offices for signatures and you're in business. You wait right here and when he goes to lunch, I'll go up and see if he approved it."

When she came downstairs, she looked furious. She had my application in her hand. She said, "He makes me so mad. He put your application in the disapprove cubby hole. I pulled it out and right now I'm taking it around to get the required signatures. You wait right here."

Before I left that office, my GI loan was approved. That woman deserves a medal. She went beyond the call of duty to help a veteran.

I love to drive so when I go on vacation I see how many miles I can put on and still do a lot of sightseeing. I had a two-week vacation coming up. I bought a brand new Plymouth and said, "We're going to Florida." Everyone was telling me, "You can't go to Florida and back in two weeks." I said, "Watch me."

I had bought a lot in a new tract and was having a new house built. I told the builder I was going to Florida on vacation and could he have my house ready to move into before I left. He said, "No problem." When it came time to leave, the house was not ready. The garage was all finished and the electricity was on. I said, "I'm not paying another month's rent so I'm moving all my furniture into the garage. I'll plug in my deep freeze and I'll be back in two weeks. Will you have the house ready when I get back?" He said, "Definitely."

This was the first year Plymouth made an automatic transmission. I got to Gila Bend, Arizona. I stopped at a convenience store for some supplies. When I came out we were not going anywhere, my transmission was out. I went next door and talked to a mechanic. He said, "This transmission is something new and I know nothing about it. If you'll wait till I get off at 4:00, I'll tow you into Phoenix to a transmission specialist." It was about 120 degrees and I think it was recorded as the hottest spot in the nation.

There was a public swimming pool about two blocks away. I told the kids, "We're going to cool off in the pool for the day." Three excited little girls in their bare feet jumped out of the car and started dancing. That sand was hot. I got some shoes on them and off we went to the pool. We stayed in the water all day, then back to the mechanic. He hooked a rope onto my car and towed us all the way to the shop for $50. This was Saturday and the shop was closed for the weekend. We put a sign on the windshield saying, "Transmission out—be back Monday." He took us to the nearest hotel. The only air conditioning was a water cooler in the window so on Sunday we went into town to an air-conditioned movie.

Monday morning I was at the transmission shop when they opened. He said, "This is a new transmission that we know nothing about, but isn't your car under warranty?" I said, "Should be, I just bought it." He called the dealer and said, "They're on their way over with a tow in." They towed me into their shop and asked to see my warranty, which of course I didn't have.

"Do you have some proof of purchase?" I said, "Wouldn't a phone call to the dealer be sufficient?" He called the dealer and said, "OK, you're covered. You'll be on your way tomorrow morning with a new transmission." We spent the day in air conditioned department stores. All the dealer charged me was $3 for the long-distance phone call and we were on our way the next morning.

I'd lost three days, but I was still determined. I had the kids' Cactus Pete tent with me and we would just pull off the road somewhere and camp for the night. If we did stay at a hotel or motel, I had a policy to never pay more than $4 a night. When we reached Florida, driving down the Atlantic coast, I was seeing hotel and motel signs reading $100 to $300 a night. I said, "Looks like we'll be sleeping in the car. I'm not camping out here…too many alligators!" I noticed most signs said underneath, "Summer rates." I pulled into a motel and said, "What's your summer rate?" She said, "$4 a night." Wow! This motel had an ice machine which was something very rare in those days, access to four swimming pools, and a private beach. If I didn't have to keep moving, I could have spent a few days there.

I drove half way out through the Keys before starting back. I had just taught Anna Mae to drive, and she had her driver's license. We were cruising along a highway with not much traffic and she said, "I'd like to drive." I gave her the wheel. We hadn't gone far when a policeman pulled her over for speeding. He wrote out a citation. He was a very courteous and friendly policeman. He said, "I want you to slow down." He handed her the citation and said, "This will not cost you anything, but you will hear from our government." A few weeks later, we received some brochures from the Florida government thanking us for visiting their state, and inviting us back with a little added note "Drive safe."

About a month after I got back, a State Farm rep came into the store and handed me a check for $50. I said, "What's this?" He said, "You paid $50 for a tow from Gila Bend to Phoenix. State Farm is reimbursing you." I said, "I don't remember seeing that in the contract." He said, "It's not there. It's something new." Seems I was still on a lucky streak.

When we got back, our house was not complete. The builder said, "My note said two weeks, but I thought I must have made a mistake because there's no way you're vacationing in Florida and be back in two weeks." I said, "I'm moving in. You're just going to have to work around me." I put the beds in the bedrooms and we ate out for a couple days. Within a couple of days, he had everything ready for me to move everything from the garage into the house except the living room. He left that to last. He had to install a fireplace and hardwood floor.

I now had a great job, a new house, and a new car. I even had a TV. I felt like I was on easy street. Carol was in second grade, Linda was starting Kindergarten. All three girls were taking ballet and tumbling and seemed very happy. The only problem was I was still stuck in a miserable marriage. I had talked to a couple lawyers and they assured me I had enough grounds to get a divorce, but there was no judge in California that would give custody to the man. They said, "She will get custody and you will have to pay child support."

There was no way I could walk away from my precious little girls. They were my joy. They were my life, and I knew if I left them with her they would not be properly taken care of. I continued to hide a little money to bail us out when she ran up a bill. I began increasing the amount, thinking maybe someday I can find a lawyer who can get me custody, because I wasn't sure I could hold out until they were grown.

Pringle was already taking good care of the help, wage wise and benefits. The union was putting pressure on him to sign a contract. They threatened to put pickets in front of the store if he didn't. Jim came to me and said, "Ralph has decided to sign a union contract. He thinks it will be a good thing. The union says we are allowed two men, a manager and an assistant manager, who do not have to belong to the union so I have hired another manager who will be your assistant. This should work out good for you. The two of you can alternate shifts. I will be free to handle other matters and you two can run the store."

This new man was a real good operator. He knew the business well. I didn't have to worry if things were being run properly when I wasn't there, but there was a problem. I won't use his real name because he was Catholic and had a lot of kids. I wouldn't want to cause the family any embarrassment, so I'll just call him Ted (not his real name).

Ted wanted my job and made no bones about it. He would come to me and say, "I probably shouldn't tell you this, but..." then he'd say some derogatory things about the Pringles, trying to stir up trouble between me and the Pringles. I said, "Ted! Why are you so intent on getting my job. You get the same pay I do, we alternate shifts, I split my bonus with you. We have equal authority." He said, "Prestige." I said, "You can't eat that." He said, "I suppose if they started paying garbage men $5 an hour, you'd be a garbage man." I said, "I'd be the first man in line, and I bet you'd be right behind me."

I figured if he's trying to turn me against the Pringles, he's probably trying to turn them against me. I just hoped they were ignoring him like

I was doing. One day Jim called me into his office. I went in hoping I wasn't in trouble for something. When I walked in, I saw the smile on my accountant's face. Big relief, it can't be bad, must be something good.

Jim said, "My brother's wife has been nagging him to get out of the business. You've noticed how his hands shake. She says he doesn't need the money and he doesn't need the stress, so he's putting the stores on the market. We can't fulfill all the promises we made to you, so we are going to have to let you go." Big shock!

I said, "I appreciate you letting me know now so I can start looking for employment elsewhere." I got paid by the week. The accountant handed me my pay check. I was on salary at $100 a week, then with a smile he handed me another check. It was for $200. I said, "What's this for?" He said, "Your vacation pay." I said, "I can't take this. I already took one week, you only owe me for one more week." Jim said, "My brother wants you to have it." Then he handed me a third check for another $200 and said, "This is to tide you over till you find another job."

I felt very pleased and started to leave when my accountant, with a big smile on his face, handed me another one and said, "Here's the big one." I noticed then that everyone in the office was smiling. I said, "What's this?" He said, "Your bonus."

I was so stunned I said, "How would you know what my bonus was? We haven't even had inventory yet." He said, "We have a good idea of what our inventory is so I was able to figure out what your bonus would be if you were still here." I walked out of there feeling like a millionaire. What a contrast between when I left Thrifty and when I left Pringles. I can't remember how much the bonus was. I think it was $400.

I was scouting around the Riverside area, hoping to find something local so I wouldn't have to move again. After a few days, I hadn't found anything satisfactory. I called Pringle Drug and talked to the accountant. I just wanted to see how things were going. I was especially concerned about him because he left a good job in Florida to come to Riverside,

California. He and his wife wanted a baby. They had tried everything and seen several doctors In Florida, to no avail. A doctor in Florida said, "There's a doctor in Riverside, California that's had some real good results."

He called Riverside and the doctor said he was pretty sure he could help them. Sure enough, they had a little girl. So naturally I was wondering would he stay in California or go back to Florida. He said, "I'm real busy right now. Why don't we get together for coffee." We got together for a nice visit. I can't remember what all we talked about. But I said, "Ted always wanted my job. Now he has it. Is he happy?"

He said, "Not very, he knows it's only till the store sells so he's scouting around for another job. Speaking of Ted, remember the night you closed up on Saturday night and when you came in on Monday morning I told you that you left the safe unlocked." I said, "I sure do remember that. I still remember locking that safe, but you say I didn't, so I guess I didn't. I'm just glad nothing was missing."

He said, "A customer came by the office a couple days later and said, 'What was Ted doing in the store on Sunday? I walked by, it looked very suspicious. The store was closed and there was Ted fooling around with the safe.' I told Jim and Jack Austin." Jack was sort of a supervisor, buyer and advertising man. After talking it over, Jim said, "Ted is a manager and he has a key to the store. We don't know what he was doing in the store on Sunday, but he had every right to be there. We can now conclude that either Ernie left the safe open or Ted left it open. I can think of nothing Ted could gain by opening the safe. Nothing was missing. No harm was done. Let's just drop it, forget, and don't mention it to either of them or anyone else."

He said, "I figured out right away what Ted was up to. He was always trying to turn the Pringles against you. I just kept my mouth shut. The Pringles and Jack are not stupid, and I'm sure if I could figure this out, so could they."

The manager of the Owl Rexall, whose name I can't remember, was what I always referred to as a gentleman manager. He had a nicely pressed suit and tie, with the appearance of a real executive. He had been managing drug stores around the country all his life. He was a sharp operator, and kept his eyes and ears open. He had a knack for knowing when to get in and when to get out. Whenever he saw an opportunity to improve his income, he never hesitated to pack up and move. He had taken the Riverside store because he knew there was no competition, and he could make some big bonuses. It was working real good for him until he heard we were going to open this big store just a couple blocks from him.

He knew Pringle's reputation, and he knew who I was and decided it was time to make a move. He transferred to the Los Robels & Walnut store in Pasadena. He told Rexall why he was transferring and told them the Riverside store would never make another dime, so they should either close it or do something to improve it. They weren't going to close it because they were stuck with a long lease.

They brought Carl Mouser in to manage it. Carl had worked his way up to manager real fast. Carl was a hard worker, but the main reason he got promoted was because he was a Northwestern football player and the top executive with Rexall was a Northwestern man and held all their football players in high regard. He was new and had to take what he could get. They took over the store next door so they could enlarge, and spent a fortune remodeling it, but they were no match for us, and we literally put them out of business.

I went to Pasadena and worked for the gentleman manager as his assistant. We worked well together. He saw a better opportunity somewhere and made his move.

In the meantime, I advertised my house for sale. I hired the escrow department at my bank. In those days, they only charged $50 for escrow. I was commuting from Riverside to Pasadena for work. It took three months to sell my house, which turned out to my advantage because I had owned it a little over six months so I only had to pay long term capital gains on the profit. A man from March Air Force base was losing his home to the 91 freeway. I sold him my home and let him assume my GI loan, figuring I would never be able to use it again anyway.

A friend of mine, Frank Castle, was building houses on weekends and evenings, so I rented one of his houses in Huntington Park. I rented a truck and Frank helped me move. We loaded everything I owned on that truck, and moved it all in one trip from Riverside to Highland Park.

When I returned the truck, I could hardly believe how small my bill was. I didn't ask for an explanation, I was just happy it was small. Months later, I was going through some old bills and discovered he had charged me for 26 miles instead of 126.

When Christmas rolled around, someone gave me a darling little puppy. I put him in a shoe box, poked holes in it so he could breathe, and wrapped it for Christmas. I put it under the tree. Come daylight, he started whining. I guess he wanted out of there. Cathy was three years old and I heard her say from the bedroom, "Some lucky kid is getting a puppy for Christmas." I don't think any of the three girls ever got a Christmas present that made them any happier than that puppy.

Carl wanted out of that store where he couldn't make a profit, so they transferred him to Pasadena. Now I was assistant manager working with the man I had just put out of business. When Carl went on vacation, there was a scorching heat wave. I ordered in a truck load of window air conditioners and electric fans. I put one of each in the aisle facing the entrance from the parking lot. When you walked through that door, you got blasted with cool air.

These were high volume items. During the two weeks he was gone, I doubled the volume over the previous weeks. When Carl got back, I showed him the figures, thinking it would make him happy. Not Carl! He always had a negative outlook on everything. He said, "You're making me look bad."

We worked hard trying to break even all year, and then make a big profit in December. We had an advantage. We were located inside an Alpha Beta grocery store with plenty of parking, and the owner of Alpha Beta was Seven Day Adventist and refused to sell liquor in his stores. We, however, had a liquor license. We got all that foot traffic coming into the grocery store. Right during the Christmas rush, the Alpha Beta had a union dispute and locked out their employees. The grocery store closed. We stayed open. We even sent some of our employees to other stores during the Christmas rush because we just weren't doing enough business. No bonus that year.

Now Carl was a much better complainer than he was achiever. I was good with figures so I drew up a plan and presented it to Carl. I showed all the figures for the previous year, showing that there was very little profit. I didn't mention the fact that the grocery store was closed during the Christmas rush. I knew that the manager negotiates every year for a new contract. I also knew that the bonus is usually a percentage of the increase in profit over the previous year. I said, "Now here is what you ask for." I put down a very large percent of the profits. "Now you do your usual complaining on how hard it is to make a profit in this store. Hopefully they will think a large percentage of practically nothing isn't going to hurt them. They just might accept it."

Then I showed him the figures on what we could really do by promoting our Christmas merchandise and displaying it out in the aisle where everyone would walk by it. Our bonus was 60/40. I showed him that his bonus should be well over $20,000 and my share would be nothing to sneeze at. He presented this at the meeting and they accepted it. Everything was going just as planned. Carl was happy. No way was his bonus going to be less than $20,000. He couldn't wait to spend it. I told him, "Play it cool. I don't spend my money until I've got it in my hands."

He didn't listen. He went way in debt and bought himself a nice big home. Then Murphy's law showed itself… if anything can go wrong it will. The conflict in Korea ended. The economy was slipping into a recession. Unemployment was increasing rapidly. Many of our customers were out of work. Most were optimistic and figured they would find a job before Christmas, so we wound up with a warehouse full of bicycles and other gifts on lay-away with a $1 deposit.

Christmas rolled around and no one was picking up their lay-away. Some asked for their $1 back. I gave it to them. Carl got mad at me. He said we were under no obligation to give them back their deposit. I said, "One thing I learned from Pringle, if nothing else, a friend is more valuable than $1. We're not going to miss that $1, and their family needs it."

As you've probably guessed, the $20,000 never showed up. His bonus for the year was about $3,000. He was pretty teed off. He resigned and went back to Chicago where some drug chain offered him the moon. It didn't take long for him to realize if it sounds too good to be true, it probably is. Carl was quite a boozer. He always took home a fifth every night. He got loaded one night, called his boss in the middle of the night, and said, "Mail my check to Pasadena, I just quit." Owl Rexall gave him his job back and he was managing a store in downtown Los Angeles.

Frank wanted to sell the home we were living in. My mother-in-law had passed away so Anna Mae and her brother Jack had inherited the homestead. We moved back into the house on 70th Street. As predicted, property values had dropped, but the only difference I could see was that my neighbors were black instead of white.

I had reached a point where I didn't think I could take any more so I gathered all the information I needed to get a divorce. I went to a lawyer and got the same reaction. He said, "With the grounds you have, I can get you everything except custody of the girls." I tried another lawyer. Now this guy was not a man I would choose to do business with. His hero was Adolf Hitler. He said he could get me custody. It seems there was a case in San Francisco where the man got custody. He said, "I have studied the case. I will present the same evidence to the judge and then refer to the San Francisco case and you will get custody."

I said, "How are you going to get the same evidence?" He said, "Let me worry about that. I know women and from what you've told me about your wife, I know her better than you do." I said, "What's this going to cost me?" He jotted down a small contract agreeing if she didn't contest, the fee would only be $110. He said, "I can almost guarantee you that when I surprise her with all the evidence, she will just give up and will not contest." I said, "Let's go for it."

In the meantime, Joe Cremo came to the Pasadena store. Joe was a little Italian, and a real sharp business man. We were already friends because we both worked for Thrifty drugs. When I was in the pricing department, he was in advertising. Joe had a knack for knowing what would sell with proper advertising. He never seemed to be wrong, so we were doing pretty well, but not enough to make us rich. I showed him the plan I gave Carl and said, "Being we didn't make a lot of money last year, if you just ask for the same contract, we can make the money we missed out on last year." Joe went for it, and the office went for it. Here we go again, heading for the big money. This is when I learned a lesson. Never shoot for the moon. If there's a lot of money involved, someone's out there waiting to take it away from you.

Now I got to thinking if I get custody, I need a nice home for my girls and I can't stay where I was. The house belonged to Anna Mae. I bought a nice home in Monterey Park. My loan didn't go through because I had filed for divorce. My lawyer said, "Cancel the divorce. After the loan goes through, re-file." Anna Mae begged me not to divorce her, made all kinds of promises on how she was going to be a good housekeeper, a good mother, and a good wife. As usual, her promises meant nothing. Nothing changed. I called my lawyer and told him to re-file.

Our district supervisor was a man I first came in contact with years ago. I was working for Thrifty as 3rd man at Florence and Miramonte in Los Angeles. He was manager of the Savon Drug Store Maywood. Savon was running cartons of cigarettes below cost. Our office called and said, "We are meeting Savon's price and we are losing money. Take a load of clerks over to Savon and buy cigarettes. If we buy our cigarettes from them, we'll break even."

It was obvious who we were. You could tell by the way we were dressed. The clerk called the manager. He said, "Take a break. I'll take over here." I had given each of the girls a $5 bill and told them to each buy a carton. They bought their cigarettes and left. I was the last in line. When he rang up my purchase, I said, "There's a mistake here. What's this extra 50 cents for?"

The manager pointed at the Sunday paper laying on the counter and said, "Isn't that your paper?" I said, "No." He handed me 50 cents and went on waiting on the other customers. When I got to the car, I checked everyone's receipt and they were all charged an extra 50 cents. I never thought of him as a crook. I just figured he knew we were competitors trying to take advantage of him and he was smart enough to make it backfire on us.

I found out what a crook the manager was when he got his son a job in the Azusa store. His son was caught stealing. The son's manager fired the other manager's son. The dad came into the store and said, "You can't fire him. He belongs to the union. You have to have three reprimands against him before you can fire him. You only have one." He made the son's manager give the boy back his job and pay him for the two days he missed. So that manager was not only a crook, but he was teaching his son to be a crook. I realized we had better watch out for this guy.

Things were going well and he must have realized we were going to have a big bonus coming so he transferred me to the Bellflower store. The manager was going on vacation and I was to run the store until he got back. He never came back so I continued to manage the store, worked my tail off, and made them a pretty good profit. As bonus time rolled around, I asked him, "How about my bonus." He said, "You're not in that store anymore." I said, "How about a bonus for the store I am in." He said, "You haven't been in that store long enough." I said, "Every store I've managed, I've increased the volume and I've increased the profit. Isn't that worth something." He said, "I'm familiar with your record, but that's no credit to you. You were just in the right place at the right time."

While running the Bellflower store, my ex-assistant manager from Pringle Drug, whom I am calling Ted, called on me. He had taken a job with a candy company and wanted to put up a nice display of his candies for the holidays. I asked him to bring me up to date on Pringle Drug. I was surprised by the following conversation because of the importance he put on prestige. I would have thought he would not have told anyone, especially me. He said, "When I turned in my resignation, they handed me a check for my week's pay. I stood there for a moment and said, 'Is this it?' Jim said, 'That's it.' I said, 'How about Ernie?' He said, 'That was Ernie'." I couldn't help but smile because I could just hear Jim saying that. He should have known he couldn't pull the wool over the Pringle's eyes.

Now this supervisor at Owl Rexall somehow managed to take over the chain as business manager. He started selling off all the stores. He made it look good by promising to keep the warehouse open so you could order any amount you needed, thereby operating on a small inventory, but you had to buy a package deal. In order to get a good store, you had to buy a loser.

Sam Vellas was a registered pharmacist and a store manager. He wanted to buy one of the good stores, but he had to take a loser with it. This crook that had just stole my bonus approached Joe and said, "Sam needs a partner. Here's your chance to go into business for yourself." Joe said, "What about my bonus." He said, "Are you going to worry about a bonus when you have a chance to go into business for yourself?"

Around this time I started going by Andy instead of Ernie. Joe thought. "Oh! Oh! He stole Andy's money. Now he's after mine. I'm never going to see that money, so I better go into the partnership." Joe and Sam became partners. Joe said, "The store in the 8700 block of South Broadway is a loser. It's a bad neighborhood. I'll run that store. I'll remodel it, bring my family in to help run it, and try hard to break even. You should be able to show a nice profit in the Morningside Park, Englewood store. I think we should do fine."

Sam said, "I'll be stuck in the pharmacy, so I need a manager to run the store. Owl Rexall is selling off their stores so a lot of managers will be out of work. I think we should hire one of them." Joe said, "Only if we can get Andy. I've worked with him and I know he will make us a good profit."

The Bellflower store was being sold so I was transferred to 6th and Main St., Los Angeles. Sam called me and said he had checked the list of managers who would soon be laid off and I was on the list. He explained the circumstances and we made a deal. I helped Joe remodel the store on South Broadway. He really needed me there because he was working himself so hard that he was really drained. On the way to work one morning, he pulled off the side of the Harbor Freeway and passed out. He didn't wake up for a couple hours.

I worked hard and long hours to keep Joe from killing himself. As soon as we got the store remodeled, I went to Morningside Park to help Sam. We reached an agreement. We would work every day on alternate shifts, taking every other Sunday off, so we could each have a day off every two weeks. Sam was good to me so I never asked for overtime. I just took eight hours of straight pay for every day I worked.

A salesman who I knew well called on me and said he had a message for me. Two partners, Marian & Brown, had bought several stores. The Bellflower Store was one of them. They weren't making any money. Brown went through the books and observed that the store had not been a loser, but profits were small. He noticed that when the books were signed by Andy, the volume and profits began to increase and continued to do so until Andy no longer appeared on the books, then there was a steady decrease and was soon losing money.

Brown went around and talked to the local merchants. Most of them agreed that the drug store was what brought shoppers into town. They said, "If we just had Andy Andrus back managing that store we'd all be better off." Brown said if I ever felt like making a move to come see him.

My lawyer had all the evidence he needed, but kept dragging it out. He had hired a private detective. Between the lawyer, detective, and some other sources, I was on the phone with private calls so much that it was interfering with my job. I met with the lawyer and handed him $300 dollars and said, "Here's an incentive. Please get this over with now. It's interfering with my job."

What this guy liked about being a lawyer was seeing people suffer. He had me in a suffering position now and was enjoying it. He called Anna Mae into his office talked to her like he was her best friend, then said, "Have you been a good girl?" She said, "Yes." He laid some pictures on the desk and turned on his tape recorder. She froze and, just as he predicted, the shock was so great she just gave in and was not going to contest.

He enjoyed making her suffer for a few days, then called her back into his office. He knew how much money I had in the bank and I had already paid him more than agreed on, so the only way he could get the rest of my money was for her to contest. He took her to lunch and said, "I'm concerned that the judge will think we pulled a fast one on you if you don't contest. If you will contest, the judge will give you custody and I know Ernie, he will not desert his kids, so you'll get him back."

She said, "I don't have any money for a lawyer." He said, "That's no problem. I have picked out a lawyer for you and it won't cost you anything." In the meantime, she had gotten a job in Culver City collating books. On the way to work, another client of her lawyer ran into the back of her. She went to the hospital, complaining of back pain. They applied a neck brace. She made frequent trips to the hospital to run up a big insurance claim. The lawyer said, "The insurance money will cover the fee. You owe nothing."

In the meantime, I sat down with Sam and we agreed we couldn't run a business this way. I couldn't take a vacation or quit because I needed an income. Trying to get this divorce and hold down a job was more than I could handle, so he fired me. This way, I could draw unemployment until things got back to normal. I talked to Brown and he said he wanted me to manage the Bellflower store and he would hold the position open for me until I was ready.

The judge wanted us to see a marriage counselor before it went to court. My lawyer said I should do it to keep from irritating the judge. This was another money grabbing farce. The counselor interviewed Anna Mae and the girls. His office gave me a questioner to fill out. I never met the counselor, but he charged me $100. My lawyer showed me the report that was sent to the judge. He laughed and said, "Is this you?" I said, "It must be someone else, it's certainly not me."

He said, "This is the conclusions the counselor came up with by analyzing your questioner and questioning your wife." When we went to court, my lawyer gave me a list of things he wanted me to say. I said, "I can't say these things. These are lies. I can't lie under oath." He said, "Why not? Everyone else does." When we finally got into court, my lawyer was throwing dirt at everyone. He was in his glory making everyone sweat. It didn't seem to matter to him whether it was Anna Mae, a witness, me, or anyone else. So long as he was hurting someone, he was enjoying it.

Finally, the judge said, "That's enough. All you can do is show more proof that Anna Mae is an unfit mother. I already know that. I do not base my decision on the mother's qualifications. I base my decision on a fact. Three little girls need a mother. I hereby give custody to the mother. Under California law, the real estate is community property. Unless otherwise agreed upon, the property must be sold within one year and the funds divided equally. I hereby give all other community property to the husband. The mother gives the father unconditional visitation rights. The mother has asked that she keep the car so she can get to work. I have decided you pay $65 a month child support for each child. If you do not agree to either, let me know. I grant you an interlocutory divorce. This means after one year either of you may file for a final divorce. If neither of you file, you will remain legally married." (The above quotes may not be accurate but it's the best I can remember).

I told Anna Mae, "The kids need the home so you can live in it until it sells. I will be living in an apartment so I have no use for any of the property. It can just stay in the house. I will pay half of the house payment, property tax, and insurance. I will give you $65 a month for each girl. Be sure you use it wisely. If there is ever a problem with the children or the property, call me. I will be there."

I went to see Brown at the Bellflower store and signed on as manager. Brown was behind me 100%. He wanted to give me full authority to build the store back up to where I had it in the past. I could see this was going to be a real challenge. It was much different than when it was a chain store. When I met Marian, I had a feeling this was not going to work. He talked, but he never listened. Marian was an Armenian who started as a salesman and now owned a hardware store, three drug stores, and some war surplus stores. He was admired by those who knew him as a real success story.

Some of his stores were losing money. I could see why. He hired managers but never let them run things. He tried to do it all himself, more than any one man could do. I rented an apartment in Bellflower near the store so I wouldn't waste time commuting. A few of my old customers were starting to come back, either to shop or just to visit because they heard I was back. Volume was increasing, but very slowly.

My biggest problem was my employees. Marian had hired most of them without considering their qualifications. They had no training. Seems they thought showing up for work, ringing up the sales, and collecting their pay was all that was required of them. I've always been a slow learner, so I figured I'd probably be a poor teacher, but I was certainly going to try.

Every morning after I did the books, I printed up a bulletin. By using past figures of purchases, sales, inventories, profit or loss and shrinkage, then comparing them with the previous days' purchases and sales, I could show our daily inventory and profit, then I put a bulletin next to it showing how we could improve. Unfortunately, most of the employees either didn't understand or didn't care.

Every month a few manufacturers would put on a drive. They would give us big discounts so the items would become high profit. Sales girls would get a commission. This always included a contest and the winning store could get some pretty nice prizes. I printed up quotas for each salesperson and stated, "This is not a compulsory quota, but if we could achieve this, you will receive a nice commission and the store would definitely win the contest." One of the girls complained to Marian. He removed my bulletin and said, "You don't upset my employees by giving them quotas." I still think it was a good idea, but maybe I just went about it wrong.

Back in those days, most drug stores included what they referred to as soda fountains. They were actually small restaurants. One thing Marian did right, he hired a good fountain manager. I don't remember who did the cooking, but the fountain manager hired some good, friendly waitresses. One problem, she was losing money. While I was working for Owl Rexall, I learned a proven formula on how to make a profit in a restaurant. We sat down together and I explained this formula to her. She caught on real quick.

I don't remember the formula, but you had to always know what the overhead was, then you had to keep a record of what every item cost. Your volume determined what your labor cost should be and what your food and supply cost should be. This was a percentage of the gross sales. There was a certain percentage you had to add to your cost on each item. I think it was 55%. This had to be figured by gross, not markup. In other words, if you wanted to make 55% gross and your cost was $1.00, you'd mark it up $1.21, menu price $2.21. Surveys showed if you charged more than that, you may lose customers to your competitors. If you charged less, your net profit was in danger.

I told her I didn't want her to lose money, but I really didn't care if she made a profit. The soda fountain is to bring customers into the store. As long as you can fill up those stools and tables for breakfast and lunch, that's all I ask, and the way to do that is low price, good food, and friendly service. She was already doing that. The only thing I wanted her to improve on was stop losing money.

From then on, the soda fountain supported itself. I made a point of always going over during breakfast and lunch to mingle with the customers, get to know them by name, and treat them like they were my best friend, which they were, because without them I'd be out of business. Most of these were repeat customers working in the area.

Two of the waitresses had a son looking for a summer job. Marian put them on as stock boys on opposite shifts. Both were real likable young men, but completely different. One was a go-getter, lots of energy. If I told him to sweep the floor, he'd grab a broom and in 10 minutes we had a clean sweep floor, and he was back helping me stock shelves and build displays.

The other was a big boy but as slow as a snail. It would take him over an hour to sweep. If I gave him a job to do, he spent the rest of the day doing what the other boy could have done in a couple hours. I decided I couldn't afford this kid. I hated to do it but I laid him off and put the other boy on full time. This was good for me and good for the store, but it caused friction among the waitresses.

"How come my boy gets fired and your boy gets full time?" the one waitress asked. She never came to me with her complaint and I was glad she didn't. How do you explain to a mother that her perfect young boy is worthless. I'd lay odds that this boy was the perfect son, probably never gave his mother an ounce of trouble in his whole life. She went over my head and complained to Marian. Marian put the boy back to work and things were right back where we were before.

Now the biggest problem of all happened. At that time, California law said, "If you are registered as a drug store, you cannot open the doors without a licensed Pharmacists on duty." It seemed all the good Pharmacists were taken. I had to call the pool to make sure there'd be a Pharmacist there every morning. They sent me alcoholics and drug addicts. I even had one that I think had lost his license because I noticed the expiration date on his license was blacked out. I couldn't let this guy fill prescriptions. Anyone can fill prescriptions, so long as there's a pharmacist there to give instruction.

I was a Pharmacists Mate in the Navy, so every time a customer showed up at the Rx, I was there to fill the prescription. This took a lot of my time, but I got through the day. The next morning, I went into the Rx and noticed he'd messed up the filing so bad no one would ever be able to straighten it out. We had a Pharmacist that stayed with us for a week. He got drunk every night and came in every morning with a hangover, but he seemed to know what he was doing, so I didn't have to watch him very close.

What I didn't know was that he had drawn money on his pay to be deducted on payday. When he left, he wanted his pay because he was leaving for Palm Springs the next morning. Brown called and said,

"When you pay the Pharmacist, be sure and deduct what he owes us." I said, "Too late, I already paid him." He said, "Get over to his apartment and collect the money." I took a couple policemen along, hoping it would scare him. It didn't work. He said, "I'm packing and don't have time for this. If you think I owe you money, file a complaint."

The policeman said, "He's right, this is not a police matter. This is between you and him," and they left, so I didn't get the money. Just to make matters worse, during the same week a young man came in the store. I knew this young man from the past. He was more mature now. When I knew him, he was in a special school because he was a little retarded. Here he was now in a well pressed suit and tie, well-groomed, and looking like a successful business man. He said he had a good job and was doing well and very happy. I was so proud of this young man. He made a small purchase and took out a check book and said, "Can I make this out for $10 over the purchase. I need a little extra cash." I ok'd the check and it bounced. Then I realized this is how he's doing so well, passing bad checks. I inquired about him from some of the other merchants. They mostly laughed it off and said, "This kid ain't so dumb. Nobody's going to prosecute him. He's handicapped. He hasn't taken any of us for more than what we'd have given him if he'd just asked."

Brown showed up the next morning with my pay check and said Marian said, "Pay Andy off. Who does he think he is giving my money away?"

Brown said, "I don't want you to leave, so why don't you take a couple weeks off and give Marian a chance to cool off, then I'll put you back to work."

I said, "I'm sorry, Brown, this is not going to work. Marian's heading for a nervous breakdown and I don't want to have one with him."

My prediction was correct. In less than two weeks, Marian was in the hospital with a complete nervous breakdown. I decided to collect unemployment for a while and work on a couple business plans I had been thinking about. Everything required money and I didn't have any. I couldn't get anyone to back me. Owl Rexall required $10,000 up front. I told Brown I would not come back to work, but if they ever decided to get rid of the store call me. Maybe we could work something out.

He offered me the Riverside store which they were stuck with. He said he'd give me the store if I'd take over the lease payments. He'd even donate some of the shelf stock. I laughed at that proposition. I killed that store and there was no way it would ever make a comeback. I finally decided that I was getting nowhere, can't go on collecting unemployment forever, and I need a better income.

Switching to grocery seemed like a good idea. Everyone except the overall store manager belongs to the union. If I could find a job in a grocery chain as non-food manager, I'd get manager wage, get all the union benefits, and start building a pension for retirement.

I took a job with Boy's Market in Highland Park. I told them I needed to be guaranteed six days a week because I needed the extra income, and I needed my day off to be on a weekend so I can spend it with my kids. They agreed to this and things were going smooth.

For a long time they worked me Monday thru Saturday with Sunday off, finally someone asked why they were paying me time and a half for Saturday when Sunday is already a time and a half day. If they gave me a different day off and worked me on Sunday, I'd have the same income and they'd save on payroll. I wondered what took them so long to figure that out.

I said that it was fine with me if I get Saturday off. No problem. I could still spend time with the kids. After 30 days, the union approached me to join. I showed her my withdrawal which I had saved all these years. She said, "This is an old one, never seen one like this before, but it just saved you a bundle of money. You are automatically reinstated."

The year was coming to a close and the home had to be sold. Anna Mae called and said she had a real estate agent who wanted to buy the house, so we set up an appointment. When I walked into the office, I looked at Anna Mae's face. She couldn't look me in the eye. I glanced at the three real estate guys and thought, "These look like Mafia to me."

They handed me a contract and a pen and asked me to sign it. I said, "I'm a slow reader so this is going to take a while." I sat there and read that contract, beginning to end, then I stood up and said, "You gotta be kidden." Then I walked out the door.

In a couple weeks, we got a buyer who loved the house and wanted it real bad. It was in escrow and everything was going fine when a big storm hit. This was a beautiful home, high on a hill with a fantastic view. There was a mud slide. The back wall slid down the hill. Part of the patio went with it. This fellow still wanted the house. He said, "I have a friend who will help me do the labor. We figure the cost of materials to rebuild the wall and repair the patio will cost around $1000." I said, "Maybe we can come up with a three-way split. I'll knock $300 off the price. I'll see if the real estate woman will pay $300 from her commission, and you cover the remaining $300 or so. He agreed to that. The real estate woman agreed, but I didn't get it in writing. Never saw that $300.

One day I saw these two beautiful women come into the store. They were talking to Joe Roberts, the overall store manager. They had just come from church and were dressed like celebrities. One of them particularly impressed me. I liked her looks, I liked the way she talked, I liked the way she moved, and those big brown eyes... like WOW! Love at first sight. A few days later, I came up from the warehouse and there she was looking at a big display of throw pillows I had just built. I immediately approached her and gave her my sales pitch, convinced her she couldn't live without one of those. She bought two of them. She had her three beautiful little girls with her, about the same ages as my three girls. She took her girls shopping, then came back in the store.

She walked up to me and said, "Would you like a kiss?" and held out her hand with a big Hershey kiss. I thought, "Corny, but cute." The girls were grinning ear to ear. A few days later, she came into to the store alone. I said, "I'm getting off at 4:00, how about having a cup of coffee with me. I'd love to get to know you better." She agreed!

I told her to go ahead and finish her shopping and I'd be at the restaurant on Figueroa Boulevard. It was only one long block from the store so I parked my car on the street between the store and the restaurant. We sat in the restaurant and talked over a cup of coffee for about two hours. By that time, we knew everything about each other. Her name was June Ward. Her maiden name was Newton. My divorce was final. She had filed, but was still debating whether to go through with it. She wasn't sure she could raise the three girls on her own. She was a Christian and believed the Bible was the inspired word of God. I was an agnostic and figured the Bible was just a book. She wasn't too happy about that.

Her car was parked in the lot at the store so we walked together as far as my car. I offered her a ride to her car. She declined. I got in my car and she stuck her head in. I thought she was going to kiss me, but she put her cheek against mine and said good night. Wow! What a sensation!

Sunday came around and I knew she'd be at the Church of the Open Door, downtown Los Angeles. I put on my suit and tie and was heading for church. The car broke down. I hitchhiked to the church. I walked into her Sunday school class and could see she was pleased to see me. A fellow a few seats away said, "Ernie." I recognized his voice. I think his name was Dick Corneal. He was the Disc Jockey at the local radio station in Riverside. He ran commercials for me when I was there. I could hardly believe my eyes. This was the last guy I would ever expect to see in church and I told him so.

Here is the story he told me. His wife and mother-in-law were

Christians and were forever bugging him to go to church with them. He was getting frustrated with this. Why should he go sit in a church with a bunch of hypocrites and listen to some preacher that didn't know what he's talking about? The Billy Graham Crusade came to town. His wife and mother-in law were attending all the meetings and begging him to just come to one meeting with them. He decided, "This guy is ruining my marriage! I'll go to their meeting and bust this guy in the mouth." After listening to Billy Graham, he became so convinced and he went forward and accepted Jesus as his savior. I thought, "Boy, if this guy could be converted, maybe there's something to this."

My top boss of non-foods wanted me to be his drug buyer. This would be a big increase in pay, but I knew my limits and told him, "I'm not qualified, I'm a good salesman but I'd be a lousy buyer. Don't want to take on a job I can't handle."

Now Barney was my district supervisor. He wanted that drug buyer job. Barney was less qualified than me, and I knew the boys would never be dumb enough to trust him with that job, but he still had hopes. The big boss wouldn't leave it lay. He kept coaxing me to take the job. I told him and Barney I was not interested in the job, but I don't think Barney believed me. He walked up to me in the store and said, "You're fired." I said, "What?" He said, "You're fired, pick up your check and leave." So that's what I did.

I spent a couple days looking for another job. I got a message that the union was trying to get in touch with me. I called them. They said, "We understand you were fired from Boy's Market. We called and talked to Barney. We asked him for what cause." He said, "I don't have to have a cause. I don't want him working for me." They said, "We put him straight. Your job is waiting for you, same position, same store, and they will pay you for the days you missed."

Barney came to me and said, "How would you like it if you fired someone and they made you give him his job back?" I said, "How would you like it if someone fired you without cause?" I could see he was plenty mad.

Now there was a salesman by the name of Sam Buoy. (Last name may be wrong). He was the honorary Mayor of Highland Park and owned a couple five and dime stores. The boss had told me to throw a lot of business his way because they wanted to be in good standing with the mayor so Sam and I got to know each other well. Sam's term was running out and he wanted to nominate me for Honorary Mayor. He said, "The whole town is behind you and will support you all the way." I said, "What does it pay?" He said, "It doesn't pay anything. We support the Boy's Home and it will probably cost you a little of your time and money." I said, "Sorry Sam, I can't afford it."

A man came into the store and said, "Are you Ernest Andrus." I said, "Yes!" He said, "I have a letter for you, sign here." I signed and he left. I opened the letter and it was a subpoena along with a predated bill for $3,000. It was from my lawyer. I had been wondering why he had never sent me a bill. I saw through his little game. That was just something I could expect out of that guy. He had checked my bank account and found out I had a balance of $3,000. So he sent this pre-dated bill to look like he had billed me and I hadn't paid, and the subpoena would scare me into giving him my last cent. I hired another lawyer to take care of this lawyer. He called and said we reached an agreement. Send him a check for $300 and this will take care of it. The new lawyer sent me a bill for $100.

I was shopping and saw a white long sleeve silk shirt for $10. Never thought I'd ever pay $10 for a shirt, but it was so beautiful I bought it. In the meantime, my car was beyond repair. A friend owned a service station one block from the store. He had an old Dodge for sale. I gave him $50 for it and said, "I've got $10 in my wallet, a $50 car, a $10 shirt, and a date with a million dollar woman. Ain't life grand?"

Of course, June was my date. When I picked her up, she was dressed to kill. A beautiful white dress that fit like a glove, high heels, and ny-lons. We went to Little Joes by Chinatown, downtown Los Angeles. The waiting room was packed with people waiting for a table. The wait-ress spotted us and said I have a table for you. We had no idea of why she took us ahead of everyone else. I nudged June and said, "It's my $10 shirt."

The big boss and Barney came into the store and said, "Come on, we're taking you out to dinner." I thought, "Here I am, being treated to dinner by a friend and an enemy jointly. The food better be good because the outcome of this meeting can't be to my benefit." We had a nice dinner and a lot of small talk, then Barney said, "I can't fire you without cause, but I can demote you to clerk and transfer you to another location." I said, "You do whatever you think fair." He said, "You finish out the week here, then report to the Long Beach store Monday morning."

The Long Beach manager was so glad to see me. He said, "I heard you were coming. So glad to have you on my team. I can only work you five days a week, but if you need the extra money, I can schedule you for Sundays." I said, "I can use the Sunday pay, but if you can't give me Saturdays off, I would prefer to forfeit the extra pay so I can spend time with my kids." Things were going pretty good.

June had never been to Las Vegas. I had a Sunday and Monday off, so I decided to take her and her three girls to Las Vegas. I went to the bank and got a loan for $100. We were off to Las Vegas. I tried to get two ad-joining rooms at the Last Frontier but it was all booked up. I tried a cou-ple other hotels with the same results. I went back to the Last Frontier, showed the clerk a $5 bill and said, "Don't you think you can find me two adjoining rooms." He said, "Slip the $5 into the newspaper", which I did, and he fixed me up.

We were having a great time. We got all dressed up, same as when we went to Little Joes. We went to see the George Burns show. There were about six in line ahead of us when he said, "No more tables." Everyone turned around to leave and he said, "I have a table for you." I nudged June and said, "It's my $10 shirt." He sat us at the table with Jack Benny and Nick the Greek.

Jack Benny was so engrossed in the show that he never even looked at us. Much of the show was aimed at our table because this was quite a combination. Jack Benny was noted as a penny pincher and Nick the Greek a big-time gambler. I thought after that I should have mentioned to Jack Benny that I saw his show on Guadalcanal during the war. I'm sure he would have appreciated that. We were having so much fun I didn't want it to end. This was the only time in my life I ever called in sick. Actually, I didn't call in sick. I called the store and told the manager I was in Las Vegas and my car was in the shop so I'd be a day late getting back. He said, "No problem, I'll put you on for Sunday and you'll still get your five days."

June was continuously quoting the bible to me. I had attended a few church services with her. Finally, I said I'm going to prove to you that this bible is not God's word. Dr. J. Vernon McGee was the pastor of the Church of the Open Door. Besides his Sunday services, he had a radio ministry and on Thursday evenings he was going 'Through the Bible in Five Years'. I picked one verse, "Seek and ye shall find." I said, "I will go to his Thursday meetings. I will sincerely seek, because I wish you were right, I just don't believe you are. If I find, you are right, if I don't, you are wrong."

I told my manager I needed Thursdays off. No problem! Dr. McGee was a fabulous bible teacher. It was hard to listen to him and still not believe. Sunday morning, I went to a Sunday School class before the service. At the end of the class, the Sunday School president gave a very sincere invitation. I thought to myself, "I'm convinced." I approached the president outside the classroom and said, "I need to talk to you." He said, "It was predestined we should talk."

I didn't know what he meant by that, but he said, "Let's step into Dr. McGee's office. It's empty so we will have privacy." We prayed together and I asked Jesus into my heart. It so happened this was on my 39th birthday. I told June later God knew what a lousy memory I have, and He didn't want me to forget when I was born again.

Things were going fine when my big boss contacted me and offered to promote me back to manager and transfer me to the Wilmington store. I had never been in the Wilmington store, so I planned on going over and check it out on my next day off. The next morning when I came to work, the non-food manager said, "Someone's out to get you. The store manager got a call this morning from the main office. He was instructed to give you three reprimands and fire you." The manager said, "How can I give him reprimands without cause." The reply was, "If you don't have causes, find some. That's an order."

I thought, "This has got to be Barney. I turned down the buyer job and I'm no longer in his district. There is no reason for him to go to all this trouble to get me fired unless it's just plain jealousy." One of the top men in the company, I heard, was a pretty reasonable man. I think his name was Fitzgerald. I had never met the man, but I wrote him a letter, explaining the situation and asked if he could get this guy off my back.

One day I dropped into the Highland Park store to talk to Joe Roberts. I told him what was going on. He showed me a bulletin signed by Fitzgerald. "If you have a union employee you want to fire and don't have cause, let me know. We have other ways." A few days later, the non-food manager said, "I hate to do this, but the store manager was looking through the time cards and saw that one day you punched in one minute late. He told me to give you a reprimand." From then on, I watched everything I did real close. I wasn't going to give them any way to reprimand me. No more reprimands.

A salesman came into the store and wanted to talk to me. I knew this salesman from the Highland Park store. I should have gotten suspicious. This was way out of his district. He said a man, whose name I can't remember, says he knows you. He used to be manager of the Hiram's Market here in Long Beach. Of course, I knew him. I never knew him well, but had met him several times. He said, "Lucky Markets have bought out Hiram's and this guy's now district non-food supervisor for Lucky's. They're building some new stores and he's looking for managers. I think you should go talk to him."

I went to see him and he offered me a job. He said, "You can go to work in the West Covina store as assistant manager until the new store is ready, then you will be non-food manager of the new store. The non-foods department is separate from the groceries, so assistant managers don't belong to the union." I said, "I switched to grocery for the extra income. It looks like this will be less pay." He said, "I'll put you on salary, same pay as you are getting now." Sounded good, so I took the job. I went to the manager at Boy's and told him I was leaving. He made sure I signed a voluntary resignation.

I never saw a time card at Lucky's. When I inquired about it, the non-food manager would say, "It's ok, I took care of it." Every payday, I was short on my paycheck. The manager would say, "The office knows about it. It will be on your next paycheck." All Southern California unions allowed a 30-day training period. You could let someone go within the 30 days without cause. As soon as the 30 days was up, they fired me. It now became obvious this whole thing was a set-up.

I went to Lucky's main office and told them they owed me money. They said they couldn't find any records. I stepped into a phone booth and called the Long Beach union. I told them what was going on. I said, "I know this is a different local, but I hope you can help." The Rep said, "It doesn't matter where you are, we will back you. Stay right where you are, and if you don't get satisfactory results within 30 minutes, call me back." I waited about five minutes when the man that hired me came from the back room and said, "I understand there's a discrepancy on your pay. How much do you think we owe you?"

I had it all written down and showed it to him. I said, "If you pay me for the hours worked, this is what you owe me. If you pay me what you agreed on, this is what you owe me." He took the one with the smallest figure and wrote me a check. A couple months after I left, I received a form from the federal government. They were investigating Lucky's Markets for unfair labor practices.

I was back looking for a job. I wanted to stay in grocery where the pay was better and I could get back in the union for the benefits. I applied for a job at several markets. The manager of the Thriftimart Grocery store, Adams & Vermont, Los Angeles came into the office and said, "I want an experienced man around 38 years old for my backroom man. I'm tired of these young guys that don't know what to watch for. I think these vendors are ripping me off." They showed him my application. I was 39 years old. He said, "I want this guy." Because of my experience as manager, he made me 3rd man. I was happy with this because he guaranteed me six days, and I really needed that extra day at time and a half.

About the same time as I went to work for Thriftimart, June's divorce was granted, then there was the one year interlocutory. So, her one year interlocutory and my one year with Thriftimart came at the same time. I took a one week vacation. We got married and went to Lover's Point, Monterey, California for our honeymoon. Monterey and Carmel have such fond memories we went back several times during our life together. When our son got married, he said, "It worked out so well for you and mom we're going to the same place for our honeymoon."

It must have worked out good for them, too. They are still married and gave me some beautiful grandkids. I stayed with Thriftimart for 20 years. Then they sold out to Safeway and I took my retirement.

The years spent with Thriftimart Groceries, Adams & Vermont, Los

Angeles were never dull. Most of the people I worked with and most of our customers were happy, wonderful people. We did have our problems. This was an old store in what was considered the ghettos. Most everyone was on welfare. I carried handcuffs in my hip pocket and used them constantly. I could write a book on my experiences in that store. During my career, I busted over 10,000 shop lifters, was held up at gunpoint four times, was taped up, tied up, and taken as a hostage, but that is what made the job exciting.

HERE'S A FEW OF MY EXPERIENCES:

I observed a man stealing a fifth of scotch. I followed him outside and apprehended him. I had a code. We only had nine check stands, so if I called for assistance on check stand ten, this meant I needed some back up and all available male help would come to my assistance. I took this man to the back room and handcuffed him to the water pipe. I called the police and was filling out a theft report. He was very cooperative until the police walked in. When he saw the blue uniforms, he went berserk, started calling them pigs, and every other insult he could come up with.

I could see this was getting to these policemen. One said, "Are these your handcuffs?" I said, "Yes." He took the cuffs off this guy and handed them to me and said, "I won't need these, I have my own", then he deliberately turned his back on this guy. I saw what was coming. The guy lunged for the cop's gun. The other policeman grabbed him in a choke hold and he fell forward, out cold. We tried everything to wake this guy up, with no results. The police called headquarters and asked for the Captain. The Captain said, "Someone bring me a bottle of ammonia", then he took a bunch of paper towels, soaked them with ammonia, and dropped them across the guy's face. He came up off the floor, looked around and passed out again.

When we went to court, the thief told the judge he wanted to be his own attorney. The judge said, "If you can't afford an attorney I'll appoint you a public defender." He said, "I don't trust public defenders. The last one I had lost my case." The judge postponed the case and I was never called back on that case. At a later date, I was witness at a juvenile court case and ran into the officer who did the choke hold. He said, "I was really scared because I was new on the force and thought I had killed the guy."

My reason for being at juvenile court ... There were two little girls and their brother who would come into the store often. I liked these kids. It was obvious there was no supervision; when they weren't in school, they were just sort of on their own. I felt sorry for them. I even bought them Christmas presents. One day the two little girls came in with their older sister. I observed the older sister filling her purse with cosmetics. The two younger ones followed suit. I was writing up a theft report, trying to put a scare into them. This was a holiday, so their mother was home. The older girl said, "We've been gone too long. Our mother's going to be worried. I need to call her." I handed her the phone. She explained to her mother what was going on.

Her mother said, "Don't admit to any thing." The older girl said, "Why are you holding us here, we didn't steal anything?" We had all the evidence. It was stupid to deny guilt, but she stuck to her story. I said, "Your mother gave you some wrong advice. You're leaving me no choice but to call the police." It broke my heart, but I sent them all to jail. Because these were juveniles, the mother was present in court. All the evidence was there and she insisted on pleading not guilty. This irritated the judge. He said, "For a not guilty plea, I'll have to set up another date. You are instructed to be back here with the children on such date." She said, "I can't afford to take off work another day." He said, "Until you teach these children right from wrong, I have no sympathy for you. Be here on that date or I'll have you picked up."

I saw a man filling a grocery bag with cartons of cigarettes. I told the manager. He went toward one exit while I covered the other. In California, if your store has turnstiles, you do not have to wait until the shoplifter leaves the store to arrest him. Once he gets past the check stands, you can make an arrest. The shoplifter was skinny and managed to squeeze through the turnstile. The manager grabbed him by his coat and swung him into a bunch of empty boxes we had stacked for customers to use. Cigarettes went flying. I slapped handcuffs on him while a couple clerks gathered up the cigarettes.

I had him in the back room when a bread delivery man went out the back door and left it open. He saw the open door and made a run for it. I ran to the door and slammed it shut, but he was already in it. It was a steel door and it cut him all down one side of his face. He was so high on something he didn't seem to feel a thing. When the police arrived, he said, "Can we make a deal?" The policeman said, "What kind of a deal?" He said, "I'm Fast Eddie." The officer said, "You're Fast Eddie? Wait till we get to the precinct, I'm sure the Captain will make a deal."

They brought him back in the store later with his face all bandaged. The officer said, "He left something here he wants to pick up." They went into the back room. He reached in behind a stack of baby food and pulled out his supply of drugs. I said, "Did they make a deal?" He said, "He gave us a list of dealers. As soon as we get them all locked up, he'll be free to go."

One night a guy walked up to me and aimed a little Saturday Night Special at me and said, "Let's go into the office." He handed me a canvas bag and said, "Put all the money in here." I said, "What about the rolled coin." He said, "Everything. Now you walk ahead of me outside the store like nothing is wrong." When we got outside he said, "Walk across the street." He had the gun in his hand under that heavy bag of money. This was Vermont Avenue, lots of traffic and many pedestrians on the sidewalk. When we reached the corner, I was thinking, "I'm not going down that side street with him. He's not going to drop that money to shoot me, and I need to make my break while there's a crowd." Then he said, "Turn around and go back, walk. Don't run." I cheated, I ran. The police brought in a guy for me to identify. I said, "You guys are good. This guy sure fits the description I gave you, but this is not him."

I was up by the check stands when I heard a crash, then another crash and tires squealing. I saw a car had just sideswiped two parked cars and was heading across the street into a service station. He slid to a stop in the service station, put it in reverse, and gunned it, came out the other entrance backwards, wide open. A little boy and a little girl were on the sidewalk. He ran right over them. I couldn't believe my eyes when I saw those two little kids get up and start running. He came across the street, over the curb, through our big window, and wound up in a check stand.

He jumped out of his car, ran out of the store, and was running down the sidewalk when some people apprehended him. One of my customers said, "He lives on my street. He just keeps doing this. Gets a car, gets drunk, and comes down the street crashing into parked cars." A man walked up to me and said, "My two kids came home all messed up and said they were run over by a car. I came down here to find out what really happened." I said, "Your kids told you the truth; it's a miracle they're alive." Another time, I was working the graveyard shift. The store was closed. A big crash and a car wound up in our store next to the snack bar. Never a dull minute.

When the Watts riots broke out, I was working the three to midnight shift. A company executive called me and said, "The looters just crossed Jefferson. You're only a few blocks away, so clear everyone out of the store, lock up, and get out of there." I closed all the check stands and announced, "Everyone leave now. The rioters are coming this way." There was a Japanese man with a full basket of groceries. He insisted on being checked out. We didn't speak the same language. I had to physically push him out the door.

I closed up and started for home. There was no ramp from the Santa Monica freeway onto the Harbor freeway north, so I always took a side street to Hoover where there was a ramp. Up ahead, I saw two cars blocking the street. A car pulled up, one moved over and let him through, then blocked the street again. I thought, "He was black, so he got through. I won't be so lucky." I was driving my wife's little German car, so I was able to make a complete turn-around in the street and head back to Vermont Avenue. I got on the Santa Monica freeway and got off at Hoover and onto the Harbor freeway.

When I got up the next morning, someone had broken the windshield on my 1960 Chevy Impala. This couldn't have anything to do with the riots, because I was in Highland Park. I was leaving in a couple days on a two-week vacation. The car was all serviced and ready to go. I found a shop to install a new windshield so I'd still be ready to go the next day. The office called me and said, "Report to the Eagle Rock store until it's safe to go back to Adams and Vermont." During the afternoon, the office called and said, "You can go back to your store now." When I got there, the National Guard had the street blocked off at Adams. They let me through so I could go to work. A neighbor told me a car pulled up in front of my house, a man jumped out of the passenger side, threw a brick through my windshield, and sped away. Years later my step-daughter told me her boyfriend didn't want her leaving him on vacation for two weeks and he was the one that threw the brick through the windshield. His name was Lucky. I said, "He was named right. He was lucky I didn't know this at the time."

There was always a big turnover of employees in frozen foods. No one liked the job. In those days, there were no doors on the freezers. They were the open casket type. There were no scanners, so everything had to be priced. If a price changed, everything had to be pulled out, repriced and put back. The frozen food man spent a lot of time in the deep freeze and had his hands in the freezers a good part of his shift. I decided to give it a try. I liked it so well I stuck with it for the next 15 years. I always maintained that anything between 7 and 107 degrees was comfortable. Putting on freezer coats and gloves was too much trouble so I usually worked without them. I'm paying for it in my old age with arthritis in my hands. My advice to frozen food men, "Wear gloves!"

I had a problem for many years with an ulcer. The doctor told me, "It's not what you eat. It's what eats you." I always worked good under pressure and actually liked it, but it seems my stomach didn't handle it too well. I took care of three things that seemed to irritate my stomach: I quit smoking, I divorced my first wife, and got out of management. Whenever I was offered a promotion, I turned it down. I was happy as third man. There was still a lot of pressure, but not near the responsibility of the store supervisor. If I had a complaint I didn't want to handle, I'd just say, "Come back tomorrow when the manager is here."

During the Equal Rights movement, we had two groups of picketers outside our store at the same time—Equal Rights and Grape Growers. The Equal Rights wanted more integration, bring more white help into the black areas and send more blacks to the white areas. I could never see where this benefited anyone. It just meant employees had to drive farther to work. The Grape Growers were demanding more pay. Caesar Chavez formed the Grape Growers union and made himself rich and famous, but I think he hurt more people than he helped. He organized the migrant Mexican workers to get them more pay, but caused them to lose their jobs. By our standards, the migrant workers were drastically underpaid, but it was so much better than they could do in Mexico so they flocked here for the jobs. I think Chavez was the biggest cause of skyrocketing produce prices. One thing you can give Chavez credit for, he got jobs for American citizens. The union wage paid better than welfare.

In 1969, on the first anniversary of Martin Luther King's assassination, one of our black clerks was scheduled to work on the graveyard shift, alone, locked in the store. He refused. He said, "I live in this neighborhood and there's a lot of tension. I will not be locked in that store alone on this night or any other night." The boss scheduled me to take his place. One of the grocery managers, who was a friend of mine, had just got out of the Army. He gave me his Army carbine, loaded it, and showed me how to use it. I worked all night with the gun under my cart. During the night, I saw a man by the front window. I thought he was inside the store, so I reached for the gun then I realized he was outside leaning against the window. I thought, "It's not too good to have this gun. Here I am almost wishing someone would break in. I wouldn't want to shoot anyone, but it sure would be fun to see their reaction if I fired this gun over their head."

I was thankful I had one night off, because this was something I would not like to witness. A very good friend of mine had taken over as head of security for the chain. He came into the store and told the manager in charge to send everyone home except for a skeleton crew. He had arrested someone who wanted to make a deal. There was a guy who was holding up stores around Los Angeles. He gave him the guy's name and explained his MO (method of operation) in detail and said he's going to rob the Adams & Vermont store tonight. He knew the exact time and every detail.

My friend brought two Los Angeles policemen in and took them into the office. One hid behind the file cabinet, the other laid on top of the cabinet with his gun aimed down over the doorway. When the store closed, the clerks were pulling their trays of money and taking them into the office. This guy showed up right on schedule, stuck a gun in one of the girl's back, and said, "Keep going." When they walked in the door, the officer shot the guy's brains out. The girl did not know the police were there, so when she heard the shot, she thought she was dead for sure.

Two women and a man were shopping. The man was carrying a baby. He walked by the cigarette display and slipped a carton under the baby blanket. He walked out of the store. I followed him out and said, "Give me the cigarettes." He gave me the cigarettes but followed me back into the store. He gave the baby to one of the women and was hanging around the check stand. I said, "I don't have time to stand here keeping an eye on you, why don't you just leave."

He reached over and flipped my tie out of my apron. I looked him in the eye and said, "I'm trying to keep you out of jail and you're not making it easy for me." The women finished their shopping and they all left. A few weeks later, I was working the closing shift. He walked up to me and said. "Remember me." I said, "Yes, I remember you." He said, "I was pretty high that day. In fact, I'm pretty high right now. Don't you have any security?" I said, "I use off duty police." He said, "Where are they?" I said, "They usually hang out up there behind those two way mirrors watching." He said, "Are they up there now?"

I knew they weren't up there now, but I didn't want him to know that, so I said, "Beats me! The meat man lets them in the back door and I never know when they are up there." He stared up at the mirrors, then left. A few weeks later, I was home watching TV when the news came on. Two men had held up the Albertson's market in Hacienda Heights.

I took quick notice because my daughter worked in that store. A helicopter followed the getaway car all the way to Compton where the police made an arrest. It was the same guy. The judge let him out on bail. He went back to Albertson's and asked for the manager. It was a different manager on duty, but he didn't know that. He stuck a gun in the manager's face and pulled the trigger. The helicopter followed him again and made another arrest. Sure glad I bluffed him out when he came into my store.

PHOTOGRAPHS

Ernie and some of his family

One of the many Legs of the run from CA to GA

Ernie with the Run Ernie Run school girls

Ernie with his RWB shirt

Ernie the Sailor

Ernie with his daughter Linda (left), granddaughter Tammy, and great grandson Justin

Ernie and his wife Susan when he started the run in CA

Ernie with his son Dan, daughter-in-law Grace, and grandchildren Danny, Amanda, Candace, and Maggy at the Prescott house

Ernie and Carlos

Ernie and June

Ernie and June with their children Donna and Danny

Ernie's restored MG

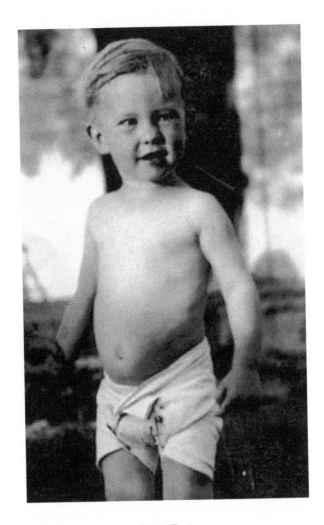

Little Ernie

LST-124

LST-325

LST-325 crew

LST-325

LST-325

Ernie's wife Anna Mae with their girls Carol, Linda, and Cathy

Prescott house

Smoke house

June's daughters Bonnie, Linda, and Susan

Ernie surprises his granddaughter PFC Candace Andrus at Marine Corps graduation
at Parris Island, NC

Ernie surprises his granddaughter PFC Candace Andrus at Marine Corps graduation
at Parris Island, NC

Ernie's route across the United States

PART 2

RETIREMENT, LIFE AS AN LST RECOVERY CREW MEMBER, AND CROSS-COUNTRY RUNNER

RUNNING ACROSS THE UNITED STATES – IN MY 90'S

WHILE WE WERE WAITING FOR JUNE'S DIVORCE TO BECOME FINAL, EVERY DAY OFF WE'D GET together with her three girls and my three girls and head off to the beach or some other form of entertainment. Those were great times with many happy memories.

One day we were sitting in her living room talking. Her three girls came in. Susan is the youngest, Linda the next, and Bonnie the oldest. Susan and Linda approached us while Bonnie stood back with a big grin on her face. Linda said, "Mom, are you going to marry Andy?"

June said, "Why do you ask?" Linda said, "Because if you don't, we're going to." This did my heart good because these kids really wanted me for their dad.

After we were married, June wanted so bad to have a child of our own. When her first two periods came around she cried. She said, "God is not going to let us have a child of our own." Someone told her, "Stand on your head after sex." She tried it and, bingo, she was pregnant. Years later, when Susan was married and had a child, she wanted another but wasn't having any luck. June told her to try standing on her head. Not sure if this is true, but I was told that she did and, sure enough, it worked. My advice to you women who want to get pregnant, try standing on your head, but remember this is after sex, not during.

A woman at work told me, "Being you two wanted this child so bad, it's going to be your love child." I still refer to her as my love child. My first marriage put me through hell. Now I was in a marriage made in heaven. Of course, there would be some problems, but when two people are truly in love, love overrules all problems.

I came home from work one day tired and thirsty. I said, "Let's go get a beer." June said, "I can't drink anymore." I said, "What do you mean you can't drink anymore." She said, "I'm having so much trouble with my veins I promised God if he'd get me through this pregnancy and give us a healthy baby, alcohol would never touch my lips again."

I said, "Wow! You made God a promise, you better keep it." She said, "Just because I can't drink doesn't mean you can't have your beer." I said, "Yes it does. I've seen alcohol destroy marriages and I made a vow that if we don't drink together, I don't drink." So, for 34 years I never touched alcohol.

We were renting in Highland Park. June was trying to sell her house. Sam, the former mayor, said he would buy the house, do some remodeling, and sell it then donate the profits to the Boy's Home. Sam said, "Do you know why you were in so much trouble with Boy's market. It was all jealousy."

I said, "I know Barney was afraid I'd get the buying job he wanted." He said there was a lot more to it than that. I said, "What do you mean?" He said, "You know Lou Mallelo." I said, "I know who he is. He's one of the big wheels with the company. I also know he'd been trying to date June. I was having dinner at June's once when he drove by, saw my car there and kept going."

Sam said, "He wasn't getting anywhere with June, then you showed up at the company picnic with her. That's not all. Barney had more reason to be jealous than just the buying job. Remember the cute little Mexican checker?"

I said, "Sure, I know her. I took her out to dinner one night. The most boring and most expensive date I ever had. She had to go to the most expensive restaurant in the county and all she did was brag about how all the Boy's market staff was trying to date her. I never asked her out again."

He said, "Well she spread it around that you two were dating." I said, "It might have appeared that way. When they had a company party at the Palladium, my car was in the shop so I took a bus to Hollywood. I was hanging out with one of the clerks and he offered to give me a ride home. He said, 'I'd sure like to get a date with that little Mexican girl. Carmen and she are hanging out together. I asked if I could give them a ride home.' They said, 'Thanks for the offer but no thanks. I bet if you asked them they'd go with us.'" I asked and they said, 'Sure!' It may have appeared like we were dating, but actually he made sure to get the cute one in the front seat with him and stuck me in the back seat with Carmen."

I had no idea all this was going on. I knew the executives were trying to make these women, but they were married. I was single. Why shouldn't I be dating?

Now we were married, June sold her house, we're going to have a baby, and I've got a good income. It was time to buy another home. When I first moved to California, my Aunt Sadie was working in a convalescent home in La Crescenta. I loved that area and always hoped I could someday live there. Every time I bought a home, I checked out La Crescenta, but never found anything I could afford. I tried again with no results.

We put a down payment on a two-story tract home in Simi Valley. The home was under construction. June was having so much trouble with her veins she said, "I don't think I can handle the stairs." We only had a $50 deposit on the home so I canceled and forfeited the deposit. We found a single story just starting construction and put a $500 deposit on it. The bank refused my loan. They said, "Some Lawyer has a claim against you for $3,000." I called the lawyer. He said, "I forgot to cancel. I'll take care of it right away."

I called the bank. They said, "You're in a good position right now. You were refused a loan for no fault of your own, so you can get the loan and go ahead with the purchase, or you can cancel and get your money back. Your choice!"

In the meantime, a friend at work said, "I just bought a home in La Crescenta. If I can get one you can get one." He gave me the realtor's card. I went to see her. She was at a meeting so while I was waiting for her I glanced through some pictures on her desk. I saw a picture I really liked. I knew how June loved beautiful things and thought she'd really love that house. When the realtor came in I said, "I'd like to look at that house."

She said, "It doesn't have the features you're looking for." I said, "I still want to look at it." She said, "The owners aren't home but here's the key. Go check it out and bring back the key." I loved the house and I just knew June would, too. I took back the key and went to get June. I let her off at the house and said, "Go around and sit on the patio while I go get the key." When I got back, she hadn't even seen the inside yet and said, "This is our house."

We went down to make an offer. We could agree on a price but I said I can't come up with that much of a down payment. The owner said he'd take a second for the balance. We loved our home. It was on a private street. Perfect for raising kids. I used to have nightmares. We were living in some big mansion and I was frantic. I wanted our little home back. We kept that home even after we had a retirement home built in Prescott, AZ. We were on a perpetual vacation between the two places. After June died, it didn't mean that much to me anymore. It wasn't a home anymore. It was just a house.

Before we got married, my oldest daughter, Carol, was married. June's oldest, Bonnie, got married before we moved to La Crescenta. We were just getting settled in our new home when June got pregnant again. She had a rough time but got through it. I walked into the ward and June was holding the baby in her arms. She said, "Here's your son." I said, "You're kidding." She said, "You don't believe me?"

Bonnie had a baby before our son was born, so our boy was an uncle when he was born. Now we had two little ones, Donna and Daniel. When we went to give the baby a bath, June's daughters, Susan and Linda, were standing there staring. Linda said, "We just want to see if you're telling us the truth."

June kept telling me to slow down. "You're going to have a heart attack." To please her, I learned to walk at 40. When Danny was four, he wanted to play T-ball. It was, "Come on, dad, let's go workout." I discovered I couldn't run anymore. I had to get myself back in shape to keep up with that kid. When I got back to running, I felt so good I decided I'd never let that happen again. I've been running ever since.

June said, "This kid's got so much energy I can't control him." Someone said, "Now that you have a boy, you can quit." She said, "I've got news for you. If he'd been the first, I'd have quit." She asked me not to repeat what she said. She was afraid it would hurt his feelings. She dearly loved that little boy.

I thoroughly enjoyed raising the girls. Now I had a son. This was a complete new life style. I loved every minute I spent with this kid. Danny always wanted his dad to be proud of him. I probably didn't tell him so often enough but I was always proud of him and I still am. He inherited his mother's disposition. When he got tired, he would sometimes get cranky. June would tell him to get to bed and they would say some pretty cruel things to each other. The next morning, he would apologize.

Once he came to me and said, "How come I'm always the one to apologize. I'm not always wrong." I said, "Because she's your mother. The bible says, 'Honor your mother and father and you will have a long life.' I think what it's telling you is if you don't, they're going to kill you." Danny could get into some pretty bad moods, but he has a sense of humor and it didn't take much to get him in a happy mood.

When Danny was a little boy, I took him fishing to a stocked pond where you had to pay a fee to fish, but you were guaranteed to catch a fish. He caught a big trout. He held it up and said, "Aren't you proud of me?" I had to pay 50 Cents per inch for the fish. The memory is well worth the money.

Here I was in my 40's and raising another family. I loved raising those two little ones. I had learned from experience that kids grow up real fast, so you have to spend as much time with them as possible or you will regret it later. I was working six days a week and trying to keep up a home. I could never afford to hire labor so between home care, yard care, car care, and a thousand other things required of a family man, there seemed to be no time to spare.

Whenever Donna or Danny wanted to do something with me, in the back of my mind was, "I don't have time for this," but I always put everything else aside and spent time with them. I have no regrets.

I was working the closing shift every Sunday so I was able to attend church. June always taught a Sunday School class, so I decided I'd give it a try. I was assigned to the three-year olds. I was more babysitter than teacher. These toddlers were a cute little group. I couldn't help but love every one of them. Most were well behaved.

The pastor's grandson was an exception. He couldn't sit still. I adored that little guy, but had to keep an eye on him. If I didn't, he'd be up to something like sneak out the door and be running up and down the hallway. At Christmas time, the toddler choir would entertain with a couple songs. They were doing just fine when the pastor's grandson got ahold of the microphone and started talking. It was difficult to understand what he was saying, but he was doing his best to preach a sermon. It was hilarious, best entertainment of the day. When they got the mic away from him, the pastor said, "He's been wanting to talk on that mic. Now he saw his chance and took it."

The next year, Danny was in the toddler group. While the rest of the kids were singing, Danny was just looking around. Finally, his eyes settled on the preacher's pedestal. I knew him well. I nudged June and said, "He's going to climb that pedestal." Sure enough, he was three fourths of the way up it when someone grabbed him and put him back where he belonged.

When the kids started school, June started working in a convalescent home. She had to work every other Sunday. She was teaching a fifth-grade Sunday School class and asked if I'd cover for her on the Sunday's she had to work. I said, "I'll sit in on next Sunday's class and see how it works." I learned then what a great bible teacher June was. I shouldn't have been surprised because she was taught by J. Vernon McGee and he's probably the greatest bible teacher the world has ever known. I knew I could never be as good as her but I was willing to try. The best way to learn a subject is to teach it.

I found that 5th graders are the greatest group because they are inquisitive, anxious to learn, and they have questions that you better be ready for because they are at an age when decisions are being made that may last the rest of their lives. When June quit her Sunday job, I took a 5th grade class of my own.

I was transferred to the Silver Lake store for a couple years. I have many memories of working in that store and one I will never forget. I was working the closing shift. I was not in charge because the grocery manager was also on the closing shift. We were checking out the late shoppers and not letting anyone else in. When the last two shoppers came through the check stand, they pulled out their guns and herded us all into the back room.

We had just received a large shipment. One of them gathered a lot of rope from the shipment. They tied our feet together and tied our hands behind our backs, then laid us on our stomachs. One held a gun on us while the other took the grocery manager into the office for the money. When I was hustling newspapers on the corner of Slauson and Vermont, there was an escape artist that would let people tie him, chain him, and apply padlocks then lay him on the railroad tracks and put a hat beside him for donations. As soon as there was enough money for a bottle of wine, he'd free himself before the train arrived. He showed me the one thing you need to know to free yourself if you're ever tied up...

He said the person tying you up is very tense so he won't be alarmed if you're tense. You simply tighten all your muscles and it is very simple to pull free. I always remembered what he told me. I had already used this procedure when working for Thrifty Drug. More on that in a bit.

I knew I could free myself easily. The meat man was lying beside me with all his equipment. I thought, "All this guy has to do is shoot all of us in the head and walk out of here." I also knew that the meat cutters knife could take off a guy's leg in one sweep, so if I hear one shot I may die in the attempt, but that guy's going to lose a leg before he gets to fire another shot. As soon as I was sure he was no longer there, I pulled my hands free and cut the others free. The manager was lying on the floor in the office. The door was locked and the robbers took the keys with them. His feet were tied with rope and his wrists bound with a metal clothes hanger. We shot a box cutter through the money slot and it landed beside him. He was able to cut the rope so he could get to the door and open it.

Back to Thrifty Drug and my escape...

I was closing one night and someone from the restaurant always had to put out an order at night in a box in the alley for the next day's requirements. This night the fountain manager was there instead of one of his employees, which I thought rather strange. I gave him the key to the back door. When he came back, there were two men with guns behind him. They ushered us into the enclosed area behind the liquor department where the safe was. It was obvious to me that this was an inside job.

One of them ordered the fountain manager to tape my closing girl. He said, "I can't do that. She's a lady." A dead give-a-way. You don't argue with a man when he has a gun. You just do as you're told. While he was taping her mouth, the gunman said, "Careful you don't suffocate her." It was a relief to hear that. If he's worried about suffocating someone, he's not going to shoot anyone. He taped up the fountain manager and laid them both on the floor. He kicked the fountain manager and said, "If anybody gets it, it's gonna be this one." Obviously, this was a show to keep me from suspecting the fountain manager.

The other gunman handed me a canvas bag and said go put the day's receipts in here. He shoved me into the liquor aisle, knocking a half pint onto the floor, breaking it. The store manager and his wife showed up at the front door and the wife was tapping on the glass with a half dollar. He was just dropping by to see how things went for the day. The gunman, thinking it was a customer trying to get in said, "Tell them to go away." Sounded like a good idea to me so I hollered, "Go away." They spotted the broken bottle, and while his wife continued to rap on the door, the manager ran across the street where an officer was shaking down a drunk.

The gunman told me to open the safe. Apparently, the fountain manager wasn't familiar with our safe. Inside the safe there is a steel box with a slot in it. We called it the juke box. All the folding money was dropped through the slot. It took two keys to open the box. I had one key, the manager had the other. I tried to tell the gunman, but he said shut up and open the safe. I thought, "If I open the safe and then they find out they can't get the money, no telling what they will do."

So I pretended to work the combination, then try to open it. Of course it wouldn't open, so I'd just start all over again. I knew just enough Spanish to hear the other gunman say, "Hit him the side of the head. Make him hurry." In the meantime, the half dollar was still tapping away so they taped my mouth, feet, and hands and left with their bag of money. As soon as I heard shots being fired, I simply pulled my hands free and freed the others. The robbers threw the money under a parked car. One got away, the other tried to hide under a parked car and was captured.

There was $300 dollars bundled which was pushed to the back where I knew the gunman couldn't see it so I thought, "Why give it to him." When the district supervisor arrived, I gave him the $300. When the recovered cash was counted, it was $300 short. The insurance company paid the $300. I don't know if the supervisor pocketed the money or if Thrifty Drug filed a false claim.

June's mood swings were getting worse. I thought it was manic-depression but the symptoms didn't fit. I couldn't figure out what brought on the moods. One night she woke up completely off her rocker. She was talking to someone in the bedroom. No one was there but the two of us. She called him Dan. Danny was in the next room and I thought she must think he came into the room. She told me later she was talking to her father. She said he was standing right there. Her father had been dead for years.

She became raving mad. I couldn't control her. I called for help. The police got there first. She mistook the policeman for a young fellow who lived next door who had been volunteering with the police department. When she discovered her mistake, she saw 666 on his forehead and started pounding on him. In the meantime, the paramedics and the pastor had shown up. The officer shoved her and she fell over the paramedic's satchel. I grabbed him and said, "Don't hurt her."

The paramedics put a straight-jacket on her and told me to follow them to the hospital. A female doctor said, "Take that straight-jacket off her." I said, "If they do, you'll be sorry." She repeated, "Take that straight-jacket off her." When they did, she came up swinging. The doctor said, "Put it back on." I was told they would keep her overnight but I had to find a mental hospital for her in the morning.

I went to the nearest mental hospital to where I lived. They said, "Do you have insurance?" I said, "Yes." They said, "We can't admit her until we clear with the insurance company." I said, "You can't reach them until Monday morning. I need a place for her right now." I said, "How much do you need? $1,000, $2,000! I'll give it to you right now. We can settle the insurance matter later."

They said, "Sorry, we can't help you, we can't accept cash if you have insurance." I said, "What a stupid policy", and called the emergency room where she was. They said, "We found a hospital which will take her and we are moving her now." I went to the hospital. She was already admitted by the doctor. They said, "If she doesn't have a psychiatrist, we can appoint one." I said, "Go for it. Get her some help as soon as possible." The doctor asked me if she'd been on drugs. I said, "No." He said, "Most of my patients wound up here because of drug use. I can rehabilitate most of them in about 30 days, but your case is different. I don't know how long this will take, but I'm confident we can help her."

I came back the next day and couldn't wake her up. She'd try to say something then doze off. I told the doctor, "I think you're overdosing her. She reacts to very small doses of any medication she takes." He reduced the medication and in 10 days she was back home, as good as new. She said some really horrible things happened during those first few days in the hospital, and she didn't know which were real and which were hallucinations.

She asked me if she tried to escape and said I did some awful things to her. I assured her none of those things were real. She said being they were all hallucinations she didn't want to tell me what I did to her. I assured her I didn't want to know and to just put them out of her mind. I took her to monthly appointments and the doctor kept changing her medication, trying to keep her from having another break down. She had a couple more break downs. I told the doctor, "I think it's a chemical imbalance." He said, "We know it's a chemical imbalance, but women have so many organs we have never been able to determine which ones are causing the problem. If I could figure that out I'd be rich."

June always wanted to go to Israel. Our pastor was getting up a group for a tour so I signed on. In the meantime, Thriftimart sold out to Safeway. Safeway wanted to put me on part time. I said, "No thanks" and took my retirement.

The Olympics came to Los Angeles. I did my first 10K run for the Olympic torchbearers in Huntington Beach. I enjoyed it so much I did another the next week, the Cañada-Crescenta Boy Scout 10K run. I enjoyed running so I just started running every 5K and 10K that came along in my area.

When it came time to go to Israel, June was getting over one of her bad spells but we went anyway, hoping this would be good for her. We flew to Amman, Jordan. One of our group's passport had Israel stamped in it so they wouldn't allow her to enter Jordan. The tour guide handed the guard $20 and said, "Grab your luggage, you're good to go." We checked into the Jerusalem hotel and I went for a jog. There was so much traffic that I tried running on a path. Big mistake! A shadow behind a bus bench prevented me from seeing a large boulder and I tripped and skinned myself up pretty bad. It was nothing serious but a lot of bandages.

We took a trip along the King's Highway to Petra. This is a very interesting city, all carved out of rocks. We saw where Aaron, Moses's brother, was buried. To enter and exit the city, we had to ride horseback through a canyon. Horses and I don't get along too well, as you may recall. The young lad leading my horse said, "I give you nice ride." He ran ahead, getting the horse into a trot. It was a struggle all the way trying to stay on that horse. The boy pointed at my ball point pen. It was one of those that came several in a package for 99 cents. I handed it to him and here came a bunch of boys all holding out their hand, I passed out all but one of my pens. I'd never seen such a happy bunch of kids.

We took a bus to Israel and as we passed Mount Nebo, the tour guide said that there is where God buried Moses. We couldn't take any pictures, even with the windows closed. We couldn't see anyone out there but they are there and they're watching you. At the border, we entered a large building. They made me take a drink from my water bottle then take a picture of the ceiling. The security was very tight. We had lunch at Jericho. We ate outside with flies crawling all over our food. We saw the remains of the wall that Joshua brought down. We went to the Jordan and some of our group put on bathing suits and the pastor baptized them. Our pastor's name was John and he was a Baptist. A German couple heard that John the Baptist was baptizing. They took it as an omen and insisted on being baptized. After we got home June said, "Why didn't we get baptized in the Jordan?" I said, "Why didn't we?" She said, "I didn't want to mess up my hair." Four years later, we went back to Israel and we got baptized in the Jordan.

I don't know if it was the flies or the food, but I was getting real sick. We took a boat across the Sea of Galilee to Capernaum. The next day our group went to the Dead Sea. I was so sick that I stayed in the hotel. I met them when they got back and toured old Jerusalem. We took in so much on this trip. Later when someone said, "We walked where Jesus walked." I corrected him and said, "We ran where Jesus walked."

We took a bus to Egypt. When we reached the Nile, we had to take a ferry across. We had to wait because they took another busload ahead of us. These were the athletes returning from the Olympics. I enjoyed Cairo. I thought it very exciting. Just to watch the traffic was unbelievable... no organized pattern. It seemed it was just every man for himself. You couldn't see the buses from the people. They were on top of the bus and hanging on the sides. We passed a zoo. I nudged June and said, "Look! The first time I've seen camels on the outside looking in."

We rode a camel to the pyramids. I went inside a pyramid and went all the way to the top. It is very hot and humid in there. When we got to the uppermost room, the guide said, "This is where they placed the dead pharaoh, along with all his riches. When they opened up the room, all the riches had been stolen." I said, "How could they get in here to steal the riches." He said, "It was probably stolen before it ever got here."

Four years later when we visited Cairo, the population had grown by a million. There was a large section of Cairo with hundreds of small buildings. This was a graveyard. These were tombs for the dead. They now had strung cables for electricity and people were living in the tombs. We took a train down to King Tut's tomb. The tomb was a fairly small cave. I had visited King Tut's museum twice. It's a two-story building loaded with what was taken out of that tomb. I asked the guide, "How could all that stuff have been in that little cave." He said it was packed in there. There were lots of boxes of various sizes. They were packed inside each other. There were lots of dolls which were supposed to be the pharaoh's servants. Much of what you see at the museum was packed in boxes.

I learned one thing while in Egypt, you eat what the Egyptians eat or starve. Not sure which is worse. We took a bus to the border on our way to Israel, the bus driver cut in front of a truck, the truck side swiped a small car. Both went off the road and the truck rolled over on its side. A woman was thrown out of her little car and was draped over a picket fence, obviously dead. The bus driver stopped, ran down to the truck, completely ignoring the women. He hollered down to the driver to see if he was all right, and said I'll get someone out here to help you. He got back into the bus, made a call for help, and then took off down the highway with his music playing and tapping on the dashboard like nothing had happened.

This was the trip when we got baptized in the Jordan. June started acting strange. I was getting concerned. We visited the Garden of Gethsemane and as we were walking back, June said, "See the bright light." I didn't see any light. She said, "It's the light that blinded Paul on the road to Damascus." I assured her there was no light. She didn't mention it again. Months later, she said she saw the light and couldn't understand why the rest of us didn't see it.

At dinner, she was acting very strange. I told the pastor, "We've got to get her to a doctor." We took a taxi to the hospital. I'm thankful to this day that I took her back to Israel because we finally met a psychiatrist who understood her problem and knew how to handle it. He was the head psychiatrist for the State of Israel. He medicated her and said, "Let her rest. I'll make a house call. You won't be able to bring her to the hospital because it'll be the Sabbath and anyone driving a car will have rocks thrown at them. I can come because I have a sign on my car showing I'm a doctor."

He came to the hotel, wrote a prescription, and said, "She is a very emotional person. These breakdowns are brought on by emotion. It can be a death in the family, a daughter getting married, or a number of other things. It appears that getting baptized in the Jordan brought this on. In the next few hours, she'll be back to normal and you can finish your vacation. Whenever she starts talking weird, give her one of these pills and she will never have another breakdown."

I said, "What do I owe you." He said, "Nothing." He handed me his sister's card in New Jersey and said, "I would appreciate it if you would send her a hundred dollars when you get back to the States." I assume this was because of the extremely high income taxes in Israel.

June never had another breakdown. She never wanted to take the pill. Whenever I saw a mood coming on, I said, "Even when you get to the point where you can't stand it, I won't make you take the pill, but when it gets to where I can't stand it, then you've got to take the pill." When things got real bad she'd say, "I don't need the pill, you take it." I'd take the car keys and walk out the door with her hollering, "That's it, just walk out on me." I'd park somewhere for about an hour then come back. She'd say, "I took your old pill. I hope you're happy." Within a couple hours she'd come to me an apologize and say, "I don't know what makes me act like that." No matter how bad things were, I never went to sleep at night without telling her I loved her. She'd say, "I don't see how you could."

We did a lot of traveling and we were always looking for where we'd like to retire. June liked the ocean. I refused to live within three miles of the ocean because the salt air created so much upkeep on home and car. I liked the desert but she couldn't stand the heat. We were both impressed with Prescott, AZ. It was high desert, one mile high to be exact, and never got too hot, or too cold. For the past 15 years, Prescott was rated as the best place to retire.

We went to Prescott to look at property. When we got there we both felt, "This is it. This is where we want to live." We did a lot of searching. A realtor took us to The Cliff Rose development. We loved the area. It was so beautiful. We went into the sales office and I said, "I want to look at the largest lots available because I need a yard big enough to give me something to do, preferably with a good view." He showed us a lot which would be at the end of a cul de sac when the street was put in. I said, "Would you be happy here?" She said, "Oh yes!" I said, "Let's go back to the motel and pray about it."

When we got to the motel, she said, "While were praying, someone's going to buy that lot." The next morning, we went back and bought the lot. We went back to La Crescenta. The sellers' market was poor at the time. I said, "Let's wait it out. As soon as we can get a good price for our home, we'll sell it and have our new one built."

June wanted to visit her mother in Chicago for Mother's Day. Neither of us had ever seen the New England States. I said, "Instead of driving, this time let's fly to Chicago, rent a car, and after Mother's Day we'll tour the New England States.

That was a wonderful vacation for both of us. We saw so much history. I love to drive and they rented us a new Dodge with unlimited mileage. When I returned it, there was over 3,000 miles on it. We covered every one of the New England States. We did the history walk in Boston, I toured the USS Constitution (Old Ironsides), took in Niagara Falls, visited the Von Trapp home from the *Sound of Music*, toured Cape Cod, saw Plymouth Rock, saw the Liberty Bell, and we took in New York and visited the Amish.

When we were at Kennebunkport, Maine, by President Bush's home, there was no one on the beach so I said, "Grab the camcorder, I'm going jogging on the beach where President Bush jogs." I told June, "I've walked where Jesus walked, jogged where Bush jogged, and when I get back to California, I think I'll get a horse and ride where Reagan rode.

When I retired from the grocery business, Ronald Reagan was running for his second term. I liked what he did for California when he was governor. His first term in office proved he was a brilliant man and had the charisma to make things happen. There was no doubt that he loved America, so I helped register voters. After he won the election, he was going to speak at a college in San Fernando Valley. He sent a personal invitation for me and guests. I took June and Donna.

When we got there, the crowd was so large I said, "We'll be so far back we won't be able to see or hear anything." June said, "Let's go try and see what happens." When I showed the invitation to the doorman, he said, "We have seats for you." They had the first three rows roped off and there is where we went. Ronald and Nancy Reagan and Frank Sinatra were on the stage. Donna said, "They look like wax figures with all that makeup."

I just wasn't ready for retirement so I took an accounting job with J & L Press in Burbank. I like working with figures so this was a very interesting job. I was using the extra income to build up my retirement fund. The company was owned by a Japanese family, Jack, his two sons, and his common-law wife. I don't remember their last name. Jack and the boys ran the shop with a good crew. They did excellent work but Jack took no interest in the financial end. He left that up to his wife, whose name was Lois, I think. Jack trusted everyone and was generous to a fault.

Lois was under such stress that she was a nervous wreck, and I'm sure she was on tranquilizers. She was no business manager. She was operating on borrowed money and kept borrowing more. The interest was ridiculously high because of bad credit and lots of debt. There was a young Mexican fellow running one of the presses. He brought his cousin in and said, "Can you give him a job?" Lois said, "Can he drive?" he said, "Yes." She said, "I can use a gofer." He said, "He can't get a Social Security number because he's here illegally." She said, "No problem, he can use your Social Security number."

IBM computers were becoming popular so Lois had a guy write a program in basic and bought a computer. This was my first experience with a computer and I really enjoyed learning to use it. Jack never bothered to get sales tax exempt numbers from his salesmen and other customers and he never collected the tax. The state sent in a woman to do an audit. Lois knew she was in trouble. She brought her daughter in to work with me, probably hoping when things got worse her daughter could take my job. The daughter was no good at this type of work and was not interested, so she hired a young Mexican girl for minimum wage.

This girl's mother worked for a local doctor. She would go to lunch with her mother and come back with a bag of drugs and other stuff which her mother was obviously stealing from the doctor. I figured this girl can't be trusted, but that's not my problem. I'll just train her the best I can. The auditor said, "You have no proof that these people were sales tax exempt. You owe the state $30,000. They sold one of their presses and laid off the night crew. I told Lois, "Before you lay anyone else off, lay me off because I don't need this job and they do."

Now I had been doing income tax returns for about 30 years, more as a hobby than for income. It was just a way to keep my mind active. One of the boys came to me to do his taxes. I asked, "How did the Mexican girl work out who took my place?" He said, "She stole $10,000 before we caught her. She was making checks out to herself." I said, "Your dad is too trusting. When I'd take a handful of checks for him to sign he never looked at them. He just signed them."

One of the employees had an IBM computer and computer desk he said he'd sell me cheap because he needed money. I bought it. There was no such thing as internet and it didn't have a hard drive. Everything was on the big floppies. I've had a lot of computers since then, but that one was the best. It did everything and I had so much fun writing programs in Basic.

My mother was getting old. I was already doing her income tax for her. She asked me to take over her finances for her. I knew very little about investing. CD's were paying well so I picked the CD which was paying the highest interest and put all the money she didn't need to keep on hand into it. My bank would inform me on Monday what the interest would be on all their CD's on Tuesday. Being my mother was over age 70.5 they would allow her to withdraw at any time without penalty, so I just kept switching CD's every time I found one with a higher interest rate. At one time, it reached 18%.

My mother had planned for her money to last until age 70, because that was life expectancy at the time. She thought I was a great investor because she was getting older and her net worth was increasing. Actually, it was only because CD's were having their heyday. My brother told me about revocable living trusts, so I went to the legal library in Glendale and learned how to write up a revocable living trust for my mother so that when she died anything in her estate would go where she wanted it to and there would be no probate and no one would have to pay tax on their inheritance.

I had managed to save up a little money and had it all in CD's. I drew up a revocable living trust for June and me. My IRA was with Thriftimart credit union and was paying 7%. I thought I could probably do better. I knew very little about investing and interest rates were dropping so I went to an investment broker with American Express. Biggest investment mistake of my life!

I took half of my IRA and trusted it to him. He sold me a limited partnership in a cable TV company and took a $500 commission right off the top. I checked out the investment and realized I'd been taken for a sucker. The partnership wouldn't mature for seven years. The only reason we put money into an IRA was to postpone the income tax. There would be no tax until the partnership sold and by that time I'd be over 70.5 and required to take minimum distributions so there was no reason to use IRA money for such an investment.

I did some studying on investments, took the other half of my IRA and did my own investing. At the end of the seven years, I had more than doubled my investment and the limited partnership paid less than 1% for the entire seven-year period. I never trusted financial advisors again. My daughter in law is now a financial advisor and she assures me that the government has clamped down and advisors are required to put customer interests first.

My brother had adopted Harry Browne's theory on how to keep your money safe and was averaging 15%, so he was keeping ahead of inflation. I bought Harry Browne's book, picked a few mutual fund families he recommended, adopted his theory, and set up two portfolios, one for my mother and one for us. I've had good years and I've had bad years, but I have averaged about 15% over the years. Harry Browne said if you have money you can afford to lose, then it would be alright to set up a variable portfolio. He gave advice on what to do and what not to do. You could make a lot of money, but you could also lose.

Someone else wrote a book on how to switch funds within a mutual fund family and make your money grow faster. (I don't remember who the author was. I think he's dead now). I decided to use my IRA's as my variable portfolio. I went to the library and got all the Sunday Times for the past three years. I picked a mutual fund family that had just about any kind of a fund you could want. I spent a couple months writing a program in basic, using his formula, then put the prices of each fund for the past three years into my computer.

I ran the program to see what would happen if I switched funds once a week. The results were better than I expected. I could see now which funds were opposite and which funds were the most volatile, so I could buy low and sell high. I transferred my IRA to the mutual funds, called on their 800 number once a week, and fed their prices into my computer. The computer would tell me what to buy and what to sell. I was retired and didn't want to spend so much time with my portfolio, so I ran the program to see what would have happened if I had switched once a month. The results were almost the same, so I switched to once a month.

It had been a couple years since we bought the property in Prescott. It was still a poor time to sell. My mother and June's mother had both died. June and I had each inherited a little money. I said, "When we pool all the money together, we have enough to go ahead and build. Why don't we have two homes? If we keep everything we need in each home, we can be on a perpetual vacation between the two places and won't have to pack anything, just get in the car and go."

At one time, my sister-in-law told June, "Someday Ernie's going to build you a mansion on a hill." June's reply was, "I hope it's a small one so the kids can't move in."

We went to the builder and picked the smallest model he had, and made a few changes to meet just what we wanted. I had owned some new homes in my life, but June had never owned a new one. I said, "This is going to be your home," so we made sure everything was just the way she wanted it. Best investment I ever made. We enjoyed living between those two homes. We were never in one place long enough to get bored.

June thought a lot about death and she said, "I want to go first. Promise me you won't die before me." I said, "How can I promise you something I have no control over?" She said, "You've got to promise me." I said, "OK. OK. I promise."

We were so happy and enjoying our life together when I developed prostate cancer. My doctor told me what my options were. I said, "If this were you, what would you do?" He said, "You're 70 years old. Normally we'd do nothing because you've got a good four years before the cancer takes you, but you're in such good health, I think you should have your prostate removed." I said, "Will it hurt to wait a month. I've signed up for a 10K run at the Whiskey Row Marathon in Prescott, Arizona, and I'd sure like to do that." He said, "A month won't make any difference."

I ran the 10K. This was the only race since I turned 70 that I didn't get an award. They had a 60 and over category. I told June, "I'm not doing any more runs for the Whiskey Row Marathon unless they raise the age category. I can't compete with those young whippersnappers in their 60's." On the way back to California to get my operation, I said, "Honey, you need to prepare yourself for this. I may not be able to keep my promise." She said, "You promised."

I said, "OK, have faith I will keep my promise." The operation went well. I never had any pain before, during, or after. He had to cut some of the nerves to remove the prostate and he removed my lymph nodes to do biopsies so this has created some problems, but nothing I can't handle.

After four years of this great lifestyle, June developed cancer and it was downhill the rest of the way. They did chemo until she couldn't take it anymore, then she went on hospice. I was her caregiver. We did everything we could to relieve her pain during those last few days. Thank God for a caring family. Our daughter Donna, and June's daughter Susan, were there at the end to help. Our son Dan, and his wife Grace, were close by to help when needed. I tried to tell June to just close her eyes and go be with the Lord, but she could see the tears in my eyes and kept hanging on. Susan was so brave. She took her mother's hand and said, "It's all right, Mom. Jesus is waiting for you with open arms. Just go to him."

She stopped breathing. It was over. No more suffering… for her, not for me. My heart was breaking. Grace showed up and took over for me and handled everything. What a blessing she was! I put on my running shoes and said, "I'm going for a run." I've always found running to be the greatest therapy, sort of an escape from reality. I ran seven miles and returned to my family. This was the second time I'd lost a loved one through cancer. Cancer is not a good way to go.

June put a lot of importance on grave sites and she loved beautiful things, so I bought a lot with a nice view at Glendale Forest Lawn, and had them dig a two-story grave. June is on the bottom floor. The top floor is reserved for me. I bought her a beautiful casket decorated with roses. Dan and Grace owned a flower shop years before, so there was no shortage of flowers. Grace helped me arrange the funeral. I heard remarks that this was the most beautiful funeral they ever attended.

I gave myself one year for mourning, changing nothing. I kept running in every event that came along, keeping up two homes, and spent hours on the computer writing programs to keep my mind active. Outside of runs, church, and family there was no social life. After a year, I decided I've got to get out and meet people so I joined a singles group that would get together for dinner, dancing, and hiking some trails.

LIFE AFTER JUNE – MORE SERIOUS RUNNING BEGINS

AL CLARK WAS ONE OF PRESCOTT'S GREATEST ATHLETES AND A FAVORITE CITIZEN. I RAN A LOT OF runs with Al. He was 10 years older than me and always came in ahead of me. We would both get 1st place because we were in a different age group. Al came to me before a race and said, "I understand you had prostate cancer. What did you do about it?" I told him I had my prostate removed and everything came out fine. He said, "They want to castrate me." I said, "Get a second opinion." He went ahead with the operation and a month later ran the Los Angeles Marathon, came back and ran the Whiskey Row Marathon. He continued running. He could still out run me.

We were getting ready to run a 10K. He said, "I'm running pretty slow now. I have to get an early start on the marathons so I can get in before noon. I have to walk part way." Into the run about a half mile, he passed me. I didn't catch up to him until in the last mile when he was walking. First time I ever beat him. Even though he was 10 years older than me, I had to tease him a little I said, "Al where's your pride, letting me beat you?"

It was downhill for Al after that but he never quit. The last Whiskey Row Marathon he participated in he just did the two-mile run/walk. I think he was 82. He died shortly after that. Every year since, they have been giving an Al Clark award to someone they think qualifies to come close to Al's performance. I mention this because 10 years later I was given the Al Clark award. I feel so honored to even be compared to this great athlete.

One Friday night after enjoying a buffet with the singles group, some of us went to the Moose Lodge because they had a live band there and a nice dance floor. There was only one empty seat. I sat down right next to Susan Fordyce who had also come from the single's group, but I had never met her. I heard her mention Roger Young to the lady next to her. I said, "Did you work for Roger Young's in Los Angeles?" She said, "Yes! Why?" I said, "Did you know my mother?" She said, "Who's your mother." I said, "Margaret Andrus." She said, "Of course I know her, but I didn't know she had a son."

My mother was the oldest waitress, with the most experience. The owner always had her handle the large banquets and the younger waitresses would come to her for advice. My mother loved to give advice. Susan invited me to her house. Roger Young's had given her a wedding shower when she got married and a going away party when she left the company. My mother's name was in both cards. We discovered we knew some of the same people. They were friends of my mother from work.

One of the friends, Rose, and my cousin Madeline used to alternate week ends and do house cleaning and shop for my mother when she was too old to do it for herself. My mother liked to take them out to dinner in appreciation. When she got to where going out to dinner was too much for her, she would give Madeline $20 and say, "Take Rose out to dinner and tell her it's on Margaret." For a long time after my mother died, Madeline would call Rose and take her out to dinner and say, "This is on Margaret."

Years had passed and I had lost contact with all her friends. Susan was still in contact with them and had their addresses, so we dropped by to visit each one of them. When we went to see Rose we said, "We would like to take you somewhere for a cup of coffee and visit." I called Madeline and said, "Put the coffee pot on I'm bringing an old friend by for a visit." It was a great surprise and a great visit with old friends. We were so glad we did this because shortly after, Rose died. Rose had cancer but didn't tell us.

Before June died, we were in Prescott. I called La Crescenta to pick up my messages. I had a message from a Tony Ganss. I didn't recognize the name, but he said. "I was Signalman on the LST 124 during World War II. We had a Pharmacists Mate from Los Angeles by the name of Ernest Andrus. If that's you, please call me." I called him and he told me he was getting up a reunion. I couldn't attend because June would not be able to handle the trip. He sent me pictures and literature and told me about the LST Association.

I joined the association and purchased a book that had just been published called *The Large Slow Target*. I was thumbing through the book and spotted a picture of Marty Pinter. I showed it to June and said, "Isn't this the guy I have a picture of walking down the street with me in Wellington, New Zealand?" She said, "That's him." I called him. Here it was 40 years after World War II and I'm communicating with old shipmates. *Large Slow Target Volume II* came out. My picture is in that one.

The LST Association puts out a newsletter called "Scuttlebutt." I read that one of the members had discovered an LST in Greece and the association was getting a crew together to go after it. My son encouraged me, when June passed away, to check into it. I called Jack Melcher, the man who was putting together a crew and said, "I'm free now, can you use another man on the crew?" He said, "I need a man in the galley." I said, "I'll work the galley. Sign me up."

I had to get a doctor's clearance and had to pass an exam. It was a pretty thorough exam covering about everything in the Blue Jacket's Manual. If I couldn't find an answer, I'd call Melcher and he'd tell me where to find the answer. Once I'd cleared all the tests, he told me to pick up my messages daily because they'd be booking me on a flight to Greece soon. A small group of eight, I believe, went over in July, 2000, and were working on the ship.

Susan and I were spending a lot of time together. I signed up for an LST 124 reunion in Evansville, IN. That's where the LST 124 was built, so it was a good place for a reunion. Susan's niece had a son who was graduating from college in Albuquerque, NM. I packed everything for my flight to Greece, just in case I had to catch a plane before I got back. We went to the graduation. Susan had to ride back with her sister while I drove on to Evansville. We met at Tony's in Saint Louis and then went to Evansville. I shared a room with Marty and it was great getting together with some of my World War II shipmates. We weren't teenagers anymore, but it sure took us back to our younger days.

After the reunion, I drove back to Prescott. Susan was preparing to go to Alberta, Canada for a family reunion. She asked me to go with her. She wanted me to meet the rest of her family. I packed all my stuff in her car and we drove to Alberta. When we crossed the border, I was driving. The car was registered in her name. The border patrol was very suspicious. He asked me several times if I had any firearms, but wouldn't take my word for it. They searched everything before letting us go.

After the reunion, we drove back to Prescott. I picked up my messages. Someone wanted me to call him for my flight instructions. I was booked on a flight from Phoenix to New York. There we were to form a group of 20 to fly on a Greek Airline to Athens and then to the Isle of Crete. Tom Cadigan from Sedona and another guy were going on the same flight. Tom's son was driving them to the airport and agreed to pick me up on the way.

The day before my scheduled flight, I received a phone call saying my flight was changed and I would have a layover in Houston. This would cause me to miss my flight to Athens. I called Tom. Their flight had not changed. I called the airline, talked to a couple people, and was told they couldn't help me. I got angry and said I wanted to talk to the manager. A courteous gentleman came on the phone and I explained the situation. He said, "No problem. I've got you back on your original flight."

The flight to Greece was like being on a cruise ship. The hostess would come by asking if you'd like something more to eat. When we arrived on the Isle of Crete, a Navy bus was waiting to take us to the ship. I picked a bunk in the troop quarters forward port side near a ladder, figuring this would be convenient. These canvas bunks are four high with a thin mattress. Outside of having someone sleeping two feet above you and another sleeping two feet below you, they are fairly comfortable. This was August, with no air conditioning, and very hot, so I didn't spend much time in my bunk. I don't remember who all was in this same compartment, but would like to mention a couple of them here.

Phil Sniderman was a nine-year-old Jewish boy in Massachusetts during the depression. He joined the Coast Guard as a drummer boy so he wouldn't have to worry where his next meal was coming from. By the time we got involved in World War II, he was 13 years old and well trained. At the age of 15, he was a Coxswain. The Coxswain is usually the Captain of an LCVP (Landing Craft Vehicle Personnel), usually referred to as a Higgins boat, so at the age of 15 he was landing troops on islands in the Pacific.

Phil picked the top bunk next to the ladder. He could leave the door open to the top deck and had the only bunk that got a little breeze. After a few days, he wasn't feeling well and had to fly home. I moved into his bunk. He had brought a lot of books with him to set up a library for the crew. The library was set up in the small stores. Don Molzahn, the only other Coast Guard man, was in charge of small stores and didn't like playing librarian. There was a cupboard in front of the galley where everyone had to walk past to get their food. I opened it and saw a bunch of books. They were all in Greek so I pushed them aside and used that for our library. The last time I was aboard, I opened the cupboard and the library was still intact.

In 2005, we took the ship up the east coast. We were pulling into the Coast Guard dock at Gloucester, Massachusetts. There was Phil on the dock waving at me. He said the reason he had to leave the ship was heart problems. Phil died a few years ago and America lost another great man that helped keep this country free.

Loren Whiting had a bottom bunk. It seemed to me that this was the hottest spot in the compartment, but he was content there. The Captain decided to secure the port side so in case of a fire it couldn't spread to the whole ship. We all moved to the starboard side, except Whiting. He refused to move. Now Loren was as great an engineer as you could hope to meet, and you sure wouldn't want to lose him. He was offered a state room if he'd just give up that bunk. He said, "Give the state room to Ernie. It'll put him closer to the galley. I prefer to stay right where I am."

If you don't know who Loren Whiting is, look on the inside of the rear door of a big semi-truck. You'll probably see his name. He invented the door. They finally got him to move. Loren was 76-years old, just six months younger than me. He had lost a lot of his hearing. At a reunion in 2003, I met one of his sons and I said, "Why do you think he was so reluctant to move." He said, "Dad is very hard of hearing and he would pick a bottom bunk as close to the engine room as possible. He would lay with his best ear down. If anything went wrong with the engine he would hear it and know there was a problem."

Loren and I were discussing finances. I said, "You can give $6,000 a year to as many of your beneficiaries as you want, tax free." He said, "My tax man told me that, so I gave him a list of 90 people." In 2003 at our reunion, I was talking to him. This was right after the 9/11 attack. He said, "I was in that building on 9/10." Loren lives in upstate New York. I think he's still up and kicking. Don't think he's kicking too hard. He hasn't done any volunteering on the ship for quite a while.

The fellow that came with Tom Cadagen, whose name I can't remember, wasn't feeling well and decided he'd better go home. Tom said,

"This ship is beyond repair. It's not going anywhere and besides I've already sailed across the Atlantic on an LST. I really don't need that experience again. I'm flying back with him. Do you want to come along?" I said, "I didn't come here to give up and go home. I'll stick it out and see what happens." I told Captain Robert Jornlin, "I've got to be home by December 15th. I have business to take care of." He said, "If we're not home by December 15th, I'll have a broken marriage."

If you're wondering why we were so determined to get this ship back to the US, here's a summary… 1,051 LST's were built during World War II. There were none left that were operational. Winston Churchill and General Dwight Eisenhower both made a similar remark that the LST was the ship that won the war. All of us had served on an LST at some time and we believe this. The LST was our home and took us in and out of harm's way and we survived. We don't want the LST to be forgotten. We want Americans to know and remember what it took to win them the freedom they have today.

The LST was Winston Churchill's dream. He knew without such a ship, Great Britain would probably be defeated. He presented this to President Roosevelt. President Roosevelt brought in John Nieidermeier to draw a diagram. John Nieidermeier's son and I had something in common. We both worked for grocery chains on the west coast. I met him at a reunion in Evansville and he showed me the back of an envelope where his dad drew the diagram.

Jack Melcher told me it would take a minimum of 44 and a maximum of 72 men to get the ship back to the US. I understand 72 signed up, but these were not young men. Time was taking its toll. By the time I arrived in August 2000, I think we were feeding 38 or 39. Some were leaving, some were arriving, and some who had left were returning. I don't think the crew ever reached the 44 mark. After searching for an LST for years, Ed Stroble discovered this one in Greece. It took several years of red tape to get the President's signature, and an Act of Congress.

Then things started to progress, but slowly. We spent four months cleaning, repairing, and replacing parts. I was working with Joe Sadler and George White in the Galley. George was a Marine, but was allowed to join the LST association because he was aboard an LST when it was hit by a suicide plane and he had to go over the side. Most of his battalion was wiped out because the plane flew right into the tank deck and the Marines were in the tank deck ready to disembark. George was topside because he had volunteered to help in the galley.

George and I were alternating shifts in the galley but he jumped at every chance to work with the deck crew. Joe and I worked good together so Joe said, "George wants to be an Ape (deck crew) so why not transfer him to the deck crew and have Ernie work full time with me." He told me, "I asked them to give you a promotion as an incentive." I said, "Joe, even if they doubled my wage, double zero is still zero so I'm content to just keep my mess cook rating."

Joe called himself a dirty old man and that's exactly what he was. Joe and I became the best of friends. He had a terrific sense of humor and never ran out of jokes. Working with him was constant entertainment. When anyone would make a remark that could fit, his favorite come back was, "I had a girl like that once." Captain Jornlin said, "It's all talk." One day Joe went to the air base for supplies. He returned in a pickup truck. An attractive woman got out and helped him unload then she wrapped her arms around him and gave him a big smooch. Several of the crew were watching. I said, "Maybe it's not all talk."

When Joe was walking across the base, someone called out "Joe Sadler." It was someone he knew from Ketchikan, AK. The guy told him that he and his wife were working on the base. The woman with the pickup was that guy's wife. Joe, another shipmate, and I took one Sunday off and got Bruce Voges, our Boatswain Mate, to volunteer to feed the crew. We rented a car and drove to where civilization began. I think it was Knossos. It was very interesting! They've uncovered the queen's palace. She had running water piped in from a spring on the mountain side into a bathtub similar to the old ones here in the US. The sewage system was well engineered. The waste water went to the orchard in the valley. This was in Old Testament times. They have a theory on how God parted the Red Sea for Moses because there was a great earthquake at that time.

Jack Melcher was our self-appointed Captain. He spent years working on this project to make it happen. We need to give him credit for working out all the details, but he was a poor Captain. He didn't get along with people. He didn't get along with the crew. He didn't get along with the Greeks. Robert Jornlin was supposed to be the executive officer. When he arrived in Greece, he was summoned to the US Embassy. Ambassador Burns wanted to talk to him. I understand that Ambassador Burns informed him that he needed to take charge. The Greeks, the US Navy and the State Department couldn't get along with Melcher and were not going to give him any support.

At morning muster, Don Lockas stepped forward and said, "Bob, will you take over and be our Captain? The crew is fed up with Melcher and don't want to take any more orders from him." We took a vote and all but two of the crew voted for a change of leadership.

I need to take a break here and explain who Don Lockas is. I don't think we would ever have gotten that ship back without him, because he was a morale builder. When the rest of us got discouraged and were ready to throw in the towel and fly home, he would say, "We're going to take this ship back to the United States and we're going to take it back on its own power." I think we hung in there because we wanted to believe him. Whenever Don introduced himself, he always said, "Don Lockas with one 's'."

Don was our master helmsman. He took me up one day on his watch and taught me to steer the ship. I did so well, Jornlin called down and said, "Is that Ernie on the helm?" He said, "Sure is." Captain Jornlin said,

"Tell Joe he just lost a mess cook." The only reason I was doing so well was because Don was standing right behind me telling me every move to make. Whenever I'd start to overreact, he'd say, "Leave it alone, it'll come back."

Don gave me some of the best advice of my life. He said, "Never shake hands with a woman." Since then, I have had thousands of hugs. We'd come into the galley in the morning and found evidence that a rat had been there during the night. Don set a trap and caught him. He took him over to the side away from the dock, said a little prayer, and gave him a burial at sea.

The Greeks used squatters in the heads. These old salts were not going to be able to use squatters. Before I arrived, the crew had already installed commodes, but they didn't flush. To flush them, you had to pour a bucket of water in them. Dominick Purruso was a policeman by trade, but did plumbing on the side and was an excellent plumber. He came with the original crew but couldn't get along with Melcher so he left.

When Jornlin took command, he asked him to come back. He returned with all his tools. He found some flush toilets. Ed Strobel bought some wine and some goat cheese and celebrated. Joe and I kept a tub of water on the stove so we always had hot water. Dominick installed a five-gallon hot water heater. Five gallons doesn't go far, but it sure was a blessing. In my opinion, Dominick was one of the most valuable men on the ship. There was always work to be done and Dominick was a man of action, never idle.

There was no biodegradable toilet paper available, so we had to save our toilet paper in a trash can. I figured the best way to keep another rat from coming aboard was to remove the temptation so every night I gathered up all the garbage and other trash and took it to the dumpster on the dock.

When we first went aboard, we were told not to flush toilet paper. The Greeks didn't want the litter in the water. Tom Cadigan said, "What about all the other stuff we're flushing into the bay." The reply was, "The fish will eat it." That night we went to Nick's for dinner. Tom said, "What's your specialty tonight." Nick said, "Fish." Tom said, "I'll have a hamburger."

As far as I know, Don Lockas (with one s) and Dominick Purruso are still among the living. Tom Cadigan has Alzheimer's. I check on him occasionally; he seems to be doing fair.

We had several experienced electricians on the crew. Don Chapman from Moline, IL was our chief electrician. I was installing some racks to hold silverware in front of the galley. A couple of the drill holes stripped and the screws wouldn't hold. Don walked by. I showed him my problem. He said, "Put a tooth pick in each hole and reinsert the screw. It will hold just fine." This was a simple solution to a major problem.

Gary Lyon from Roseville, MN was a guy who knew everything there was to know about generators. He was retired as head electrician for Minneapolis. His expertise probably saved the ship. There was a unique individual, one of a kind, by the name of Bailey Wrinkle from McKinzie, TN. He carried his equipment in a wicker basket. The crew referred to it as "Bailey's Easter basket". Bailey's basket disappeared. He was frantically searching for his basket. Boats (Bruce Vogus) asked us to boil an egg for him. He colored it and put it in Bailey's basket. The next morning at muster, Captain Jornlin said, "We have a package here, I think it belongs to Bailey Wrinkle." Bailey shouted, "You found my basket." Bailey was fond of that egg. He carried it around in his basket until it started to smell, then he called a small group of us together and held a little service and gave it a burial at sea.

I was trying to learn some Greek and I said, "This is a hard language to learn." Bailey said, "I only speak one language and that's Southern." Don Chapman, Gary Lyon, and Bailey Wrinkle are all dead now.

Dick Meyers was one of our Helmsmen, a football player from Lincoln, NB. He was teaching me to play cribbage. Don Lockas said,

"Let me play. We can play three man." I said, "I don't know how to play three man." Don said, "We'll teach you." I had no idea what I was doing, but I skunked one and double skunked the other. Don never played cribbage with me again. Dick Meyers was only 75. His girlfriend was about 90. She had a son. Her son was Gary Lyon. Dick was instrumental in getting Gary to join our crew. I don't think we could have ever gotten the ship across the Mediterranean without him.

Boats came to me and said, "We're painting over the Greek helicopter pad. Would you like to get in on it?" I was painting away when Boats said, "You're not staying within the lines." I said, "I'm a Hospital Corpsman. When we prep for an operation we don't stay within the lines. We just paint the whole area."

Joe and I spent long hours in the galley, seven days a week. Only a couple of the crew took time off to go to church on Sunday. Joe knew I was a Christian, so he purchased a tape recorder and some tapes, so on Sunday while we're working in the galley, he'd play gospel music and say, "This is your church service."

Joe was up by 0400 every morning preparing and planning for the day. As soon as everyone had eaten and things were pretty well put away, he'd go somewhere to relax. I would stay and wash all the dishes and swab the aisle in front of the galley, then swab down the galley. They had cleaned the grease off the galley deck before I arrived, but only enough to give them working space. They didn't bother to clean the grease from under the fixtures so I'd take a shovel and a bucket and scrape up grease and haul it down to the dumpster. The grease was about four inches thick under everything. This was such hot work that I'd work until I couldn't handle any more, then I'd go down where we had an electric fan and let the fan blow on the back of my neck until I got cooled off.

When they finally got the engines running, we took it on a shakedown cruise. We cruised around for several hours on the Mediterranean. It was a great success. We had a happy crew with not a dry eye on the ship. We were all set to go, but we didn't have enough money left for the fuel, and the State Department would not let us go.

British Petroleum donated the diesel. We just had to go over to Athens to pick it up. We still had the State Department to deal with. Ed Strobel came down from the helm and Jornlin said, "Ed, you didn't have to do all that zigzagging. There's no submarines out there." The LST has a flat bottom and no keel, so it's inclined to drift. If you're not familiar with this, you're bound to overreact, and Ed was pretty good at overreacting.

Ambassador Burns wanted to see the ship, so they planned a big party. It was quite a shindig. I think the whole US Embassy was there, plus a couple Greek Admirals. The US Admiral had other commitments, so he sent several Master Chiefs from Great Britain, Spain, and Italy. I had a nice chat with Ambassador Burns, then I had lunch with the Master Chief group. One of them said his dad lived in Salome, AZ. I said, "I drive through there often. I'll stop in and see him and tell him I met you."

After I returned home I did just that. His dad said, "His mother and I were separated and he was shuffled back and forth between the two of us and wasn't getting any discipline. He was a wild kid and always in trouble. The Navy really straightened him out. Just what he needed."

There was a dog that hung around our ship. If she tried to come up the gangway, they wouldn't let her come aboard. The crew would throw her treats. If any other dog came near, she would chase him away. She got to know the whole crew and she would follow us into town and back. We were in Souda Bay, so the crew named her Souda. Paul Stimpson and I were going into town for a little sightseeing. Souda was tagging along and making some little noises. I said, "She's talking to us." Paul said, "What's she saying." I said, "How should I know. I don't speak Greek." Paul is dead now. His death came as a shock because he was one of the healthiest, strongest, toughest men I ever knew.

Norvel Jones was our Corpsman. We called him Doc Jones. He was never an actual Corpsman, but he was a fireman and had a little experience. He couldn't do any minor surgery but probably knew enough to handle most anything that was apt to happen. He told me his medical experience was minimal because most of his patients were dead. He couldn't do any labor because of a bad heart. I don't see how he ever managed to get on the crew. He had been pronounced dead twice on the operating table and survived. He was determined to make this trip and stuck it out all the way. He spent most of the time relaxing in his sick bay. He relieved Molzahn occasionally in the small stores. Later, after the ship got underway, Jornlin used him as lookout because there was no labor involved. He liked this and seemed good at it. Norvel Jones is dead now. They couldn't bring him back this time, but he got to fulfill his dream.

Bill Hart was not so lucky. He had a bad heart and he couldn't do labor. He had to sleep on a mess hall table. He helped us in the galley for a while, but even that was too much for him. He was a good planner and good to have around when problems occurred. I said, "Bill, this ship isn't worth your life. Why don't you give it up and go home?" He said, "No, this is something I want to do." I wasn't the only one concerned, because Jornlin sent him home. The long flight from Athens to New York was too much for him. He died at the airport. He probably would have had a better chance on the ship. I wrote an obituary for him and George White proofread it for me and corrected all my grammar.

John Michaud was an eighty-six-year-old Motor Mac (Motor Machinist Mate). John was up and down that ladder into the engine room several times a day. He took me down into the engine room to see what he was doing. The ladder top to bottom is at least 20 feet. The engine room was flooded right up to the walkway with a mixture of salt water, diesel fuel, and engine oil. I said, "John! You can't even walk into town without stopping for a rest. One of these days you're not going to make it to the top of that ladder. This ship's not worth your life. Don't you think you should go home and increase your life expectancy?" Doc Jones said, "John's not taking his heart medicine like he should, and his blood pressure is scary." Eventually, Captain Jornlin sent John home.

In 2003 when we took the LST up the Ohio river to Evansville, John and his family were on the beach waving at us. He would be about 90 years old then. Our crew lined up along the rail and saluted him and blew the fog horn.

I think it was Veteran's Day when Captain Jornlin announced the State Department was not going to allow us to go. A disheartened crew were making plans to fly home. Then came a cablegram from the Ambassador's office. I didn't see the cablegram but I think it read something like this, "The reasons the State Department are giving for not letting you go are not good reasons. You guys are going."

When we finally got the paperwork and took possession of the ship, we took a moonlight cruise to Athens. British Petroleum gave us 40,000 gallons of diesel fuel and the Hellenic Navy donated four LCVP's from their scrap heap to hang on our davits so we'd really look like an LST.

We got word that Ambassador Burns was coming aboard, so we dressed in our dress uniforms and waited. I have bad veins. The Ambassador was an hour late. After standing on that hard deck in my dress shoes for an hour, a vein busted in the side of my foot. This turned into a nightmare. It took us 13 days to get from Athens to Gibraltar because everything went wrong that could go wrong.

By that time, I was developing a lot of cellulitis. I was on my feet about 14 hours a day and we hit a couple storms. The ship was rolling and bouncing. It has been said that an LST will rock in dry dock. One of the engines went out on us so we were running on one engine. It seems we only had one generator that worked and it didn't work all the time. The generator would die and the engine would die, leaving us at the mercy of the sea. The ship would drift into the trough and take some big rolls. Joe and I were trying to fix lunch. We're getting out the dishes when the soup took off across the stoves. We let the dishes go and grabbed the soup. The ship began to roll the other way. We were gathering up the dishes when the soup started back the other way. We grabbed for the soup. Too late! All the soup dumped into the French fryer. Joe said, "Twice I've made soup. Twice I had to throw it out. No more soup!" We served cold cuts for lunch.

Problems with the steering was an everyday occurrence. When the steering would go out, they would blow the fog horn. That was a sign for a crew to rush to the after steering where it could be steered manually. Once or twice, we had to make a complete 360 degrees to get back onto course. We flew a flag warning other ships we were out of control. Ed Strobel came down from the helm. I said, "How did we do today?" Ed said, "I think we lost 10 miles." Every time the ship got into a trough, Joe would start swearing, calling the "stupid" crew every profane name he could come up with. As soon as they got the ship back on course, he was all praises for what a great crew we had. I said, "Joe, would you rather be setting at home watchin' TV or out here rocking and rolling on the ship? This is what I call living."

When we reached Gibraltar, I went to a doctor. He gave me a prescription and said it will heal in a couple days. The next day it ulcerated and caused a big hole in the side of my foot. It looked like a gunshot wound. Signs of phlebitis were developing and I went to another doctor and got another prescription. The doctor said it should heal in a couple days if I could keep my foot above my heart. I asked, "Where do I get the Rx filled?" He said, "Safeway market." What a surprise to find a Safeway market on Gibraltar. Great Britain has socialized medicine, so there was no charge.

The wound was looking ugly so the Skipper called the British Navy doctor. He made a house call. I don't think he came to see me, I think he came to see the ship. He said he wanted to see me at his office at the hospital to do some tests. A young man was interviewing me for the History channel but I can't remember his name. He took me to the hospital and had the camera on me all the way through the hospital. Some nurses wanted to know what was going on. "He said he's an important man." The nurses disappeared, guess they didn't want to get filmed without makeup. The doctor asked if I was diabetic. I said, "No." He said, "I can't take a chance. I'm going to take a blood test." When the result came back. He said, "Good, no diabetes, we don't have to amputate." He wrote Captain Jornlin a letter, put it in a sealed envelope and said, "Give this to your Captain." The letter wasn't sealed when I gave it to the Captain because I opened it. I couldn't wait to see what he said.

He recommended that I not sail across the Atlantic where there would be no way to receive medical help for a month. I started packing. In the meantime, Glenn Gregg came aboard looking for me. He said when the fellow whose name I can't remember returned to New York, he told him what we were doing and he wanted to get in on the action. Glenn was a roving reporter. He signed up to work for Linda Alvers on the History Chanel Documentary and asked if I would talk to Captain Jornlin. He would like to sail the rest of the way on the ship. I told him about the money we each put up. He said, "Money's no problem." I said, "These old guys need help, they don't need a passenger." He said, "I can work." I talked to Jornlin and he said, "If I let him on, all the other reporters are going to want on. I can't have reporters bothering these men. They have too much work to do."

The way I heard it, Jornlin talked to his wife Lois and she said if you have a young man that's willing to help, you'd be crazy not to grab him. Anyway, I flew home and Glenn sailed on the ship.

I was back in Prescott for Christmas. I told the doctor I wanted to get back on the ship. He said OK, but keep that foot elevated as much as possible. Susan drove me to Mobile, AL while I kept my foot on the dashboard. The ship pulled in right on schedule, 10:30 AM January 10,

2001. I think there were somewhere between 9,000-10,000 people along the banks, on the piers, and on the balcony at the Convention Center. What a great welcoming party. Two fire boats led the way, spraying red, white, and blue water.

I got back on the ship as soon as it docked. Don Lockas (with one s) presented me with an American flag all properly folded and said, "We flew this flag for you on January 1st and marked the date, longitude and latitude on it." I think Loren Whiting donated the flag. I have a lot of flags donated to me while I was running coast to coast flown over the US capital in my honor and some state flags flown over their capital. I treasure every one of these flags, but the one that means the most to me is the one flown over the LST 325.

The ship arrived in Mobile on January 10, 2001. Mobile named the crew that brought the ship into Mobile the Gold Crew because they were wearing gold dress uniforms. There is a plaque on the ship listing the gold crew. My name is not on the plaque because I was not on the ship when it pulled into Mobile. I got back on the ship as soon as it docked. I was wearing my gold uniform. The Captain and the crew included me in their Gold Crew.

Susan asked Jornlin why he included me in the Gold Crew and not the others that left the ship in Gibraltar. He said, "They deserted us. I can still see Ernie's nail prints on the rail as he left the ship." There were a lot of others who helped get that ship in shipshape and getting it back to the US. There is another plaque listing those. My name is the first on the plaque, only because my name starts with "A". Volunteers immediately started coming aboard to help restore the ship. These are called the Blue Crew because they are mostly dressed in blue work cloths. What's left of our Gold crew are getting too old to be much help.

Thank God for the Blue Crew. They are doing a great job. All I can tell you about bringing back the LST 325 is what I witnessed personally. If you want the full account, get it from the Captain, the man who faced and solved all the problems and with a determined crew, and accomplished the impossible. Read his book *Bringing Back a Hero* by Robert D. Jornlin or go on YouTube and type in "The Return of the LST 325".

In September, 2001, the LST Association had a reunion in Mobile. We had a ceremony, I think it was a recommissioning. I quote here one thing I remember Jornlin said in his speech. "If the Navy should ever need us, we are available."

SUSAN AND I GET MARRIED, AND THE LST IS STILL A KEY PLAYER ...

SUSAN AND I WERE SPENDING SO MUCH TIME TOGETHER, I SAID, "WE MIGHT AS WELL BE MARried." I proposed and she accepted.

The LST 124 group were anxious to see the LST 325, so I said, "Let's have our next reunion in Mobile. I'll host it and I can show you the ship." We agreed on a May reunion. I told Susan, "We're having a reunion in Mobile. Why don't we get married on the ship?" She agreed, so I called Captain Jornlin and asked him if he would marry us. He said, "I'd be honored but I don't think it will be legal in Alabama." I said, "I'll make it legal." We got a license in Arizona and were legally married by one of the Baptist Church pastors. My brother was best man for the second time. He was best man when I married June. At the end of April, we were all packed and ready to drive to Mobile when I got a phone call. As soon as I heard my granddaughter's voice, I knew. Carol, my oldest daughter, had just committed suicide.

When June died, I was alone, still living between my two homes. Twenty days later, Anna Mae died. Within a twenty-day period, all my children had lost their mother. Carol had been trying to stay beautiful all her life. She had been taking prescription drugs to keep her weight down for so many years that she was finally suffering side effects, both physically and mentally. She could no longer hold a job. Vanity had destroyed her life and finally killed her. She wanted to come with me to Prescott. We had some great times sight-seeing and hiked a few trails, including the Grand Canyon.

After she died, her daughter showed me a log she kept, saying it was the most fun she'd ever had in her life. She wanted to just go on living with me. I told her that was not possible. She was on welfare in California. She had no income, so she needed that help. I told her she could live in my California home, but she wouldn't be able to keep coming to Arizona. I got her into a hospital. Got her a hip replacement, some reconstruction on her jaws, and some dentures. She asked me if I was going to marry Susan. I said, "I'll never get married again."

She stayed in the California home until my son Dan and his family needed a place to live because the home they were going to buy was selling at a price that was too high, so they had to move. I told him to move into my home until he found something else. Then I decided to sell him my home. Seven people in one house wasn't working, so Carol moved in with her daughter.

My son and his family were living in my La Crescenta home. It was on a private street and a great place to raise children. That's where he grew up, so he wanted to buy my house. I sold it to him at a very good price and they raised their family there.

When Carol heard Susan and I were getting married, I guess she figured any hope of coming home to live with Daddy was scuttled. She called me and said, "Dad, remember what you always told me, "Never say never."

It was just a couple days later that I was informed of her death. She was in such poor health I wouldn't wish her back, but my heart was broken. This was my first born, the apple of my eye. She was 57 years old when she died, but to me she was still my beautiful little girl.

I called Tony Ganns and Captain Bob and told them I'd be a day or two late but didn't plan to change anything. We drove to Corona, California for the funeral and drove from there to Mobile. It was a beautiful wedding on the LST. I had shipmates from World War II and shipmates from the LST 325 there. Susan's son Rod came from Lake Tahoe, California, to walk his mother across the deck and give her away. Her granddaughter, Joyce, from Alaska came down to be the Maid of Honor. Joe Sadler came down from Alaska to be my best man. Instead of *Here Comes the Bride* we had a tape of Elvis Presley singing the *Hawaiian Wedding Song*.

You can see our wedding on the LST 325 website—Archives May, 2003 "A wonderful wedding on the LST." We had the reception at the hotel where we were staying. Joe and I cut the wedding cake. Captain Jornlin gave a presentation of bringing back the LST 325.

Susan sold her home and we moved into my home. I had already bought another lot because I needed a bigger garage. I had a high clearance truck, and an antique MG besides my family car. We went to the contractor that built my home. He had retired, but his son was running things. We picked a model home and then started changing everything. With modern technology, this was no problem. It was all done on a computer.

Susan stayed home to make sure the construction was going the way she wanted it, and I went back on the LST. We were taking the ship on its first cruise since restoring it. They left without me, but I caught up with them at the dock in Saint Louis. We were there for the Fourth of July. They were shooting off the fireworks from a raft close by, the biggest display of fireworks I'd seen since the invasion of Saipan.

We gave tours there then sailed up to Evansville. There were so many people who came to see the ship, some stood in line for hours then got turned away and came back the next day. When we closed for the day, I had the gangway watch with another shipmate. We had orders not to let anyone on board. A car pulled up and a fellow said, "I have my uncle here. He's a World War II veteran. He missed the ship when it was in Mobile and there's something on the top deck that he welded on his ship during the war. He had me drive him all the way up here. He brought along his welding equipment and wants me to take a picture." My shipmate said, "We can't let you on board." He said, "We can't stay overnight. I have to get back to Mobile." I said, "Bring him aboard." They got their picture and left. I said, "So put me on the report, they can court martial me. It'd be worth it. Did you see the tears in that old guy's eyes?"

At the end of one of my tours, a young lady came up to me and said, "Did you say you were on the LST 124?" I said, "Yes." She said, "Where did you go aboard?" I said, "New Caledonia." She said, "When?" I said, "January, 1944." She said, "My dad went aboard the LST 125 in New Caledonia, January, 1944." I said, "When we went from the transfer unit to the dock there were only two of us on that jeep and neither of us knew what an LST was. I was going on the 124. He was going on another LST. I don't remember which one. It must have been your dad." She said, "I know it was him, because you are an angel that was put here just for me." I said, "I may be an angel in your sight, but I don't think the crew would agree."

She said her dad never talked much about the war, but she knew he served on the LST 125. Her dad died and she heard about this LST coming to Evansville so she came to see what her dad's ship looked like. Her name is Susan Bloom. She has become so attached to that ship she could probably sail it herself. She adopted me now as her father, so I guess I acquired another daughter.

When I finish a tour, I say "Let me tell you my favorite sea story. It's about our Captain. Everyone said it was impossible to take this old ship back across the Atlantic, but he did it. The Coast Guard said he couldn't take the ship up to Evansville, but here we are. But the best thing he did, was he performed a wedding right where we're standing and that was my wedding." I told them I was on my honeymoon. When they asked, "Where's the bride?" I said, "Home supervising the construction of our new home. She says the ship is my first love."

We planned to take the ship up the east coast in 2004 to celebrate D-Day + 60. I flew into Mobile. I was working in the galley with Frank, whose last name I can't remember, but he's a little chubby Italian with a great personality. His wife was there helping us supply the ship for the voyage. We were all set to go. The Coast Guard wouldn't let us go. They said the ship wasn't safe. We donated all our perishables to charity and went home. They put the LST in dry dock and took care of everything the Coast Guard required and planed the trip for 2005. I missed the ship when it left Mobile in 2005 because I was in the hospital having my gall bladder removed.

I flew to Washington, DC. The ship was docked in Alexandria. I took a taxi to the ship. I worked in the galley with Joe Lewin, who served on the LST 1138 during the Korean conflict, and when I got caught up in the galley, I gave tours. A young man that was volunteering on the ship took a load of us to see the World War II museum. I wasn't able to enjoy it because I was developing some phlebitis and my leg was starting to swell. We sailed up the coast and docked at a Merchant Marine dock, gave tours there and on D-Day + 61 we had a memorial service on the dock. I think there were about 20 veterans there that were at Normandy on D-Day.

Ambassador Burns came aboard. He was no longer Ambassador. He was serving as second in command under Condoleezza Rice. I told him what had happened to my foot. He said, "I know. I heard all about that." My step-daughter Susan (MY little Susie) drove up from Connecticut. I was so thrilled to see her. I gave her a tour of the ship then we spent some time together at Cape Cod. She spilled ice cream on her blouse so we shopped for a blouse. My leg was getting worse so Captain Jornlin called a cab to take me to a hospital on Cape Cod. The fellow, whose name I can't remember, who bunked right under me was not feeling well. Jornlin asked him to go with me to the hospital and get checked out. He refused. The hospital put me through a lot of tests. Their biggest concern was blood clots, but they found none. When I got back to the ship the other fellow had suffered a heart attack. They took him to the sick bay at the Merchant Marine base. They put him in an ambulance and were rushing him to the hospital when he died.

We sailed up to Boston. As we came into the harbor, a fire boat escorted us in spraying water. We docked one dock over from the USS Constitution (Old Ironsides). I attended a memorial service on the dock next to the USS Constitution. I rode in a Dukw with some other members of the crew representing the LST 325 in the Bunker Hill Day Parade. The LST 325 escorted the USS Constitution on its turnaround. Instead of sailing on the LST, I sailed on Old Ironsides. They gave me a 40 MM shell for a souvenir. I said, "We have 40 MM shells on our ship. Can't you give me a cannon ball?" I was in the galley when Susan Bloom walked in looking for me. She presented me with a book she had written about the LST 125. If I can find the book, I can add a lot to this book because the 124 and 125 were sister ships engaging in the same invasions from January through April. I've forgotten the names of some of those Islands.

The LST 325 originally only had two davits to hold LCVP's . The Greeks added two more. The crew removed two of them, thus restoring to original and reducing the amount of upkeep. They kept two LCVP's, sold one, and couldn't get rid of the other because the side was caved in and was beyond restoring. They were sorta stuck with it. Jornlin said they wanted $4,000 to haul it off. Before the ship left Mobile, Spielberg's crew came to see the LST. He wanted to use it in his movie *Flags of Our Fathers*. His crew saw the damaged LCVP and said they could use it in the movie. They were just going to blow it up, so the condition didn't matter. Jornlin sold it to them for $5,000, giving us a net profit $9,000.

He agreed to lease them the other two for the movie. The crew put the damaged LCVP on the top deck and with the other two on the davits, sailed to Boston.

Clint Eastwood called and asked if we were going to let them use the LST in the movie. Jornlin said, "No! We took a vote and determined we couldn't take a chance on anything happening to it." Clint said, "That's all right, our special effects guys can take a tanker and make it look like an LST. No one will know the difference."

He wanted us to bring the LCVP's to Washington, DC. Again, Jornlin said, "NO! We just came from there. We have no intension of stopping there on the way back. This is a long cruise and the crew are anxious to get home." Eastwood sent a big truck to Boston and they lifted our LCVP's from the ship to the truck with a big crane.

We sailed up the coast to Gloucester. We tied up at the Coast Guard dock and there was Phil Sniderman waving at me. Glucester was a great liberty port. The crew was enjoying it so much I think they stayed an extra day. I wasn't able to get ashore because my leg wasn't getting any better. I told Captain Jornlin I was going to have to jump ship again. I took a taxi to Boston and flew back to Arizona. I thought it was the steel deck that was causing my leg problems, but all the doctors agreed it was the long flight right after surgery. I now have doctor's orders, "Whenever flying get up and walk around every hour."

Back at the hospital in Prescott, I went through all the same things as Cape Cod, fearing blood clots. The doctor applied una boots, changing them once a week. When I took a shower, I had to seal my leg in a plastic trash bag. I was used to this, having been through it a couple times before.

We were planning to take a holiday cruise to Hawaii. My cousin Madeline, her daughter Bonnie, and Susan's sister LaVerne, were going with us. Susan's brother had never been to Hawaii. His wife had Alzheimer's and didn't even know who he was when he visited her, so he decided to go with us. He bought a new suit and was real excited about this.

I was in Evansville giving tours on the LST. Susan was helping in the gift shop. We were staying at a motel. I got up early and went for a run. I received a phone call. It was LaVerne. Their brother was killed in a freak accident. We started for home and planned to stay overnight at Tony Ganss' home in Saint Louis. On the way, LaVerne called and told us when the funeral was. I said to Susan, "We can make it." We got an early start from Saint Louis. I drove fourteen hours a day and arrived in Beiseker, Alberta, Canada the night before the funeral.

When we left for our cruise, we drove to San Diego and got a hotel room for the night. Joe Lewin was living in San Diego so we got together and shared dinner at a nice restaurant on the wharf. Our cruise ship and the US Midway were at the same dock so I did a quick tour of the Midway. I would have liked to have seen more, but had to get back to the cruise ship. When we got to Hawaii, my daughter Donna and her man Chris were there on vacation. They had a rented car so we did some sightseeing. We went to the Arizona battleship memorial. It is completely submerged now. When I was there in 1944, it was resting on the bottom but sticking way up out of the water. I was told that one of our LST's was still visible at West Lock but I couldn't go see it. I was told it was a restricted area.

I START MY SERIOUS RUNNING CAREER ...AT AGE 87

I KEPT MYSELF IN SHAPE BY RUNNING EVERY OTHER DAY, FROM THREE MILES TO SEVENTEEN MILES. The farthest I had ever run was 18 miles when I was 69 years old. That was on a high school track and it just about did me in. Twenty years later, I ran seventeen miles with very little difficulty. I think what made the difference was the high school track was all level, therefore I was using the same muscles the whole way. The seventeen miles was in the hills of Prescott. I ran my first one half marathon, The Whiskey Row Marathon in Prescott, considered one of the most challenging in the country, when I was 87 years old.

A friend, Ken Ekman, told me about a runner from Great Britain who was running across every nation. He had just run through Prescott and Ken put him up for the night. I thought, "That would really be a fun adventure, maybe I should run across the United States." Susan's niece ran the Ragnar two-hundred-mile relay from Prescott to Phoenix. We were there to see her off. Everyone was having so much fun, I tried to get on a team for the next year, but couldn't find a team.

The following year, I was running a seventeen K on the Peavine Trail, Prescott, AZ. Ken was organizing the run and I told him I sure would like to run the Ragnar Del Sol. He said, "You may be in luck. There's a gal getting up a team and she's running the trail today. I'll introduce you."

So I was introduced to Stephanie Fricke, the team captain. She said, "I'll take it up with the crew." She called me later and said, "The crew voted for you 100%. You're in."

I did my first Ragnar 200 mile relay when I was 88 which was the most fun run I'd ever done. Because of my age, they featured me in their Ragmag magazine. People were asking for my autograph and wanting their picture taken with me. I thought, "If an 88-year-old gets this much attention for a 200-mile relay, how about a 90-year-old running coast to coast." I decided right then, I'm going to do it. I was just going to do it for the adventure. Then I thought, "Maybe this is our chance to raise enough money to get the ship back to Normandy for a memorial service."

I had two years to make my plans. I mentioned something about it to Captain Jornlin and he said, "It will never happen." I said, "Well, I can try."

I did my second one half marathon at the age of 89. Before I started my coast to coast run, I ran the 10K for the Prescott Fire Department. Being I was the oldest runner, they had me ride on top of a fire engine during the Christmas parade. I ran the 10K for the Skull Valley Fire Department. I ran that run the year before and got held up by a big bull on the road. Glad I didn't run into him again. I came in dead last, but I was not alone because a group that finished ahead of me came out and ran in with me.

They furnished the runners a pancake breakfast. While I was enjoying my pancakes, the announcer said, "We are now going to give out the awards. The first award goes to the world's greatest runner." I assumed it would be the one who came in first. He called my name. This is biggest and best trophy I've ever received.

I didn't tell Susan my plans until I had it all figured out. She said, "I wish you wouldn't." I said, "It's something I really want to do." She said, "OK," and we sat down and started making plans. At first, she was going to go with me. We bought a new Winnebago motor home and a tow car. I had decals put on both, showing runners, including this old man, a picture of the LST, and a twin 40 mm gun. We started getting the house ready to sell.

I used a ruler to find the nearest distance across the US and determined that would be San Diego, CA to Brunswick, GA. That was as the crow flies. Not being a crow, I had to run a couple hundred miles extra to find highways I could run on. I drove to San Diego to find the best place with the least sand to run across for my starting point. A life guard told me Mission Beach. I checked it out. It was a perfect place to start.

On the way home, I drove through Yarnell, AZ. The next morning, a fire swept through Yarnell, killing 19 of our beloved firemen. I belonged to the Prescott Antique Auto Club and we had just finished restoring Prescott's # 1 fire engine. One of our members was a retired fireman and still has his license. His grandson was one of the firemen that was lost in the fire. In the next parade, he drove the fire engine with the 19 names on the side.

Before I started my coast to coast run, I ran three more Ragnar two hundred mile relays. One in Las Vegas, another in Del Sol, and the Southern Cal run from Huntington Beach to San Diego. The captain of the Southern Cal team was a Hospital Corpsman stationed in San Diego. Most of our team was Navy. The plates on our vans said 'for government use only'. My first run was through Corona.

My daughter Linda lived in Corona at that time so she was there at my start and finish.

My wife, Susan, was losing her eyesight and decided not to try living in a motor home, so we started looking for an assisted living retirement home. There was a new one just a few blocks from our home. They had room for her. This was luxury living. I had an auctioneer come and take everything except what I wanted to take with me. I had a couch in one of the bedrooms that made into a bed. I stayed there while clearing everything out. I could have all my meals with Susan because she was so close and she could come up to the house any time she wanted.

Our next-door neighbor, Maddee Curran, was in real estate. She agreed to take over, get the house ready to sell, and put it on the market. I hired the fellow to redo my landscaping that had done it originally because he was so good and I didn't want anyone else touching it. I drove my RV and tow car down to El Cajon, CA and camped at the Sunland RV Resort. While I was gone, Maddee was so good to Susan. She took her shopping, took her to the doctor, and was right there for her for anything she wanted.

I turned 90 on August 19, 2013. And I planned to start my run on October 7, to get across the desert before it got too hot. My brother and his wife drove down on October 6th, and brought Susan with them. I rented two adjoining rooms at the Best Western. I was able to spend two nights with Susan before they headed back. On the October 6th run, Channel 10 news filmed me running and announced what I was doing, but they never told how to get in touch with me or how to help.

Cathy, Linda, Carl (Linda's husband), and Janet Dalton (a friend of the family I hadn't seen in many years), plus Susan, my brother, and his wife, were all there to see me off. It seems I was the only one that believed I could do this. I ran alone while everyone else went to breakfast. Carl was at the finish to get me back to my car. Cathy stayed with me in the RV for two weeks at the start, which was a big help. She could drop me off at the start, go find a Starbucks and pick me up at the finish. I called the captain of my Southern Cal team, whose name was Sarah Weaver, I think, and she got some sailors out there to run with me.

Jessica Edmond was my first runner. What a blessing she was! She ran Legs 2, 4, and 6. By then I had a lot of runners showing up. I had to run alone Legs 3 and 5. After that, I never had to run alone until Leg 14. On Leg 6, Jessica brought along five sailors plus her 9-year-old daughter Sydnee and 11-year-old Samantha Merrill to run with me.

Two of the sailors that really kept me inspired were Jeremy Merrill and Christopher Stubbs. Jeremy stuck with me for five legs and Christopher six. They had a shipmate who was at the Isle of Crete, Souda bay at the time. He googled me and saw that I had spent four months there getting our LST seaworthy. He said, "Looks like an omen. I've got to run with this guy. My home is in Texas so when he gets to Texas, I'm going to put in for leave." (I can't remember his name off hand maybe I'll come up with it later). When I reached Texas, he had been transferred to Japan. He flew home and drove five hours to run with me. He presented me with some gifts donated by his running club in Japan and left. He holds the record for traveling the farthest.

For Leg 9, I was running through Ramona, California. An article came out in the local newspaper. Mike Gesualdo called me and said his 11-year-old daughter had never met a World War II veteran and he wanted her to meet me. He showed up with his family of three, along with 10 others, plus a couple who joined in along the way. This was in 2013. He ran a total of eight legs with me. On Veteran's day weekend in 2014 and 2015, he showed up with some of his shipmates, and he was at the finish. He has become a true friend. He picked up some of my belongings which were in storage and held them for me until I got settled in California, then delivered them to me. He bought a trailer and drove me to Prescott to get my classic MG out of storage. One of the runners at Leg 9, Terry Blue, was wearing the same Whiskey Row Marathon shirt as me. We had never met in Prescott, but we had run in the same race. We became friends. She ran six legs with me.

Leg 11 was another special one. Fourteen sailors off the USS Pearl Harbor (LSD 52) ran with me. I just have to mention Amy Prodan, because she seemed so special. She was just a 19-year-old sailor. Not only a beautiful young lady, but stood out in a crowd with her pleasant personality and friendly nature. What impressed me mostly was her devotion to family. I knew her home was in the Phoenix, AZ, area so when

I was running through the area, I contacted her and let her know where and when I would be running, just in case she happened to be on leave. She showed up with her family and it was another great run with some wonderful people. She said, "I won't be able to run the next leg with you because I'm celebrating my 20th birthday by sleeping in." Before I wrote this, I contacted her to see if she is still in the Navy and what's going on in her life. She is still in the Navy and is a Rescue Swimmer Instructor. She is only four hours away and plans to come do another run with me.

During Leg 17, Larry Shriver from Banner Queen Ranch near Julien, CA ran with me. He ran two other legs with me. On Leg 21, he brought along his twin boys, age 13. Legs 20, 22, and 23 I had to run alone and he showed up to drive me back to my car. I visited their ranch and met his beautiful wife. He was a true friend. I was running up a hill east of Julien, CA. A man pulling a cart with a big sign "LOVE LIFE" was walking the other way. I hollered over, "Where you going?" He said, "I'm walking the 48 states. Where you going?" I said, "The Atlantic Ocean." He said, "Let's get together and take some pictures." His name was Steve Fugate. He said he had already walked across all 48 states several times and was now walking all of them in succession. The next morning I wasn't running and I knew about where he would be, so I met him and said, "You should reach Julien about 1:30. Stop at Granny's Kitchen and I'll buy you lunch. I brought some maps along and maybe you can give me some advice."

I told the owner of Granny's Kitchen what I was doing so she brought her whole crew out for a welcoming party. Our lunch was on the house. While we were eating, she called a TV station in San Diego. They drove all the way out and put us on nationwide TV. Steve was hiking the Apalachian Trail when his son committed suicide. His daughter was so broken up over her brother's death she was on tranquilizers. She eventually took an accidental overdose and died. He had now been walking nearly 16 years trying to stop young suicides. He was having a lot of success. He would tell people attempting or thinking suicide, "Your life is not yours to throw away. It belongs to your family and friends. It is a selfish thing to do. Think of the broken hearts you're leaving behind." Steve finished his walk, then wrote a book. I told him that people kept telling me I should write a book. He said, "I hope you do so, you'll see what it's like to sit in front of a computer for two years when you're used to pounding the pavement."

There were two things Steve taught me which were a great help. Always Google drive, never Google walk, because It will take you on some trails you will regret and there will be no place to park cars... and never give up your space. The car coming toward you is not going to hit you. He doesn't want to get blood on his car and if he pulls over, all the cars behind him will pull over. If you give up your space, he won't pull over and neither will the other cars. I ordered Steve's book. He said he has walked over and back across the U.S. nine times and I have now inspired him to do it again. This is his tenth trip and will come to about 50,000 miles. It's October, 2017 while I'm writing this and he's walking across Louisiana. If you're interested in his book it's *Love Life* by Steve Fugate. There's a nice article about our meeting on page 259.

I was camped at the Leaping Lizard RV Ranch near Borrego Springs, CA. I got a phone call saying Susan had a mini stroke and was in the hospital. I called her and she said, "Don't worry about me. I'm fine. At 8:00 PM, another phone call came. She had a major stroke and was in a coma. The manager of the RV Ranch, Susan Baker, was a wonderful friend. She had already volunteered to get me back to my car when I had to run alone. Now she had me leave a key to my RV in case of an emergency and said she would look after it until I got back. I got into my Dodge Dart and headed for Prescott, AZ. I had to detour because of road construction. Took me all night to get to Prescott.

Susan was in a coma. She couldn't see, talk, or swallow. She did move her right leg and right arm. She had a fully charged hearing aid and could hear. I took her hand and said, "If you know who I am squeeze." She squeezed. The doctor said he could keep her alive artificially but she would never improve. She had told him that she did not want that. I held her hand for a week until she stopped breathing. We had a nice memorial service for her at the First Baptist Church. I went back to the California desert to continue my coast to coast run. I have always found running to be great therapy.

I was 90 years old and outlived three wives. My first marriage was miserable, but if I had it to do over, I wouldn't change a thing. She gave me three beautiful daughters and I loved raising them. Through those daughters, I have grandchildren and great grandchildren. Life is good. My second marriage was made in heaven. June was the love of my life. She had three daughters the same age as my three. Six girls to raise now and loving it, then we had a girl and a boy of our own. The older girls were starting to leave the nest. Starting another family was a blessing. Donna is still my love child. Dan was my only boy and how I loved raising that kid. He sure kept me on my toes. He's probably the reason I've lived so long. His energy was what got me back to exercising and now he has blessed me with four beautiful grandchildren. My third wife, Susan, was the best wife I ever had. She made my eighties the best years of my life. We were both retired. Nobody had to go to work. We could do nearly everything together.

When I got back I had to run a few legs alone. The other manager, Starr Hutchinson, drove miles to get me back to my car then gave me two checks—one to sponsor me and one for the ship. After some of my runs, I stopped in Brawley for breakfast at Brownies diner. An article came out in the local paper. After that, all my meals were on the house and the owner sponsored me. On my 33rd Leg, I was in the middle of the

California desert. Jim Blair and Jeff Middleton, friends from my Ragnar runs, showed up. In the meantime, I moved my RV to Sans End RV Park in Winterhaven. One of the campers, Stan Bomak, a trucker from Canada, joined me. We'd drive to the start and he'd take the car to the finish and do some rock hunting until I got there.

Stan knew the U.S. like a book. I told him I planned to finish at Brunswick, Georgia, but couldn't see any way to reach the Atlantic Ocean. He said, "Run across the bridge onto Saint Simons Island. You'll love it there and you can run right into the ocean." Great advice! I couldn't have found a better place to finish. By this time, I had made so many wonderful friends and I was not even out of California.

I could not find a way from California into Arizona on Google without either getting onto an interstate or going as far north as route 66 or going into Mexico. I was running across the U. S. so Mexico is out, there were no pedestrians are allowed on the Interstate, and I had no intention of going that far north. I said, "I'm heading for Yuma." I was told there was no way I could get to Yuma on foot. I said, "I'll find a way."

I talked to the Highway Patrol. They didn't know any way. I went into a Shell station. The girl on duty said, "Talk to the Border Patrol. They know every road." She put my flyer up in the station and said she'd make some inquiries. She said that the Border Patrol comes in often for coffee. I drove to the border and talked to a patrolman. He was very rude. This was the first person since I had started my run that was unfriendly. I tried to give him one of my flyers. He refused it and said, "I don't care who you are and I can't help you."

The next time I went into the Shell Station, a couple Border Patrol agents were there having coffee. The girl introduced me to the female patrolman. She said, "I know a way. I drive it often." It was only a block away so I went right over to check it out. It was obvious she had a 4-wheel drive because there was no way I could drive through that sand so I parked the car and walked it. It went through all right, but by the time I got back to my car, a vein in the side of my foot busted. This was the same area where I had the busted vein before. I drove to Prescott to have my doctor look at it. He said, "It'll heal. Don't stand, sit, or lay down for long periods of time. Just keep moving. When you do sit or lay down, elevate your foot above your heart." I followed his orders.

It was three weeks before I had to run through the sand. It had healed by then. I ran 1.66 miles through deep sand and then it got worse because the street hadn't been repaired in years. Another three miles of broken concrete followed, but I got through. My next run was across the bridge into Yuma. A TV reporter was out there filming me when I crossed into Arizona. I got rid of all my TVs years ago. I had a big TV in my RV but had no idea how to use it. A camper pulled in next to me. I mentioned it to her and she came in and got the TV working for me. I said, "I was running as fast as I could across that bridge but that old man is moving slow."

The owner of the Shangri La RV Park in Yuma contacted me and said he'd be honored to have me stay at his camp free of charge. I thanked him for his kind offer but I was ready to move beyond Yuma. He said I'll notify other camps and see if I can get you some free stays. There was no way to get from Yuma to Phoenix without getting on the Interstate, so I had to head north. What's a couple hundred miles when you're running coast to coast. I took Highway 95 north to Quartzsyte.

Mark Wrathall, another one of my Ragnar runners, got his family up at 2:00 AM and drove all the way from Corona, California to run with me. Two days later, Jim Blair did the same thing. Jennifer Jones, publisher of the Desert Messenger, brought Ed Foster, the mayor of Quartzsyte, out to meet me by the Welcome to Quartzsyte sign. I met Gunny Saint Germain, a retired Marine, when he came to run with me on Highway 95. Gunny has a small military museum.

On the next run, he brought along a fellow Marine, Carlos Cano. I was a hospital Corpsman during World War II. The Marines have always told me that the Corpsman is the Marine's best friend and Carlos was definitely a best friend. He ran 44 legs with me in eight states. I stayed at the H&H RV Park in Quartzsyte. I made a lot of friends in Quartzsyte. Larry & Peggy Sparks were always there for me when I needed a volunteer. They showed up again in New Mexico when I needed an escort through a tunnel on Mt. Cloudcroft. They've also been here to visit me in California. Peggy's sister, Joan, and her husband, Warren, were there for me in Quartzsyte also and came to visit me in Tallahassee, Florida.

Ed Foster, mayor of Quartzsyte, asked me to bring my car with the Coast2Coast Runs decals on it to the car show. I met some interesting people at the car show. A man in his 90's whose name I can't remember, is in the Guinness Book of World Records and holds the record for the one-hundred yard dash for his age group. The manager of the Patton's museum asked me to do a presentation. I agreed. He would contact me when he was ready. He wanted to do some advertising and get a group together, hoping to get me some support.

Gunny brought the Vietnam Wall to Quartzsyte. He gave me a table so people could meet me. The mayor gave a speech. I told him there was one remark in his speech that was not true. He said no one respected the Vietnam veterans when they returned. I said, "The World War II and Korean veterans respected them." He said, "Then why didn't you do something about it?" Good question! Those were the baby boomers. Those were our kids in Vietnam and those were our kids demonstrating. Rather than take sides, we just stayed out of it. It was easy for me. I didn't have a son in Vietnam and none of my kids were demonstrating.

The owner of Black Rock RV Park contacted me and offered me a free stay so I moved my RV from Quartzsyte to Black Rock. When I reached Bouse, AZ, Joan Fradenburg started showing up. Joan was the captain of the team when I ran my second Ragnar Del Sol. She also ran with me in the Whisky Row Marathon, Prescott, AZ before I started the coast to coast runs. She ran a total of 15 legs with me between Bouse and Payson. Since then I was on her Ragnar team again and she ran with me again at Whiskey Row. I am now signed up to run on her Del Sol team again.

On Leg 62, some of my family from Chicago showed up. My step-nephew John Gibson and his son Danny ran with us. His wife Vicky and his sister Debby and her husband Dick were volunteers. We ran from Salome to Wenden, 5.27 miles then to breakfast and a little family reunion.

I moved my RV to the Cactus Ranch Trailer Court, Wickenburg.

Leg 63 was a 4.21 mile run east from Wenden, AZ. Stephanie and Mark Fricke and Erick Johnson showed up for the run. These three have been true friends and have run with me many times in Whiskey Row marathons, Ragnar Relays and Coast to Coast runs. I was running into Wickenburg on a Saturday, ending right on the corner of the street Joan lived on. She said she couldn't run with me because she was running a 10K. After my run, I went to the 10K finish to see how Joan did. She said, "There's a 96-year old woman here who just did the 5K in her cowboy boots." I said, "I've got to meet that woman." She was right in front of us so Joan said, "I want you to meet Ernie Andrus." She said, "I know who he is. I was hoping to meet him at the American Legion. I was in the Navy."

When I stepped in front of her I said, "I know you. We flew together to Washington, DC on the Honor Flight. You were dressed in red, white and blue." She gave me a picture of herself dressed in her cowgirl outfit in the parade. Before I left on my coast to coast run my brother had commented "Whatever happened to that 93-year old woman that went on the Honor Flight with us?" I said, "She's probably dead." I sent my brother the picture and said, "Here's our dead woman, just did a 5K in her cowboy boots."

We were concerned about our next run. There was a blind curve, fast traffic, and no shoulder. We were trying to find a way to detour and avoid that curve, but no luck. Thirty-five people I had met on the highway walking from the Pacific Ocean to Washington, DC walked around that curve with no mishaps, so I guess we can chance it. Fortunately, we didn't have to. There was an article in the newspaper that morning. A World War II LST sailor lived near our starting point. He wanted to meet me and show me his album. He was at the start. I said, "How about escorting us around the curve then meeting us back here for breakfast and you can show me your album." A perfect plan.

I moved my RV to Eagle View RV Resort, Fort McDowell. This is on the Indian Reservation. It cost me almost $900 for one month. I took it because it was the most convenient. The camper next to me was owned by Bo of Mercurius Creative and he looked at the decals on the side of my motor home and said, "You don't have a website. Can I sponsor you? This is what I do." He set up my website (coast2coastruns.com), gave me an $1,800 three-year contract and marked it paid in full.

I was parked on highway 60 east of Aguila, waiting for Joan. A fellow stopped to see if I needed help. I told him what I was doing. He said, "I'd love to run with you but I have to get to work." He pulled up his pant leg and showed me his artificial leg and said, "Vietnam, but I can still run." I was running into Sun City when Rocky and Dianne Hill showed up. Rocky is one of my shipmates from the LST 325. They didn't come to run. They came as volunteers and to join me for breakfast. Rocky's not a runner. He's a swimmer. He agrees with me that the surest way to win a race is outlive your competition.

As I ran through the Phoenix area, several Ragnar friends ran with me. I was concerned about a run along Shea Boulevard, toward Highway 87. No shoulder, lots of traffic, and a blind curve, again. I had four runners, all Ragnar friends, plus John Murphy on a bicycle. Erick Johnson ran ahead with an American flag. I observed that when he held out the flag traffic moved over, so after the run I went to Target and bought some flags. Most of my runners and I have been carrying flags ever since. From the Pacific to the Atlantic, I never had a traffic problem.

Steve Hartman of CBS news and his cameraman, Bob Caccamise, flew in from New York to film me on the road. They then flew to Evansville IN to film the LST. This went worldwide on TV and on YouTube. They filmed me again running into Waco, TX and again at the finish on Saint Simons Island, GA.

I received a call from Hoop LaHa in Connecticut wanting an interview, said they would send someone to interview and take pictures. I said, "Are they going to come all the way from Connecticut?" She said, "No! We have connections in Phoenix." They did a very good video. It went viral on the internet and drew a lot of attention.

Leg 78 was a 6.02 mile run along West Thunderbird Road from 51st Avenue to 7th. I had 11 runners. This was the leg where Amy and her family showed up. There was another special runner by the name of Kendall Jordan on that run. She ran two more legs with me and said she was graduating and meeting her family for a Hawaiian vacation, but she would have to come back to pick up her car so she would run with me again. She showed up for Leg 92 and brought me a souvenir from Hawaii-an Arizona battleship shirt. It was a real blessing to have her along. This was a 4.95 mile run and all uphill. This was the first time I had to take a break. We found a nice guard rail to sit on for a couple minutes.

I was driving back and forth trying to find a good place to finish and start a run. I had my cruise control set on 65. I overlooked a reduced speed sign and got my picture taken. Lousy picture! Nowhere near worth the price. I received a citation, "Excessive speed, 65 in a 45." I went into Payson to pay the fine ($233). The clerk had the morning paper laying beside her with my picture on the front page. She said, "Don't pay the fine. Talk to the judge. He's a reasonable man." I said, "The court date is in July and I'll be a hundred miles from here." She said, "Go to traffic school so it won't be on your record." I said, "Same problem." She said, "You can do it on the internet." I said, "I spend half my time on the computer now. I have too many other things to think about. I better just pay the fine." The insurance increased on both my car and RV for three years. That ticket cost me about $1,500. For a real scenic drive, try highway 87 between Phoenix and Payson. As the elevation changes the scenery changes, but beware, they take lousy pictures.

The morning I was running into Payson, I had one runner, Bobby Doss. She saw the newspaper article and remembered me from the Del Sol 200-mile relay so came out to run with me. Two ladies on bicycles approached us from the other way to join us to the finish. They said there was a welcoming party waiting for us at the finish. This was a 4.78 mile run, mostly uphill, so we were 20 minutes late arriving. There was a mud run taking place nearby and all but one of the welcoming party had left. The one left was a retired colonel. She waited for us because she wanted to take some pictures.

I drove along the Mogollon Rim looking for a camp to move into. The first one didn't have an available space. He said, "Try my neighbor." I pulled into the Mogollon RV Park. I mentioned to the manager that some camps had given me a free space. When I mentioned Shanrgri-La RV Resort in Yuma she said, "I used to be at the Shangri-La. He owns this camp, too. I'll call him and see what he says." She called him and he said, "Tell him we're proud to have him at our camp and give him a free space." While I was camped there, I met some wonderful people. There were two families, the Wilkies and the Grants, who volunteered to get me back to my car when I ran alone. And both families sponsored me.

Leg 95 was a 6.03 mile run on highway 260 out of Payson. Seven runners came all the way from Tucson. They were military, something to do with helicopters. Lisa Brody from Phoenix joined us. After the run, we went to Denny's for breakfast and took some pictures. Leg 96 looked like I would be running alone. A gal that Lisa worked with said, "You can't let him run alone. You gotta go up there." The two of us had a great 5.19 mile run. I said, "Everyone's been buying my breakfast, this one's on me." Back to Denny's we were for some great fellowship and some more pictures. When I bid her farewell, I felt rather sad like I just made a very special friend and now I'm going to run off and leave her and probably never see her again. To this day, every time I see a Denny's, I think of Lisa. The story of my coast to coast runs, make friends then run off and leave them.

Jimmy Danko, an artist in Los Angeles, contacted me. He said, "My girlfriend and I only have one car between us. She's going to be out of town and suggested I take advantage and go run with Ernie, so that's what I'm going to do. I'll drive to Payson on Wednesday, run with you on Thursday, do some sightseeing Friday, and run with you again on Saturday." I said, "Where do you plan to spend the night on Wednesday?" He said, "I'll either get a motel or sleep in the car." I said, "No you're not! I have a bed in my RV I never use. You can spend the night here."

He spent the night Wednesday and ran with me Thursday. This was a 4.06 mile uphill run on highway 260 from Christopher Creek loop to the 260 trail head. Gail Watts from Glendale met us at the start. She had her mother-in-law with her. She left her mother-in-law in the truck and ran about one mile with us then went back to her truck. On the way back, she picked up odds and ends along the road, made them into a great art piece and mailed it to me. I have it hanging in my living room. I love it!

Jimmy went to the Grand Canyon and came back Friday night, spent the night, and ran with me on Saturday. This was one of the roughest runs of them all. It was only 3.32 miles. A steep climb from the 260 Trail Head to the Mogolon Rim Visiting Center. I took two breaks before we reached the top. There was no shoulder facing traffic but a nice shoulder with traffic, so we ran with the traffic. Jimmy tagged along behind, holding out a flag.

The next run was 4.57 miles starting at the Mogolon Rim visiting Center ending at Rim Lakes Recreation area. David Steel from Surprise,

AZ called and said he would be there to run with me. I Googled the running club in Surprise and found there was a Daniel Steel in the same town. Sounds like brothers to me. When he arrived, he said, "I brought another runner with me." Her name was Kristin Steel. I asked her if Dan was David's brother. She said, "No, he's my husband. David and I never met until this morning, but we were friends on Facebook. David called and said I'm going to go run with Ernie. Would you like to join me?" Kristin was a 100-mile runner. I thought how ironic. Here's a 100-mile runner running with me on Leg 100. She ran with me again two weeks later.

The editor of Runner's World contacted me and asked if I'd consent to an interview. I agreed. Aron Gulley showed up and brought his wife along. An ideal team. Aron is a reporter and his wife is a photographer. Aron said the editor wanted him to get right down there before some other magazine got ahold of me. Aron ran an 8.33 miles leg with me east out of Heber, AZ while his wife followed along in the car getting pictures. Aron said, "We stopped for a cup of coffee on the way and met a retired Navy man who has little gift shop. He wants to meet you. Said he has something he wants to give you."

We stopped by on our way back to my car. The owner was Richard Vian. His shop was called Everything Under the Sun. He gave me a red Support Our Troops shirt. I've worn the shirt every Friday since then. Aron put together a great article. He contacted me a couple times. He was disappointed in the editor. After rushing him to get the article, she kept putting off running it. Once a month, a woman would call me and go over everything, saying she wanted to make sure there were no mistakes. I told her there were two mistakes. First, I was referred to as a soldier, which I wasn't. I was a sailor. Second, it called me a medic. Medic's are Army. I was a Navy Corpsman. When it was finally published, six months later, the same two mistakes were still there. I was featured in the March 2015 issue of Runner's World. I never dreamed Runner's World had such a big distribution. I gained 4,000 Facebook friends from that one article.

I moved my RV to the Elk Lodge, Show Low, AZ. Keith Rieger of Surprise Running Club called and said, "My girlfriend and I are driving to Albuquerque. We would like to buy you breakfast in Payson." I said, "I'm way beyond Payson. How about lunch in Show Low?" He said, "Fine! What's your favorite restaurant?" I said, "Jack in the Box." He said, "We'll meet you at the Jack in the Box at 1:30." I was waiting at the Jack in the Box when a couple came in. The man was wearing an LST 325 shirt. I gave him one of my flyers and said, "Have you visited the LST 325?" He said, "My brother lives in Evansville and he took us to see the LST." His wife wrote me a check. Keith and his girlfriend came in, we had a great visit. He bought me lunch and gave me a $50 Jack in the Box gift certificate.

July 12, 2014, Leg 108, Robyn and Harry Fowler and Frank Millerd drove up from Tucson to run with me into Show Low, 5.52 miles. We went to the Sweetheart Café for breakfast, gave the waitress a flyer. She showed it to the other waitress who was the owner. She said, "What can we do for you?" I said, "It's all right there on the flyer." The two waitresses went around to all the customers and took up a collection. They raised $150 for sponsorship.

Leg 109 was a very pleasant 5.46 miles through Show Low. A large part of the run was on a paved walk/bicycle trail. My Ragnar friend Erick Johnson showed up to run with me, which made it very special. My daughter Linda had recently retired and said wherever I was on July 17, she'd be there to run with me. As a complete surprise to both of us, my granddaughter, Tammy, and great-grandson, Justin, flew in from Minneapolis and we had a four-generation run out of Show Low. My son-in-law, Carl, was our volunteer to get us back. Justin, like most kids, got a little bored doing the same thing and was saying, "Are we there yet?" He said, "I think I'll go get in the car with grandpa." I said, "If you do and I get in the Guinness Book of World Records, I won't even mention you." So he finished the run.

I had previously stopped in at the Stanford General Store on highway 61 and got acquainted with the owner, Jon Dahl. He was having a barbecue with a live band on the weekend, raising money for the volunteer fire department. He put up a table for me so I could promote my coast to coast runs. The following Saturday, I would be running past his place on highway 60. He was located just a short distance up highway 61. He asked if I could finish my run at Standard General Store and he would advertise and recruit some runners and raise some money for me.

My plan was to run approximately five miles on Thursday. The Thursday run was the one Linda was running with me. She had asked if I could shorten it a little. She wasn't sure she could make five miles. This turned out perfect. I shortened the Thursday run to 4.77 miles and adjusted the next two accordingly. This made the Saturday run a 10K, 6.23 to be exact. He drummed up four runners. Charged them $10, $1 for each K. Jon did a lot for me. He raised over $200, plus gifts and meals and escorted me on three runs.

Susan Esker, another 100-mile runner, from Surprise, AZ, showed up for this run. Jon Dahl and Billy Ray Smith were escorts. More about Billy Ray later. I have a prized souvenir from this crew. They picked up a cover from a Toyota gas cap, wrote on it "7-19-14. When you feel like you're out of fuel, just open the door and we'll be your fuel! Thanks Ernie." They all signed it. I have it hanging on my wall right under Gail's masterpiece.

I moved my RV to Avery Lance RV Park & Bar-B-Que, Springerville, AZ. He gave me a free space and free meals. My dentures couldn't handle his Bar-B-Que but they made a delicious macaroni and cheese. I had macaroni and cheese every night. Billy Ray was a local disk jockey. When he came to Avery's, he set up a large TV screen, put a picture of the LST 325 on the screen, and between Karaoke's, he introduced me to the crowd. While I was there, Carlos Cano showed up. He'd just returned from Alaska and had a freezer full of salmon. Avery cooked up some salmon for him and he donated some to the restaurant. When I moved, they gave me a good supply of macaroni and cheese.

I met K and T Nez, who are sisters, in the parking lot. These were Indian girls. T (Tiata) had served in the Navy for six years. She said, "I've been waiting for you to get here so I could run with you." The whole family (two sisters, mother and father) ran with me for two legs. The VFW in Eagar couldn't do enough for me. They supplied me with one runner, a few escorts, and made donations to both me and the LST and kept asking, "Is there anything else we can do for you?"

Al Oltesvig escorted me into Springerville and had his family at the finish for a welcoming party. He did this again later and his grandson Brandy, who I think was 12 years old, handed me a one dollar bill and said, "I want to sponsor you." I met a Navy vet at the VFW. He said, "You're from Prescott, maybe you know a shipmate of mine. His name is Al Puknat." Al was a member of my Navy Vet Breakfast Club. Small world!

On August 7, 2014, Leg 119, we crossed into New Mexico.

Carlos and I moved our RV's to the Pie Town RV Park, NM. They gave me a free space. I met a lot of interesting people at Pie Town. The owner of Pie-O-Neer Pies, whom I think is named is Kathy, has a video on her on Youtube channel—Pie Lady of Pie Town. There's two pie restaurants in town. They alternate their hours so there's always one open. Pie Town is on highway 60 just east of the Continental Divide. Carlos had already run five legs with me in western AZ. He ran another five legs here in eastern AZ and western NM. He had to leave to get his dog, Jack, to a vet.

August 18, 2014, Leg 124. This was a 9-mile run with the last two miles all uphill on Highway 60 from 601 junction to Omega. We had an escort named Kim Carr so before we started up the hill I took a little break and sat in his car. Carlos has had nine operations on his feet. About halfway up the hill, I said, "How's your feet?" He said, "Hurtin'." I said, "Why don't you go get in the car for the rest of the way." He said, "Failure is not an option." When we reached the finish, he said, "No more nine mile runs."

I met a woman at the restaurant who was on her way to Albuquerque to run a marathon. She was a school teacher. She was running a marathon a month for the year. The next one after Albuquerque was Pikes Peak. I said, "You have to have a doctor's clearance to run Pikes Peak." She said, "I already have it and I'm good to go." There's a route comes through Pie Town which is mostly dirt. European's fly into Canada, rent motorcycles or bicycles and ride from Canada to Mexico. There was a fellow working on a beat up looking bicycle and I think he was from Norway. I said, "How far do you think you're going to get with that piece of junk." He said, "I went to a junk yard in Canada, bought a frame and built my own bicycle. I'm riding it all the way to Mexico."

August 19, 2014, was my 91st birthday. My brother and his wife were driving from Prescott, AZ, to help me celebrate my birthday. I said, "The closest motel is 16 miles away. It's an old motel, all remodeled. It's very nice and has a restaurant." He booked a room and when he went to breakfast the waitress said, "Are you here to help your brother celebrate his birthday?" He said, "Yea! Are you going to bake him a cake?" She said, "I don't bake cakes." We were sitting in my motor home having ice cream when the waitress showed up with a tray of fresh baked cupcakes. She said, "I thought a 91-year old man should have cake for his birthday."

I dropped into the Pie-O-Neer for a piece of pie and asked if there was any place in town I could get a haircut. The waitress said, "We have an employee here that cuts hair. I'll have her get in touch with you." Lisa Trease showed up at my RV and gave me a free haircut.

A reporter from Socorro called and said he'd like to get an interview. I said, "I'll be having breakfast at the truck stop in Datil on August 30th." He said, "I'll meet you there." This was Leg 129, a 5.46 mile run ending at the post office in Datil. I had four runners. These were going to become the best friends a man could hope for. Tara Waldrip, Dennis Parent, Ruby Mendez Harris and Harrell McClellan. The reporter showed up for the interview. He said, "I just interviewed a retired Marine that's walking coast to coast. He'll be passing through here shortly."

The next day I was driving along highway 60 checking out my next legs. I saw this guy pushing a bicycle with his gear fastened on it. I figured this has got to be the Marine. We had a nice chat and he said, "I'll be passing through Pie Town tomorrow. I'll stop by for a visit." He said he was feeling depressed sitting behind a desk in an office 40 hours a week. He decided he had to make a change and get out into nature, so he packed up his gear and started walking across the U.S. He asked, "Have you seen the toaster house?" I hadn't even heard of it. It was a short distance from the RV park so we walked up to see it. Fascinating! The yard and trees and all through the house were old toasters. He took advantage of the RV park's shower and continued on his way. I don't remember his name.

A short distance from town there is a museum with several acres of windmills. From August 28 to September 6, I only had to run alone four times and I always had an escort or volunteer to get me back to my car because Tara was making sure I had support. Tara ran with me four times and Dennis, Tara's boyfriend, ran twice. He was stationed in San Antonio so he had to come a long distance. Ruby ran twice and Harrell ran three times. Tara's parents, Bruce and Jan, and their dog, ran once. Tara and I dined out twice. This all happened through Socorro, but this was not the end. Tara asked, "Where will you be for Thanksgiving?" I said, "Near Hope." She said, "Our farm is at Artesia. That's just a few miles away. We'll come run with you and then have you over for Thanksgiving dinner."

I met a clerk at Smith's market in Socorro. He was a member of the

City Council. He invited me to their meeting. I met the Mayor, Chief of Police, and the Commander of the Disabled American Vets. The police escorted us into town and the sheriff escorted me out of town. The Disabled American Vets sponsored me and made a donation to the ship. I said, "This is sorta in reverse, I should be supporting you."

I moved my RV to the Midway RV Park a little south of Socorro. The manager, George Conklin, gave me a space for a month and only charged me for a week and volunteered to get me back to my car whenever I need it. Dennis and Tara flew down to Jamaica for a barefoot wedding in the sand and a honeymoon.

Jane Peranteau drove over 100 miles each way from near Albuquerque twice to run with me. She has authored several books. She had just published her first novel, "Jumping!" She gave me a copy. This is a story that goes beyond science fiction. Science and the human mind cannot fathom anything beyond time and space, but that's where this book takes you. It's not a spiritual book following any religious belief. It's something she had to concoct out of her own imagination.

I moved my RV to Mountain Springs RV Park and stirred up a lot of dust getting to and from this camp, but the view was worth it. The manager had me come and visit his mother in Alamogordo. She was a World War II Navy nurse and was one of the few women that actually went into the war zone at Okinawa to fly out wounded. She was nearly 100 years old and her son said my visit really made her day.

I moved my RV to the Boot Hill RV Resort at La Luz. The Alamogordo news ran a story on me so I started getting some runners from Holloman Air Force Base. I was working on my computer and looking out the window when I saw a woman walking along the highway and trying to flag down a ride. No one was giving her a ride. Finally, I couldn't stand it any longer so I got in my car and picked her up. I said, "Where can I drop you off?" She said, "I'm trying to get to the convenience store to pick up some groceries." I said, "Do you have money for groceries?" She said, "I only have a few cents but I'll make out all right." I handed her a couple dollars and said, "This may help a little." I noticed as she walked toward the store she spoke to a couple ladies coming out of the store. One of them handed her some money. I guess she did all right.

My youngest daughter, Donna, and her man, Chris, came from Jackson, WY, for a visit and did a couple runs with me up the highway toward Cloudcroft. I took them to see White Sands which is so unique and beautiful. We went to the New Mexico Museum of Space History. I put on a space outfit and had my picture taken running across the moon. I gave the clerk a flyer. The local radio office was in the same building. When the news guy came in she showed him the flyer. He said, "I just saw this old guy with a group of runners with him running up Highway 82. Wondered what was going on."

For my next leg I was live on the local radio station while running up the mountain. Larry and Peggy Sparks pulled in and camped next to me. They showed up at just the right time because the next run was through a narrow tunnel. We needed an escort. Cloudcroft was the highest elevation of my trip at 8,868 feet.

Saturday, November 8, 2014, Veterans Day weekend, Leg 159. On Highway 82 I started at the two-mile mark to truck ramp sign and ran through Cloudcroft to the truck stop. I picked up a police escort on the way. Mike Gesualdo and three of his shipmates came from four different states. There were a total of nine runners, counting me. We went to Big Daddy's Diner for breakfast. They took some pictures. I haven't been back since, but I imagine our picture is somewhere on the wall.

Leg 161, with temperatures below freezing, was an 8.19 mile run. There were two runners with me, Sam Madrigales and Jessica Kienbaum. We took a break at the Barn Door Restaurant to defrost, then finished the run. I stopped on the way back for breakfast. I stood with my back too close to the fireplace and my sweats got so hot they melted. The owner took our picture. Said she was going to put it on the wall.

I was driving down highway 82 from Cloudcroft before daylight, at one below zero and ice on the road, I was moving slow. An elk came running out of the woods and right into the driver's side. I think it was a female. Didn't see any horns. She left some hair on my destroyed side view mirror. I looked in my rearview mirror and saw she was chasing me so this was another reason for thinking it was a female. If you mess up a woman's hair, she's going to get mad. I pulled into the Mayhill Café. The door was caved in on the driver's side. If you think it's easy to get out the passenger side from the driver's seat, try it when you're in your 90's!

It looked like I'd be running alone with no one to get me back to my car and the temperature was 17 degrees, so I decided to have breakfast and wait until about 11:00 when it wouldn't be so cold, and maybe I could drum up a runner or volunteer. A couple guys got their tools and worked on my door. They got it so it would open and close. One of them said, "Why don't you go talk to those two guys sitting by the window. Maybe they'll run with you." They said, "Sure, we'll be glad to go for a run."

These two were rancher Ronnie Wilbanks and his hired hand John Battle. This is all I knew about Ronnie Wilbanks until I got to Artesia and Bruce Waldrip told me he had called Ronnie and told him I would be running through his town. He said, "Ronnie owns that café and almost everything else in Mayhill. He was once the richest man in New Mexico."

I moved my RV to Rio Penasco RV Park, Mayhill, NM. He gave me a free space. This is where I met Jay Tysver, who became a true friend. My toilet was stopped up. He got a plumber's snake and unplugged it for me.

Carlos showed up on his Harley, pitched a tent next to my RV, spent the night, ran with me the next morning, then headed for Corpus Christi. He said there was a storm heading that way and he wanted to get there before the storm hit.

When I was ready to move my RV to the Shawna RV park in Artesia, my car was in the shop and I was using a rental. I couldn't tow the rental car with the RV as it was not equipped for that. I couldn't drive both my RV and rental car. Jay offered to help. He drove the rental while I drove the RV. I didn't have to take him back because his father lived in Artesia. His dad met us at the RV park. Jay was going to spend a little time with his dad and his dad would give him a ride back.

Leg 167 was Thanksgiving Day, 2014. There were four runners, Tara and Dennis Parent, Sandy Smith, and Chelsea Willeves. We ran 7.14 miles, then I returned to my RV for a shower and a little rest then went to the Waldrip farm for dinner. They are great people and they had great food. There was lots to be thankful for.

For the next three weeks, I had crowds of runners. The morning we reached the city limits of Artesia, I had 17 runners. Brandi Shutterly got the whole town excited. The next couple runs through town, everyone came out of the shops to cheer and welcome me. The welcoming party ran into the hundreds. Brandi got the whole Shutterly tribe out to run with me and the Waldrips were always there. Bruce was a deacon at the Baptist church. I attended his church a couple Sundays.

Melissa Guthrie of Redline Fitness ran with me four legs, donated a nice warm jacket with a hood, and treated me to a concert. Kallie Waldrip, Tara's sister, came down from Portland, OR. She said she had to come before I got too far away because she was the only one of the family that hadn't run with me.

I moved my RV to H & H RV Park on Highway 180 in Texas, 7 1/3 miles east of Hobbs, New Mexico. Once again, I had free space. I planned to run Leg 177, which was 3.34 miles on December 20th, then drive to Odesa/Midland airport to fly out for Christmas. The Waldrips were coming to run with me. My clutch went out and I pulled off to the side of the road and called the Waldrips. Bruce stayed with my car and waited for the auto club to tow it into Tate's Dodge dealership in Hobbs. Jan drove me to the airport.

Bruce called the airport and told them to watch for a World War II vet in a red jacket and make sure he doesn't miss his flight. When I walked in, I heard the announcement but no one paid any attention. I was that told because I was late, my seat had been sold. I gave the clerk a flyer. She said, "Wait right here. I'll see what I can do." She came back and said, "The Captain said he has a seat for you," so I caught my flight.

I spent Christmas week with my daughter Cathy. Cathy knew I'd want to keep in shape so she had set up some runs on the Sacramento River trail. Fifteen runners showed up to run with me plus a crowd of well-wishers. The TV cameras were there and we got some good coverage. Damian Platoch in Connecticut had said he wished he could run with me but I was too far away. When he heard I was running the Sacramento River trail, he said, "I'm familiar with that trail and I'm going to be in Redlands, CA during Christmas week." He showed up and ran with us.

Getting back to the airport in Texas was a nightmare with eleven hours of delays. Arrival time was supposed to be 2:00 PM Sunday but we didn't get in until 1:00 AM Monday which was too late to get a rental car. There was a group of people there who had flown in for a funeral. One of them said, "I booked some rooms at a motel. I won't need them all. You're welcome to one." I was scheduled to do a 7.99 mile run Monday morning, which I postponed for one day. I caught a taxi Monday morning back to the airport where I could rent a car. Tate Dodge dealership had my car for a week. I assumed it would be fixed and ready to go. When I got there, they hadn't even looked at it. I told them I had to turn in the rental, so I need a loaner. They rented me a loaner for $35 a day.

Bruce met me Tuesday for the 7.99 mile run. It was freezing out there on that highway. We ran six miles and then caught a ride to his car to warm up, then went back and ran the other two miles. I called the Dodge dealer every day and always got the same run around…the mechanic was working on a transmission and would get to my car as soon as possible. When I complained, I was told, "I'll have the mechanic call you." I never got a call from the mechanic.

I got snowed in at the RV park and my water pipes froze up. I came down with the flu and developed phlebitis in one leg. A neighbor gave me some bottled water. Olga Rojo showed up at my door with her 11-year-old daughter Alexus who is nicknamed Charlie. These two were angels from heaven. She drove me to the hospital in Seminole. It was the middle of the night and the equipment needed to check me out wasn't available. They said, "You'll have to come back in the morning."

She took me back to Hobbs, New Mexico and put me up in a nice motel room. She came back the next morning to take me to the hospital in Hobbs. They put me on an antibiotic. She took me back to my RV and sent Glynn Briswell of RV sales, parts and service out to see me. He brought a helper with him and went to work on my RV. They defrosted the pipes, winterized it for me, and added a few parts to make sure I didn't have any more problems. They did this all for free and wanted to know if there was anything else they could do for me.

That evening Olga showed up again with Charlie and grandma. Charlie had gone through grandma's pantry and brought me a couple boxes of food and other supplies.

January 4th, since I wasn't able to run Leg 177 when my car broke down, I went back to run it. Olga and Charlie ran with me. We left Olga's car at the finish and took my loaner to the start. About a mile up the road, Olga realized she left her keys in my car. She went back for her keys while Charlie and I ran to the finish, so Olga got in a couple extra miles that day. Olga was always there for me when I needed a friend.

She said, "You now have a family in Hobbs." We got together for several breakfasts and a couple dinners.

I met Mark Bowman at the camp and we became friends. He ran a total of seven runs with me until I ran off and left him. Carlos came back. He parked his trailer on the Walmart lot in Seminole and did some more runs with me.

I was still getting the run around from the Dodge dealership. This went on for six weeks! A Ragnar friend of mine, in Dallas, called Tate's Dodge and said, "Why aren't you getting his car ready?" The reply was, "There's a part on back order." She said, "When will you get it?" The reply, "We don't know." She said, "What's the part?" The reply, "A fly wheel." She said, "What's the number?" She was given the number. She put out a nation-wide search. She called them back and said, "I found one in Missouri. It's being shipped. Now get his car ready."

In the meantime, I had talked to Bruce. I told him they were charging me $35 a day for the loaner and running up a big bill. Bruce said, "Tate goes to our church. I'll talk to him and maybe we can get some answers." He called me back and said, "Tate's going over to Hobbs and talk to the manager. In a couple days, my car was ready. I went to pick it up. They charged me $300+ for the loaner. I put it on my credit card. I said, "Didn't Tate come over and talk to the manager." She said, "Just a minute, I'll ask him." The manager came in and said, "Tate said you're not charging him for the loaner. I'll pay for seven days, Chrysler will pay for seven days because it's under warranty. You'll have to eat the rest. Guess I'll have to eat it. Give him his money back." All it cost me was a few nights sleep and some shattered nerves.

When I went to check out of the RV camp, the manager called the owner. He was a little unhappy because he had only offered me one month free and I wound up staying two months. He still wasn't going to charge me, but I said I ought to give him something, so I had her put $200 on my credit card.

I was finishing one run at the New Mexico/Texas border. I drove up to the border to check the distance and there was a man with a bicycle hauling gear and a little dog. Another man was talking to him. The man with the bike said he and his dog live on the road, camping out along the way. The other man handed him a hundred-dollar bill and said, "I'm sure you can use this." He walked over to me and said, "What are you up to?" I gave him a flyer. He handed me a hundred-dollar bill and said, "I own a thriving oil refinery here and I like to help people whenever I can."

When I ran into Texas a group of well-wishers from Hobbs were there to see me off. Mark was running with me. A woman asked me how long it would take me to get across Texas. I said, "You can have a baby by the time I get there." It took nine months to get across Texas, and wonderful memories to last a lifetime.

When I ran through Seminole there was a welcoming party of about 300. The kids at the school were all lined up along the fence waving flags and chanting "USA, USA." It was a great feeling to see the patriotism among these young students.

Olga was having a birthday party for Charlie. She was turning 12. I was invited. I called my daughter to see if she had a small shirt left. She was all out of small. One of my runners said, "I can get you a shirt made in time for the party." She took me to a shop. She came up with a beautiful RUN ERNIE RUN shirt. I said, "Can you make me 20 in assorted sizes and colors?" She said, "No problem." I said, "When can I pick them up?" She said, "I'll deliver them to your RV." When she showed up I said, "How much do I owe you?" She said, "Nothing, this is my donation." She handed me some money and said, "I already sold half of them."

Carlos and I went to South Ridge RV Park in Big Springs, TX. The manager, Jackie Jackson, wasn't there so we left a flyer on the door, along with a note saying I need a space for a month. She called me and said, "I'll have a space for you. It won't cost you anything. If the owner won't give you a free space, we'll take up a collection."

Carlos moved his trailer to the Walmart in La Mesa. I moved my RV to the Walmart and parked next to Carlos. We had several runners join us between Seminole and Lamesa. Through Lamesa, it was just Carlos and me. A man came out of a parking lot and handed me a hundred-dollar bill but I didn't get his name. A few blocks later, three women driving by stopped and said they were from Seminole and missed me when I was there and they just wanted to make a donation. I'm continuously amazed at the generosity of the American people.

The next day we drove our campers to the South Ridge RV Park. Carlos helped me hook up then headed for home. He ran six legs with me through Seminole and Lamesa.

Jackie introduced me to some other campers, the Herron's and the Abbe's. They became very good friends, Jackie Jackson and Vickie Herron did some escorting while the kids ran with me. Vickie did one run with me. Her two boys, Nicholas 10 and Noah 12, ran three legs. We were getting a lot of rain so I had to rearrange some of my running days. Big oil trucks splashing water across the shoulder was a problem.

I notified the media and the American Legion that I was coming through Big Springs and was completely ignored. The only one that responded was a TV station. I think it was from Odessa. Jackie couldn't understand why, so she made some phone calls. She got the whole town excited. Leg 208 started at interstate 20 and ran on highway 87 through Big Springs for 7.66 miles. A whole crowd showed up at the start, the newspaper, radio, and TV, the Chief of Police, and so many more. I was overwhelmed. A woman presented me with a Quilt of Valor made by Kim Thompson. It looks great on my bed.

I had a police escort, 13 runners and more joining in on the way and many welcoming me on the street through town. A lady from Lupe's Flowers handed me a long stem rose which I carried to the finish. When we reached the VA hospital, there was a welcoming party of about 200. They had me stop to take some pictures. This just goes to show if you blow your own horn you get ignored, but if someone else gets excited, people take notice. From Big Springs through Sterling City and to Robert Lee were all fun runs with lots of runners.

I was doing a 5.31 mile run along highway 87 with two beautiful young ladies and a 12-year-old named Anahi Paz. A guy pulled up on a Harley Davidson and said, "Thank you for your service" and handed me four $100 bills. I asked his name but he didn't give it to me. He said, "I'm an oil field worker from New Mexico and I just want to show you I appreciate what you're doing."

When I left the South Ridge RV Park, I stopped at Casey's Campers in Big Springs. He filled up my propane for free. I moved my RV to the Wild Cat RV Park, Robert Lee and was given free space. Carlos was riding his bicycle 300 miles, pulling a trailer, to come run with me. He was coming up highway 83. I was in Ballinger checking out my next few runs so I drove down and picked him up. This saved him one day of peddling. The owner of the Wild Cat RV Park put him up in what he called his motel. It was just a couple trailers fastened together with a porch added.

I moved my RV to The Texas Ranger RV Park in Santa Ana. I find no record so it must have been a free space. A policeman who was camped there came by and told me there was a tornado heading that way and I should secure my RV and go up to the big building until it passes through. None of the other campers were concerned. They said the tornados always pass by on the other side of the mountain. The policeman said, "That's usually true, but they weren't here in 2003." I followed the policeman's suggestion and the tornado passed on the other side of the mountain.

Leg 227 was a 7.12 mile run east from the Colman county line on a desolate highway. It looked like I was going to be running alone and have to hitchhike back to my car. An Angel showed up ... Angel Stepankiw, who was a blessing from heaven. She ran four legs with me and made a sizable donation.

We ran through Bronte, ending at Lee Farms. I had seven runners running with me. I felt so honored when we ran through town. Every shop had their flag flying. I think the welcoming party was more than the town's population. The whole school turned out. Two girls ran in ahead of us with a big sign reading, "Welcome Ernie Andrus." The kids fell in behind and ran around the corner with me and then back to school. When we reached the finish, Lee Farms had a big truck there blowing its horn.

One of my runners, Jodie Arrott, invited me to come back to the school for lunch and speak to the 4th and 5th graders. This is my favorite age group, so I was delighted. These kids took so much interest in everything and had lots of questions. One girl mentioned Adolph Hitler and the girl sitting across from her said, "Who's Adolph Hitler." I said, "This is why we need to teach history to these young ones. No one should forget Adolph Hitler because there's others like him in this world and they need to be stopped before they get power."

These kids wanted to know all about the depression, the war, and my run. A little boy came to me after the meeting and asked if there was going to be another war. I said, "I hope not, but don't let that stop you from joining the military. It not only will be good for you, but you'll be trained and ready in case your country needs you." Jodie said, "My father is the county judge. He is in Ballinger and said he will make sure you have escorts all through the county." When we reached the court house he had all the town officials there to greet me. On one run he showed up personally because he wasn't sure I had an escort.

Carlos did four runs then said he needed to head back to Corpus Christi, but he wasn't going to pull that trailer again so he shipped most everything home and folded up the trailer and put it in my trunk to pick up the next time.

I moved my RV to the CC RV Park, Early, TX and got free space again. He had enlarged his camp and the new spaces were too far from the tower so I couldn't get on his Wi Fi. I could either take my computer to the laundry room or go across the highway to a picnic table next to the tower.

When I ran through Bangs, the whole high school turned out. The highway was lined with hundreds of people waving flags. I had two escorts. The Chief of Police, Jorge Camarillo, in front and a patrol car in back. A car pulled up next to the Chief and slowed down, apparently to ask what was going on. A driver, looking at the people instead of where he was going, rear ended him, right alongside the Chief of Police.

Leg 233, was on highway 67 through Brownwood, 6.57 miles. There were 16 running with me, including two of my Ragnar friends from Phoenix, Erick and Teresa Johnson. I had fire engines, police cars, sheriff cars, and ambulances for escorts. At least another hundred runners joined in along the way. Twenty young girls ages 15-17 joined me to the finish. They were all wearing bright red RUN WITH ERNIE shirts. They said their coach made them qualify. They had to run an eight-minute mile then they got a shirt and got to run at the finish.

A bus load of preschoolers was parked in the bank parking lot. Each child had drawn their own flag on a piece of notebook paper and was waving it. I made a brief stop to talk to them. The little boys were more interested in the fire engine than in me. The next day they had a BBQ at the court house square. The mayor, Stephen Haynes, presented me with a proclamation declaring the 8th day of May 2015 as Ernie Andrus Day. They took up a collection to sponsor me. The total came to $1,435.20. I met a Marine Veteran in a wheelchair. I told him I was a Navy Corpsman in world War II and the Marines always told me, "The Corpsman is the Marines' best friend." He said, "That's very true. My Corpsman is still my best friend to this day. He pulled me out of a creek in Vietnam."

Robyn McDonald of Early, TX ran three legs. At the finish of the final leg, she cried because she couldn't run with me anymore. She was such a sweetheart.

I was still camped in Early and drove to Goldthwaite. On the way back, I blew a tire. I discovered my Dodge Dart didn't have a spare, just an air pump. What good is an air pump when you blow a tire? I called the AAA. Two hours and still no AAA. A local rancher stopped and said, "We have to get you off the highway before dark." He went home and got his equipment. He tried squirting some stuff into the tire but it didn't help. He inserted a plug and got enough air so I could drive back into town where he knew a church pastor who had better equipment. When he tried to put in enough air, the whole side blew out.

I saw the AAA cruising along the highway and flagged him down. He apologized for the delay. They sent him east of town instead of west. I was towed all the way to my RV. A neighbor helped me remove the wheel and took me to a tire shop. I didn't want to risk this again so I bought five new tires. He installed the one. We went back, put it on the car, and drove back to have the other three installed, then I went to a junk yard and bought a rim and had the other tire installed. Now I have a spare and hope I never have to use it.

I moved my RV to the Gatesville RV Park in Gatesville.

A little east of Star, Sergio Gamino showed up. He was a real blessing. He ran nine legs between Star and Mexia. When he wasn't running, he was escorting. When we ran through Gatesville, Mary Fae Grimes, Sergio's girlfriend, showed up. She ran six legs with me. She was like a mother hen looking after me, making sure I was all right. Frank Cash showed up just east of Evant and ran four legs and did some escorting. On D-Day, June 6, 2015, we ran into Gatesville. There were fifty runners besides me and three escorts mostly in RWB (Red, White & Blue). We went to brunch at the steak house and Frank presented me with many gifts, including a new pair of shoes, complements of the RWB.

I stopped to fill up with gas just a couple blocks from the RV Park. It began to sprinkle. Just as I drove up to my RV, a tornado came through. I couldn't get from my car into the RV and had to wait it out in the car.

We lost power for a few hours, but no damage. I was doing laundry at the Valet Cleaners and Laundry in Gatesville and one of the machines didn't work. I went to the cleaners next door to complain. I gave him a flyer. He marked the machine out of order, transferred my laundry to another machine, and deposited the money. He handed me two nice laundry bags and said, "Next time you have laundry put them in the window before 8:00 AM and you can pick them up after 5:00 clean and folded, no charge." I dropped in to Ronny's Barbershop and he gave me a free haircut.

I wanted to move my RV to the Home Place RV Park just west of Mexia. It was self-service ... put your check in the box and pick a space. I wanted to talk to the owner to see what kind of a deal I could get, but I wasn't able to get ahold of anyone. Mary Fae said, "Let me handle this for you." She called me and said, "It's all arranged. You just go ahead and move in. She gave me a nice discount and I paid it. It's yours for free." A beautiful young lady, whose name I don't remember, in the RV park said, "I want you to meet my friends at the VFW. There was a big sign out front reading "WELCOME ERNIE ANDRUS WORLD WAR II VETERAN" and they gave me a nice donation. My daughter Cathy came to spend ten more days with me.

Carlos showed up on his Harley. He did two more runs with me and then he led the way on his Harley. Cathy and I followed up to Dallas. My Ragnar friend Meltem was putting on a special event called, "Ernie is in town running by Dallas." We had a party at the American Legion with a fabulous dinner and a local bakery that went all out, serving so many beautiful, mouth watering pies! The next morning, we did a 5K run in the local park. I didn't get a count but there were lots. Carlos left because he was riding into Washington, DC, with thousands of other bikers called Rolling Thunder.

A few days later, a TV station wanted to put me on live. A driver picked me up and took me to Dallas. When I went on TV there I was sitting right next to the young lady who was interviewing me. Actually, I was in Dallas and she was in New York. Modern technology is amazing. Carlos came back and did two more runs.

June 14, 2015, was Leg 245, with six runners. One in particular, Patrick Kerwin, said, "When you reach Waco, I'll get some support from the firemen." I didn't know it at the time but he was Fire Chief at one of the stations. He did four runs and some escorting and had me over to his station once for lunch. Stephanee Corbet contacted me and said she was bringing a friend and they were coming from Oklahoma to run with me. When she got there, I said, "I know some Corbets." She said, "I know! I didn't know who you were when I contacted you, but I called my aunt in Kansas and told her I was going to run with a 92-year-old man by the name of Ernie Andrus who's running across the U. S." She said, "We know him." Stephanee is the granddaughter of the Dale Corbet mentioned earlier.

Leg 251 was on Thursday, June 18, 2015. Fifteen runners! We were running from the Cedar Chest Antique Mall on highway 84 to Waco. Patrick asked me to end the run at the fire station on Speegleville Road. I agreed because it was only a short distance off highway 84 where I had planned to finish. He said, "When we get there, go around back and enter through the back door." When we got there, the Color Guard were standing in full uniform. A large welcoming party was inside, including the media. There was a chair for me to sit down, a few speeches, and some awards. You can't beat the Texans when it comes to southern hospitality!

I was concerned about how I was going to get through Waco. I wanted to stay on highway 84 but that didn't look possible. With fire engine escorts, it turned out to be no problem. From the fire station into Waco we had 23 runners. As we ran through eastern Waco, it looked like someone had thrown handfuls of coins along the highway. My daughter said, "Someone heard you were picking up coins and got here ahead of us." On highway 84 east of Waco, Linda Slbodick with her large poodle (both dressed in red, white and blue), along with two of her friends, ran with me. This was the second time for Linda and her dog because she was in Dallas for the "Ernie is in Town" event.

I moved my RV to the Cedar Grove RV park, Fairfield. I don't find any information so it must have been a free space. I was filling up my RV black tank to flush it out and got talking to some neighbors. Forgot all about it until we saw water pouring out under my RV. I ran and shut off the water. Everything was flooded. The neighbors and I gathered up all the towels we could find and cleaned up the mess.

July 17, 2015 the Fairfield VFW put on a dinner in my honor and had an auction. They raised over $1,500 dollars.

Mary Birdsong, a 77-year young chick, drove all the way from Austin to run with me three times. The first time it was just her, Carlos, and me. The second time it was just her and me. When I was running into Fairfield, she was afraid I'd be running alone so she drove up the day before, got a room in a motel, and ran with me the next morning. It turned out I had 21 runners and a World War II veteran in a wheel chair join me for that run. After the run, she suggested we go to breakfast. I turned her down because I had a 12:00 engagement and wanted to shower first. This has bothered me ever since. If I ever get back to Texas, I'll buy her breakfast even if I have to drive all day and stay in a motel overnight!

July 18th I ran through Fairfield with the 23 runners and a wheel chair. There was a big sign reading "WELCOME ERNEST ANDRUS WORLD WAR II VETERAN." They were having a fair in town and invited me to come back at 12:00. They had a table set up for me so I could meet the town's people and maybe raise some more support. I raised another $145. This was the engagement I turned down a breakfast for. I think my priorities were in the wrong place.

Jeremy Shipley, sheriff of Freestone county, stuck with me through the county. He ran five legs with me. Kenneth Brown, my daughter-in-law's uncle, whom I had never met, came up from Texas City and parked his RV next to me. He ran with me on July 25th and had me over for a steak BBQ. He left the next morning because he had to get back for work. It just happened to be Jerry Brown's birthday, my daughter-in-law Grace Andrus' father, so I contacted him and said, "Your brother and I are celebrating your birthday with a steak BBQ."

We moved my RV to Champ's RV Park in Huntington.

I left highway 84 onto Highway 298 and ran through Elkhart then turned left onto highway 21 east and ran through Alto. Then I turned right onto highway 69 ending at Hicks Pole Company. Hicks had coffee and donuts waiting for us. Carlos was back and ran three more legs with me. I had my 92nd birthday so Carlos brought me a bunch of goodies he knew I liked. They were so good that I overate. I guess I was allowed this on my birthday.

There was a nice turnout of runners from Alto to Lufkin. As we ran into Lufkin, the sheriff of Angelina County was our volunteer for the day. He dropped off his daughter and her husband to run with me, Briana and Bryan Harkness. I think the sheriff was Greg Sanches. Along the way, a beautiful young runner out for her morning exercise joined us for a short distance. Briana picked up a little stray kitten and handed it to her. They agreed the kitten should be named Ernie, so there's a cat named Ernie in Lufkin, TX.

I needed some replacement parts for my RV. The Angelina MFD Housing gave me a discount on parts and Zachary Brogan delivered the parts and did the labor for free. The commander of the VFW in Lufkin, Alfred Navarro, couldn't do enough for me. He took me to dinner a few times, had me as a guest for a dinner and dance at the VFW, and took me around to various merchants for donations. The Huntington Market & Deli got up a one mile walk in my honor and raised a nice donation.

Lisa Wise of Brookeland, TX ran five legs with me between Lufkin and Jasper. Lola Rose from Zavalla did five legs as well. She only ran part way on the first three, but held in there to the finish on the last two.

We moved my RV to Whispering Springs RV Park, east of Newton.

The run into Jasper was one of the most outstanding receptions so far. The commander of the American Legion was Roy James. He is also commander of Texas Honor and Remember and asked me to finish at the Walmart. I had seven runners on my team, one of which was the Walmart manager, and a deputy escort, Glenn Blank. The High School band was playing as we reached the finish, with a fire engine flying a flag a hundred feet in the air. Part of the parking lot was roped off and filled with well wishers waving flags. They had a grandstand set up for me and a chair. The media was there, and we had about two hours of speeches, each presenting me with some kind of a token. I can't begin to name all the awards I received. They are all displayed in my living-room now. Jasper county judge, Mark W. Allen, presented me with a proclamation and said he posted a copy at the county court house for future generations to see.

I met Carson George, the author of *Forever 22*. I was given one of his books. He has an Honor and Remember Wall, which I saw, with the names of every Texan who has given their lives for the county. It is a traveling wall, like the Vietnam Wall. I was offered a free night at the bed and breakfast, a hotel where Generals Patton and Eisenhower stayed. I was told that my name has now been added to the famous people who stayed there. If that is true, what an honor to be mentioned along with two great generals.

We crossed into Louisiana and Carlos came back for a couple more runs. We moved my RV to Vera's Dependable RV Park, which turned into a nightmare. I picked it for convenience because it was right on the highway. The people who had the space before me stole all the electric attachments. The handyman said, "No problem. I'll get you all hooked up." He was no electrician. He ran 220 into my 110 and blew out my microwave and some other electrical things. The person in the next space let me plug into her RV so I could have electricity. One of my runners brought an electrician by and he wired me up so I could get by until I got someplace to replace parts.

We ran through Merryville, took highway 110 through Singer, and started Leg 299 at Singer School RD. All the kids were out there to see me off.

We took highway 110 to Longville, turned right on highway 171, and ran past the Beauregard schools. There were about 1,500 kids out there cheering me on. The school sent some high school runners on a bus to the start and a deputy to escort us. We had 13 runners plus a few more who joined in along the way. The assistant principal of the high school, Missy Adams, invited me back to the school and fixed a nice breakfast.

I called the owner of Vera's Dependable RV Park and left a message saying, "I'm out of here. This place has been nothing but a headache. Whatever refund I have coming, give it to the neighbor for using her electricity."

I moved my RV to Caribbean Wellness and RV, Opalousas, LA and had a free space. I pulled into Reedgas and they filled me up with propane. No charge!

Dwayne Hodge from Ragley, LA was a faithful friend who ran ten legs with me, from Longville to Opelousas.

We took my RV to Courvell's RV Parts and Service to replace the microwave and other blown out parts and for a complete service.

On November 14, 2015, Mike Gesualdo and three of his shipmates came to run with me in celebration of Veterans Day. These swabbies come from all parts of the United States for their annual reunion. This was Leg 315, 4.81 miles on highway 190 ending just five miles west of Krotz Springs, LA. It was so great to spend time with these guys again.

I was moving my RV, pulling my tow car through Opelousas. I went over some railroad tracks. A pin busted and the tow bar came lose. Two guys in a truck stopped to help me. They removed the tow bar. It couldn't be put back on because it was bent. I drove the RV to the Home Depot parking lot. One of them drove the tow car while the other drove their truck. The driver told me to take my tow car and tow bar to the South Louisiana Community College and they could probably fix it. I explained my problem to the instructor. He called out a few of his students and said, "Here's some good practice for you guys." He showed them what needed to be done and they went to work on it. After several tries, they got it to fit. The instructor said, "No charge! Safe travels!" And I was on my way. I moved my RV to Livonia but don't remember the name of the park. Tom Taylor of Maurice paid for the space.

The next run was 5.34 miles, ending at the Citgo station in Krotz Springs. We had seventeen runners and a great welcoming party, which was quite a turn-out for a small town. I need to mention two very special young ladies here because I'll be mentioning them later. This was Wendy Landos' second run with me and Shila Crow's first. When I ran out of Krotz Springs, I had 25 runners. The police escorted us across the bridge and said, "I can't let you run on this next three and a half mile bridge. It's too dangerous so I've opened the gates so you can run on the old highway." This was only a quarter of a mile farther and no traffic. There were lots of mosquitoes and a lot of hunting dogs barking. I think everyone enjoyed this run, which was 6.74 miles.

The next run was 5.69 miles, ending at Livonia. A remarkable young lady by the name of Paula Francis contacted me and said she would be there to run with me. Paula is doing the Happiness Walk USA, well over 8,000 miles. You can follow her on The Happiness Walk USA on Facebook. This was my first encounter with Paula, but not the last. She was in New Orleans and met Marvin Cooper from Mississippi there and told him she needed a ride up to where I was running, so he brought her and ran with us. It was *pouring* rain. Marvin said, "We can't run in this." I said, "Don't worry! It never rains on me. When I start running, the rain stops and doesn't start again until I finish." He said, "I can't depend on that." He went to the Dollar Store and bought a bunch of Ponchos. We put on the ponchos and started running. The rain stopped. We never got a drop of water on us the whole way.

For the four runs after Krotz Springs, Mel and Sybil Comeaux were always there to either, run, volunteer, or just to enjoy a breakfast together. The Comeauxs are Shila Crow's parents. This family has become very special. They had me to their home for Thanksgiving and back again twice for special Christmas celebrations. Shila gave me a King cake and still sends me King cakes for special occasions.

I needed to cross the bridge over the Mississippi River into Baton Rouge. They were doing some painting so one lane was closed. Deputy Rick Barnett said he would be patrolling the bridge but couldn't help me because he would be on the other side but he would try to get a State Trooper to escort me. Wendy Landos was concerned that I wouldn't have a way back to my car so she drove up from Krotz Springs. The State Trooper, Brian Lee, called and said, "We can't do this during the rush hour. I'll meet you at the foot of the bridge around 9:45 and escort you across." So we drove to the foot of the bridge and waited for him. I put a sign on the back of Wendy's car saying, "Walkers ahead" and a flashing light on top of her car so I had two escorts.

As soon as we got across the bridge, the trooper said he had to leave because he was due in court. It was a pretty dangerous route from the bridge to the finish. The trooper warned Wendy and me to stay as close to the right as possible and be careful at the ramps. We finished with no problem, but Wendy said it was pretty shaky for her. She drove me back to the start and escorted me to the foot of the bridge where my car was parked so I got in my full 7.02 miles.

A friend I had met in Krotz Springs, Webster Reed, is a Gold Star father as his son was killed in action January 28, 2005. He told me there was a man, Chris Ring, swimming the entire Mississippi to bring awareness to the Gold Star families. He invited me to go with him to meet this man in Baton Rouge. Baton Rouge was making this Chris Ring day and because the mayor was out of town, they declared him honorary mayor. What an amazing young man! I said, "I can't imagine doing what you're doing." He said, "I can't imagine doing what you're doing."

I moved my RV to the Nite RV Park, Baton Rouge.

December 7, 2015, Pearl Harbor Day was Leg 325. This was ironic as the leg was the same number as the ship I'm trying to raise money for. I wonder why so few people pay attention to this day. It's the day president Roosevelt said will live in infamy. I have more than one reason to remember December 7th. On that day in 1941, the Japanese attacked Pearl Harbor and on that day I made my decision to join the Navy, which was to change my life forever. On December 7, 1963, I married the love of my life, June Newton Ward, which was another life changing event. On this day, December 7, 2015, I had a lovely lady from Thibodaux, LA by the name of Valerie Sepulvado running with me to help me keep my mind on things of the present and still reminisce on things of the past.

John Martin, a San Bernardino County, California fireman, flew in, rented a car, got a room in Hammond, then drove to Baton Rouge to take me out to dinner. Three policemen came in. John told the waitress "Put their meal on my tab." I soon learned this is typical of John. He has a high regard for those who serve. John said, "I'll be running with you on Thursday through Hammond. I'll spend tomorrow paving the way for you," and he sure did. I had six runners on my team with Terry Cannon, Deputy Sheriff and Miles Miller, Hammond Policeman, escorting, and the fire departments had their engine out front with the uniformed firemen standing at attention. When we reached the intersections, motorcycle police were there holding up traffic.

I took off Christmas week and flew to Jackson, WY, to spend Christmas with my daughter Donna. A volunteer, whose name I can't remember, took me to the airport and said she'd be there to pick me up when I returned. It snowed the whole week. One day the sun came out, I think it was Christmas Day, so we went for a three-mile run on the Elk

Reserve. When I flew out of Jackson, the pilot asked if he could introduce me. I received a hearty welcome, then they moved me to first class and served a nice meal. When I got off the plane in Atlanta, I went to the desk to get directions to where I could catch my flight to Baton Rouge. I gave her a flyer. She said, "Would you like an earlier flight? I can save you two hours." I said, "I would love that." She handed me a voucher and said, "Here's twenty dollars for food, complements of Delta." Then she said, "Don't go away. It's a long way to the gate. Don't want you to get lost. I have someone coming to take you there." A young fellow showed up with a wheelchair and wheeled me to my gate. I said, "I hope no one recognizes me. This would be bad for my image." I called my volunteer and informed her of the time change. She was there waiting when I arrived.

My next run was December 28. I hadn't had time to drum up some runners so I was running east on Highway 190 all alone, no runners, and no escort. Michelle Ginsburg took highway 190 to work, just out of curiosity, knowing I would be running along there. She expected to see a whole bunch of runners, a marching band, and police escorts. She parked her car and ran along with me. She called John Crosby, her boyfriend, who came and took her back to her car and then joined me. He called his sister to meet us at the finish so we'd have a way back to our cars. Michelle told John, "We can't let this happen again. We've got to do something about it."

John started contacting the sheriff department in every county I ran across, giving them my schedule in hopes that I'd never be without an escort. He kept this up all the way to the Atlantic Ocean.

My next run was 6.8 miles, ending at the Gulf Bank, downtown Covington. The bank had a large parking lot so I went in, gave them a flyer, and asked if it would be all right for us to park some cars there the morning of the run. They said, "No problem. We've got plenty of space." I don't know who did all the canvasing, John, Michelle, or the bank, but forty-three runners showed up at the start. We had three deputy sheriffs and two Covington police cars for escorts. While running, one of the runners, I think it was John but not sure, said, "How are you fixed for shoes?" I said, "I'm about due for a new pair." He said, "What do you wear?" Then he made a phone call. When we reached the finish, a gentleman from Varsity Sports said I have two pairs your size. He handed me two pairs of running shoes and a couple shirts.

The mayor was there and presented me with a key to the city. The bank had taken up a collection and donated $132. The next run was just as exciting with 46 runners, four police escorts and a marching band. The finish was at the Tammany Parish Animal Control. They had hot coffee waiting for us.

I moved my RV to the Sunrise RV Park, Pearlington, Mississippi.

My next run was to start at the Tammany Parish Animal Control. I was camped about 50 miles from there and overslept. I never use an alarm and this is the only time I overslept. I didn't have time for anything so I skipped my morning exercise and my morning coffee. I didn't know how to get to the start from this new location, and it wouldn't be daylight for another half hour, but I knew how to get to Covington, so I drove to Covington and then to the start. I was a little late but no one seemed to mind.

We had nine runners waiting at the start and three deputy escorts. We ran highway 36 to highway 41, 6.95 miles. The lack of exercise and coffee took its toll. I was pooped, ready to collapse, but it was still fun because I had such wonderful company, and now friends I will never forget.

Thirty runners, two deputies, and a Pearl River policeman met me at the 36/41 junction. It was raining. I said, "Don't worry, it never rains on Ernie." We had a slight mist for the first mile, then it cleared. We ran 5.71 miles through Pearl River. I counted ten welcoming signs through town, mostly neon, and lots of people on the street cheering. We finished at the Shell Station. There was a crowd there to welcome us, including

Joseph McQueen, Mayor of Pearl River. He presented me with a key to the city, plus a personal donation. I did a presentation at the elementary school… I think it was the Cyprus Cove. I love those fifth graders.

We had nine runners on highway 190 to the 90, ending at the Pearl River Fisheries. One of my runners was Michael Maenza, owner of MMI Culinary Services. When we reached the finish, his chef was there and we had a picnic on the spot. He supplied me with enough prepared food to fill up my freezer. He said, "When you reach the Atlantic, I'll be there to feed everyone for free." I said, "There may be a lot of people." He said, "Bring on a thousand, no problem." He wasn't able to fulfill his promise because when I reached the Atlantic Ocean, Louisiana had a flood and he was busy feeding the flood victims.

On January 16, 2016, I crossed into Mississippi. Out of nine states, this is the only one Carlos didn't run with me. I followed highway 90 all the way across Mississippi. The scenery along the Gulf was outstanding. I told a Mississippi policeman I really didn't need an escort along the Gulf because there was a nice paved trail to run on. He said, "You can do that but we want to get in on the action." All the way across Mississippi, I had lots of runners and more escorts than I could keep track of (deputy sheriffs, city police, fire engines, and others).

When I ran across the Bay Saint Louis Bridge from Waveland to Pass Christian, MS, I had a record of 67 runners. There were more, but they didn't fill out waivers so I don't have a record. A few of Ainsley's Angels were in the group. Willy, a twelve-year-old, completely paralyzed, was pushed in a stroller. At the finish, I autographed a little flag and gave it to him. Everyone was taking pictures and little Willy started laughing and just kept laughing. Here's a little boy who can't even move, but he was happy. Life is worth living, regardless of circumstances. I received a Facebook message saying, "Willy has us get out the flag every day so he can look at it."

John Crosby and Michelle Ginsberg stuck with me for 17 legs through Louisiana, Mississippi, and Alabama, doing everything for me they could and they were there for the last two runs at the finish. When I got too far away, they turned it over to Nathan Hill and Lisa Trim. In the meantime, they went to Las Vegas and got married. These two were meant for each other. They have so much in common. Both are race drivers.

I moved my RV to Howard's RV Park, Grand Bay, AL, and got a free space.

I leaned on my laptop and cracked the monitor. I went to Best Buy and bought a new laptop. They charged me to transfer information from my old computer. The guy did more harm than good. My computer was useless! I was afraid to take it back to Best Buy for fear I'd get another guy like the one who had messed things up. True friends, Nathan Hill and Lisa Trim, both of which stuck with me for 13 legs, including the finish at the Atlantic Ocean, handled all the detail work for me so I could concentrate on my running. Nathen is a computer guy. They drove all the way from Long Beach, MS, on Sunday and spent the day fixing my computer.

Leg 350 was on February 11, 2016. I ran five miles and entered Alabama just west of Grand Bay, 7.01 miles total. The next leg ran through Grand Bay with 5.87 miles. The following leg was 7.07 miles ending in Theadore. Carlos was back running with me again for three more legs.

I contacted Captain Hal Pierce. He was the Navy Port Coordinator who welcomed us and our LST into Mobile. He did a lot for us then and for the next few years while the ship was in Mobile and he had us back for the 10-year reunion. We were treated royally. Now he was going all out for me again, getting Mobile excited. He invited me to a meeting and dinner. I can't remember what the meeting was, something to do with Mobile. I met a lot of important people there.

I moved my RV to Parkway Mobile Home and RV park, Loxley, AL.

Leg 353 I ran from Theadore to Mobile, ending at the Skyland Mall. We had a large welcoming party at the mall. I was flooded with gifts. Council member John Williams was at the finish. He said, "I'm going to run with you on Saturday." I said, "I'll believe it when I see it. Other politicians have said they were going to run with me but none has ever shown up." He said. "I'm going to show you that some politicians do what they say they will do." True to his word, he showed up on Monday with 26 more runners. He ran part way on Saturday then came back Monday and ran a full leg. He also showed up for my birthday dinner in Brunswick, GA, and ran the last two legs into the Atlantic.

Leg 354 was 6.37 miles along Hwy, 90 through Mobile and I had 27 friends, old and new, running with me. I won't attempt to name them all but I do want to mention a very special one, Kaye Barnett. This was the beginning of a friendship with memories that will last for a lifetime. John Crosby asked Barry Booth, a local dentist, Vietnam veteran, and coordinator for the Mobile Honor Fight, to do what he could for me. He was instrumental in what took place Monday.

Monday's run, Leg 355, had 15 runners and two police escorts. The police closed the Bank Head tunnel while we ran through. A nice size group and the Patriot Riders Motorcycle Group were at the tunnel exit to greet us. After the run, we all went to the Battleship Memorial Park, had the best cheeseburger ever, and then met in the aircraft pavilion for a great reception. There were reporters from TV, newspaper, radio, and lots of important people. There were many gifts. A man, whose name I didn't get, gave me a silver dollar with the date 1802. Don't know what it's worth now, but it probably could have bought a farm in 1802.

Carlos ran so many legs with me and he always finished ahead of me so I presented him with a big first place blue ribbon. Bill Mueller and his wife Jean ran a couple runs with us. They are members of the Blue Crew on the LST 325. The Blue Crew, as I mentioned earlier, are the volunteers who have been working on the ship since it arrived back in the US. Bill and I were shipmates on the 2003 river trip.

On Leg 357 I had 18 running with me, including Barry. A few of us went to breakfast. A 105-year-old veteran met us there. Don't remember his name. Barry invited us to attend the Republican convention in Mobile. He picked us up and took us there. They had a great dinner and a standing ovation for both the 105-year-old veteran and me. Robert Bently, the governor of Alabama, came to my table to shake my hand. He was still denying any wrongdoing at that time, but a few months later he pleaded guilty and resigned. I don't think shaking my hand was his wrongdoing. Something more serious, it seems.

I moved my RV to The Arrowhead RV Park in Marianna, FL.

Joan McClenny missed me when I ran through Covington. She contacted me and wanted her grandson to meet me. She took me to a nice Mexican restaurant. After a long run, I needed to get off my feet but I was running out of supplies and needed to do some shopping. I went back to my RV and freshened up. She went home and then drove all the way back to take me to Walmart. I rode in a motorized cart while she pushed a cart and we loaded up with supplies. She helped me carry everything into the RV and put it away. She ran six legs with me in Louisiana, Mississippi, Alabama, and Florida. She had to get up in the middle of the night and drive through four states just to run along. Since I finished my Coast to Coast run, she came to visit me in California. Joan is another friend I'll never forget.

Florida showed the least interest of any state I ran across, but the sheriff departments and city police were wonderful across the Florida Panhandle. I always had plenty of escorts. I had lots of runners, but they were mostly from out of state. I was running through Pensacola when a tall man ran up behind me and said, "Hi, Uncle Ernie." What a surprise! This was my nephew's adopted son, Anthony Anderson. The last time I saw him, he was a little kid. This guy stood about 6 feet 3 inches.

April 23rd, Leg 381 had 10 runners, four escorts, and was a 5.78 mile run east of Bonifay. Gabby Gross who had already run two previous legs with me was having her 10th birthday and her grandmother, Kaye Barnett's birthday was in just two more days. They wanted to celebrate by running with me. They drove all the way from Mobile, AL. I picked up a birthday cake from Walmart and left it at the restaurant where we'd be having brunch, so we had a brunch birthday party. You can see why Kaye Barnett and I became good friends. This was her ninth run, and not the last.

We ran through all the little towns on highway 90 through Jackson county. These were all fun runs because I had so many friends for company, both runners and law enforcement.

I moved my RV to Lakeside Travel Park, Tallahassee.

When I ran through Gadsden county, Sheriff Morris A. Young was at a meeting. One of his deputies asked ,"Have you heard about the 92-year-old veteran that's running across the United States? He's on the highway right now and will be running past here in a couple days." Sheriff Young came out to the highway and ran to the finish with me, in full uniform. He ran with me the rest of the way across Gadsden county and had all his deputies either running or escorting. He was running for re-election, no pun intended. All along the highway I saw signs reading,"Keep Gadsden county Young."

I got a notice that the Whiskey Row Marathon in Prescott, AZ was giving me the Al Clark award. I felt so honored to be receiving this award that I wanted to be there in person, so I took a week off and flew from Tallahassee, FL to Palm Springs, CA. My daughter Linda and her husband Carl picked me up at the airport. The Whiskey Row marathon group knew I was coming so they signed me up for the 10K run. While in flight, my big toe was hurting. When we got to my daughter's house, I took off my shoe and saw a toe nail had split and was poking into my toe. We went to the emergency room and the doctor removed the toe nail so I wasn't able to run the 10K, but it was great to be there for the presentation and visit with old friends.

When I got back to Tallahassee, my toe was fine and I was able to continue my runs. A couple picked me up at the airport to get me to my RV. This same couple had me to their home a couple times for dinner and to spend the night while my RV was being fumigated, getting rid of the bugs I picked up in Louisiana. I can't remember this couple's name, and that bothers me. The lady of the house asked me if I had heard of J. Vernon McGee. Of course I'd heard of him. I attended his Through the Bible in 5 Years at the Church of the Open Door in Los Angeles and received Christ in his office on my 39th birthday. Dr. McGee has been dead for many years, but he taped his messages and they are still being heard throughout the world.

The first week of June, Carlos was back and brought his uncle Martin with him. Carlos had fallen off a roof and broke his back. He was wearing a back brace, but he and his uncle still ran two legs.

When we ran out of Tallahassee, the heat was getting to us. We were praying for rain, then a storm hit us and we got drenched. Boy did that feel good. Carlos came by to pick me up to go to Denny's for dinner. Somewhere along the way, my keys fell out of my pocket. Fortunately, I had another set hid away at the RV.

I moved my RV to the River Park RV Park, Valdosta GA, with the help of Carlos and Martin.

First, I took highway 90 to Monticello, turned left on St. Margaret's Church Road and right onto Ashville Rd. Then I took Ashville to highway 221, and turned north into Georgia. Finally, I took Highway 221 to Quitman, Georgia, turned onto highway 84 east to Valdosta. Tom Wheeler ran with me into Georgia and stayed with me all the way through Valdosta. When we ran into Quitman, he led me to the Peach Shed at Lawson's Farm where I could get a blueberry shake ... delicious! At the finish of the next leg, a shake was waiting for me. One day I drove to Lawson's for a shake. On the way back, my clutch went out. Seems the mechanic at Tate's didn't clean out the hydraulic fluid well enough. I had to replace everything again, including the clutch and fly wheel, only this time it wasn't under warranty. Ted Dickerson was another faithful runner through Florida and Georgia.

When I picked up my car and returned the rental, Hertz shuttled me back to my RV. The driver was 90 years old. He had another passenger. The passenger was a truck driver from Russia. He was so impressed with what we were doing at our age he made a phone call and said, "Do you mind if I interview you?" He said, "You are now live in Moscow. Our people have some questions." It seems there was more interest in a 90-year-old still holding a job driving shuttle than in a 92-year-old running. He asked me, "Who won the war, the US or Russia?" I said, "Russia did their part." He repeated, "Russia did their part" and asked me no more questions.

My daughter Cathy took an early retirement and came to join me for the rest of my journey.

I moved my RV to Laura Walker State Park, Waycross, GA. Here I had free Space and a beautiful spot on the lake. Dan and Renee Krajar from New York arrived and parked near us. They stayed for about a week and ran three legs with us, so we had great company and fond memories. Cathy and Renee did some sightseeing and took some pictures of alligators.

From Valdosta to Waycross there was some pretty hot weather but I had lots of runners and plenty of escorts, along with lots of road construction which looked more like road destruction. A deputy sheriff would go ahead and hold up traffic until we got through while we had plenty of escorts—fire engines, patrol cars, and other emergency vehicles.

My granddaughter, Robin Levesque, and great-granddaughter, Sierra Levesque, came to run with me in Waycross. It was Sierra's 9th birthday, so we went to a nice restaurant to celebrate. From Waycross, the number of runners kept multiplying. Here are some of the faithful runners across Georgia. Mary Woodruff, Jennifer Smith, Cathy Ratledge, and Beverly Lavala. Mary is a retired teacher/coach. The school kids call her Coach. She was always there to help any way she could. She arranged for me to give a presentation at a couple schools.

I took some time off in June of 2016 and met my son, Dan, daughter-in-law Grace, and grandkids Danny, Amanda, and Maggy, on Perris Island. My grand-daughter, their middle daughter, Candace, was graduating Marine Bootcamp as a Private First Class. We surprised her when I showed up. I told her that as a Corpsman, I was a Marine's best friend.

August 1, 2016, was Leg 421 which had six runners, all repeats except one young lady by the name of Kathy Williams. (Well to me, 66 is young!) She is a military child and gave me an autographed book she wrote called "Dear Dad." I highly recommend this book. I found it so interesting I could hardly put it down. (Publisher's note: We published Kathy Williams' book, and I served under her father in Vietnam. You can order both Kathy's and Ernie's books at www.deedspublishing.com).

I moved my RV to The Golden Islands RV Park, Brunswick, GA. I think the Chamber of Commerce arranged for my space, at no charge to me.

Carlos was back to run the final three legs with me into the Atlantic Ocean. He ran a total of 44 legs with me in seven states. Since then, he came to California and ran with me, making it eight states.

Chandra Capps Kendall, Saint Simons Island, along with Tom Purdy, the pastor of Christ Church, Woody Woodside, the president of Golden Islands Chamber of Commerce, and many others arranged for the biggest welcoming party to ever take place on the island. Cathy arranged a birthday dinner on Friday evening, August 19th. Family, friends, and runners from across the country were there for the finish. Many came to the dinner. A total of 16 of my extended family were there for my birthday and to run into the finish with me.

Years ago, someone by the name of Sandy Martin from Alabama became a friend on Facebook. I sent him a message saying, "I know there are a lot of Martin's and a lot of Navy vets in Alabama, but just thought I'd mention we had an officer from Alabama by the name of Martin on the LST 124 during World War II." To my surprise, that was his father. He showed up at the dinner and presented me with a nice framed picture of the LST 124. It's now hanging on the wall in my living room. I only spent a year and a half on that ship, but the memories are for a lifetime. She was a great ship, took us into harm's way and out, and never let us down.

It's because of those memories that I went to Greece to help bring back the LST 325. I could see only two things different between the two ships—the location of the sick bay, and the 325 has openings from the tank deck to slide a stretcher through. The 124 did not have those. We had to tilt the stretchers and carry them up a steep ladder.

My step-daughter, Sandy Suelzle, flew down from Canada and Chandra put her up in her home. Her daughter, Joyce Bishop, came in later and was welcomed into the Kendall home also.

I only have a record of 186 runners at the finish, but I know there were more who didn't register, and there must have been about a thousand more who joined in along the way. About another thousand were along the way cheering.

There were two fly overs. One was planned. I found out later who the other was. We were having dinner in a nice restaurant when the owner came to our table and said, "My wife wanted to run with you but we were out of town and didn't get back in time so I flew down low so she could get a good look of you running into the ocean."

Bud Badyna, better known as Backward Bud, ran several legs with me. He is in the Guinness Book of World Records many times for breaking records running backwards. He painted a patriotic picture including the LST 325 on a half-inch thick, two feet by four feet board and carried it to the finish. It is also displayed on my wall. A jeep was waiting for me at the finish to rush me to a veteran's home for a shower and then back to the beach where a tent was set up. There were lots of speeches, lots of awards, and a ceremony including just about everything, even the color guard. The proclamations and certificates of appreciation I collected across the US covers a whole wall of my living room. I knew that my age would draw attention, but I never realized being a World War II veteran would create so much interest.

Kaye Barnett showed up at the finish and ran the last two runs. This made a total of 18 legs. She brought another one of her granddaughters with her, Marleigh Daigle, a little three-year-old girl. I've had younger runners, but she is the youngest to finish a complete leg. I guess all the excitement kept her from getting bored.

In the late 1930's, I read about someone's dream of building a highway from the tip of South America to Russia. I thought, "If this ever happens, I've got to drive it." It will probably never happen because of the ice problem at both the tip of South America and the Aleutian Islands. During World War II, they built the highway from the US to Alaska in order to move war equipment to Alaska. So through the years, driving the Alcan has been on my bucket list. I decided as soon as I finished my coast to coast run, I would drive my RV to Alaska. My step daughter, Sandy, lives in Alaska and she didn't want me driving that highway alone so she flew to Georgia to be at my finish and to help me drive to Alaska. She insisted on doing the driving.

She drove the RV all the way from Brunswick, Georgia, to her brother's farm at Lacombe, Alberta, Canada. She said her brother, Lonnie, wanted to go with us. When I told him this, he said, "I didn't say I wanted to go. She said this is what we're going to do." They decided the logical thing to do was leave the RV at the farm and travel in his truck. That was a wise decision because there was so much road construction, driving that RV would have been a disaster.

Since I finished my Coast to Coast runs, I have continued to run three days a week. I continue to post on Facebook before and after every run so I had several runners join me in Canada and Alaska. The round trip was fascinating. The trees were changing color and we saw lots of wildlife. After we got back to Lacombe, Lonnie helped me drive the RV to California. When I married my third wife, Susan, I inherited another wonderful family and I feel so blessed.

When I arrived in California, I camped at the Country Hills RV Park in Beaumont. I continued my three day a week runs. A few of my old friends and some new ones, including two of my daughters and a great-grand-daughter (Sophia, five years old) came to run with me. On October 31, 2016, I moved into my new home in Sun Lakes Country Club and continued my three days a week runs. In November, the Pro Football Hall of Fame, Canton, Ohio invited me to be their speaker for the Patriot's Project. A car picked me up at my door and drove me to the airport. Someone was waiting at the airport to take my luggage and escort me to my plane.

When we arrived in Ohio, a car was waiting to take me to the hotel. There was a nice room, meals, room service, and a buffet party and dance which were all paid for by the Pro Football Hall of Fame. I have a daughter, Linda, June's middle daughter, and her husband, Jim, living just a few minutes away so I was able to get together for a nice visit. I did a morning run and two locals showed up to run with me. I met some real heroes there. One I was really impressed with was Shilo Harris, author of "Steel Will (My journey through hell to become the man I was meant to be)." He autographed one of his books for me and this is one of my most prized souvenirs.

I don't know why they picked me as the speaker. I was never cited for anything heroic beyond the call of duty. All I did was a fun run across the US in my old age. Paula Francis, the Happiness Walker, walked up to my front door, stayed overnight, and joined me and my family for the Veteran's Day walk. After breakfast, she continued her walk for 10 miles, then turned around and walked another 10 miles back to my house and spent another night. The next morning, we went to breakfast and I dropped her off where she turned around the day before so she could continue her walk to the Pacific Ocean.

My daughter, Linda, lives at the Sun Lakes Country Club in Banning, California. I bought a home in Sun Lakes for three reasons: 1. It's a beautiful community. 2. It's so nice having my daughter close by. 3. I have a grandson with a precious little two-year-old living just 20 minutes away.

My daughter, Cathy, comes often to help with her new grandson. I gave her a room in my home so she's a part time resident. How neat is that?

Carlos came to visit and do another run with me. When Paula reached the Pacific, Carlos drove me down and I was there to run with her through Santa Monica and to the beach by the pier and Carlos was there to give me a ride back.

2017 was an interesting year. I ran three days a week at the Sun Lakes Country Club. I participated in the Veterans Day Walk and did three 5K's, a 10K and three 200 mile relays. I celebrated my 94th birthday by running a 200-mile relay from Spokane, Washington, to Sand Point, Idaho, which was a beautiful spot to finish a run. My step grand-daughter, Joyce, lives in Spokane so she ran with me. Some friends shared their glasses and we were able to see some of the eclipse. Paula took some time off for the holidays to take care of some business, then came back to Santa Monica to continue her walk. My daughter, Linda, and I met her at the Santa Monica pier and joined her for the first part of her continued walk.

As I write this, I'm back in Sun Lakes running three days a week. I'll run six miles tomorrow and next week I'll be in Wickenburg, AZ to run another Ragnar Del Sol 200-mile relay. They've named the team "Ernie and the Road Runners."

NOTE: AS OF PUBLICATION, ERNIE, AT AGE 95, IS BEGINNING HIS SECOND RUN BACK ACROSS THE US FROM GEORGIA TO CALIFORNIA.

ERNEST ANDRUS WAS BORN IN AUGUST, 1923 IN WOLF RIVER TOWNSHIP, DONIPHAN COUNTY, Kansas. He spent his early years living on a farm with his parents and two brothers. Later the family moved to California. He lived through the Great Depression and served in the U. S. Navy during World War II. During the war Ernie served on an LST (Landing Ship Tanks). After retirement in 1984, he took up running. Ernie was part of a group of shipmates that went to Greece to locate an LST, refurbish it and bring it back to the US on its own power. Today it has a home in Evensville, IN where it is open to the general public for tours. Because of his love for running and his love for the ship, At the age of 90, Ernie decided to run across the United States, from coast to coast to try to raise funds for the ship. Ernie completed his cross country run one day after his 93rd birthday.